Elite Politics in an Ideological State

Elite Politics in an Ideological State

The Case of Pakistan

ASAF HUSSAIN
Research Associate, The Islamic Foundation
Leicester

First published in 1979

© Asaf Hussain 1979

Wm Dawson & Sons Ltd, Cannon House
Folkestone, Kent, England

British Library Cataloguing in Publication Data

Hussain, Asaf
    Elite politics in an ideological state.
    1. Elite (Social sciences)—Pakistan 2. Pakistan—
    Politics and government—1971—
    I. Title
    323.3   HN690.5.Z9E4

    ISBN 0-7129-08609

Printed litho in Great Britain
by W & J Mackay Limited, Chatham

Contents

List of Figures and Tables   *page* 9
Preface   13
Abbreviations   17

1 THE IDEOLOGICAL STATE   19
   The Mughals and the Feudal State
   The British and the Colonial State
   Islam and State Formation
   Islam and the Ideological State

2 THE POLITICAL SYSTEM   33
   Political Stratification and Political Elites
   Political Alliances and the Social Structure
   Power and the Political System

3 THE LANDOWNING ELITES   44
   The Feudal Mode of Production
   The Rural Power Structure and the
     Political System
   The Feudal Political Order
   The Politics of Agrarian Reforms
   Conclusion

4 THE BUREAUCRATIC ELITES   61
   The Colonial Heritage
   Elite Recruitment
   The Emergence of the Administrative State
   Political Rule by the Non-Elected Leadership
   Political Participation During Bureaucratic Rule

     Elite Conflict and Decentralization
     Conclusion

5   THE RELIGIOUS ELITES   79
     The Religious Elites
     Islamization of the Ideological State
     The State Religion and Islam
     The Future of the Nizam-i-Mustafa

6   THE INDUSTRIAL ELITES   93
     The Industrial Elites
     Ethnic Structures and Economic Power
     Economic Power and the Political System
     The Capitalist Mode of Production
     The Industrial Elites under Bhutto
     Conclusion

7   THE PROFESSIONAL ELITES   111
     The Professional Elites
     The Democratic State and Elite Factionalism
     Constitution-Making and Ethnicity
     The Parity Principle and Economic Development
     Political Legitimation and Political Opposition
     The Rise of the Awami League
     Regime Oppression and Political Accountability

8   THE MILITARY ELITES   126
     The Contextual Linkages
     The Officer Corps and Military Ideology
     Praetorianism and the Political System
     The Ayub Regime (1958–1969)
     The Yahya Regime (1969–1971)
     The Military under Bhutto (1971–1977)
     The Zia-ul-Haq Regime (1977–)
     Conclusion

9   THE ONE–PARTY STATE AND POLITICAL
     CONFLICT   146
     Party Ideology
     The State Machinery
     The Political Instrument
     Elite Factionalism and Political Conflict
     The Elections of 1977
     Conclusion

10 ETHNIC NATIONALISM AND IMPERIALISM 161
  Imperialism and Ethnicity
  Conclusion

EPILOGUE 169
NOTES AND REFERENCES 173
SELECT BIBLIOGRAPHY 201
INDEX 206

List of Figures & Tables

Figures

1 The ideological state—Pakistan   *page* 31
2 The power structure of the political elites in Pakistan   37
3 The Central Secretariat   67
4 Constitutional map of the Bhutto regime   152

Tables

1 Representation of elite groups in the political arena, 1947–1978   35
2 Historical origins of elite groups, 1947–1978   36
3 Landownership in West Pakistan, 1959   55
4 Estimate of tenants benefited by land reform, 1972–1976   59
5 Representation of the Civil Service of Pakistan in East Bengal and West Pakistan, 1948–1967   65
6 Social and business backgrounds of the twelve big houses   95
7 Control of manufacturing assests by industry, 1968   96
8 Development expenditure of Pakistan, 1947–1970   101
9 Trade balances for East and West Pakistan, 1948–1967   102
10 Private investment in East Bengal and West Pakistan, 1963–1968   103
11 Industrial investment, 1970/71–1976/77   108
12 Professional elites in the Legislative Assemblies of Pakistan, 1947–1969   112
13 Main characteristics of West and East Pakistani professional elites   114

14 Approximate ethnic group strength of the Pakistan
    military officer corps   *page* 129
15 Votes cast in the Presidential Elections, 1965   137
16 Defence expenditures as percentage of total govern-
    ment expenditures, 1948/49–1971/72   139
17 Results of the General Elections to the National
    Assembly, 1970   141
18 Results of the March 1977 Elections   157
19 Elitist transformations of Pakistan   162
20 Number of U.S. officials stationed in Pakistan,
    1948–1971   164
21 Foreign economic assistance to Pakistan, 1950–1970   166
22 Elite group distribution in the Federal Cabinet
    (5 July 1978)   170
23 Elite group distribution in the Federal Cabinet
    (22 August 1978)   170

DEDICATED
with love
to
Amina Hussain
Freda Hussain
Nadia Hussain

Preface

Pakistan's civil war of 1971 cost a great deal in terms of human misery, death, destruction, defeat, humiliation and the disintegration of the country. This boo was the result of an intense personal experience that I went through at that time, while I was living in the United States. The deep concern that I felt, perhaps shared with thousands of my countrymen, was not only for the safety of relatives and friends but also for the future of the country. After only twenty-four years of existence the country had split into two. How long could the new Pakistan remain as one state? Such questions plagued my mind as it became increasingly difficult to assume or pretend that it would. Such concerns directed my attention to the structure of Pakistan's political leadership, the type of political system in operation and whether, after the civil war, it was proceeding towards the integration of the state or was creating conditions conducive to insurgencies and ethnic nationalism.

Before I left Pakistan for the United States, I had worked as an officer of the Central Superior Services of the Government of Pakistan. As an 'insider', I had a very good idea of how the bureaucracy worked and the extent of its power. The bureaucracy, however, was only one group that worked as a political directorate. A thorough research of almost all the books, papers and articles published on Pakistan indicated that other such groups were frequently referred to as well. These included the military, landlords and industrialists and others who had played a significant role in the politics of Pakistan. But a comprehensive study of how many such groups there were and how they operated in the political system of Pakistan was lacking. A brief sketch of how this book came to be written may be of help to the researcher in the field.

The first field trip to Pakistan for this purpose was made in 1973, when my main focus was the highest decision-making body—the Central Government Cabinet. The occupational backgrounds of all Central Cabinet Ministers since 1947 were checked and the model that emerged from these data on the various political elite groups is discussed in chapter 2.

Elite studies have used various methodologies to identify elites. These have included the positional, reputational and decision-making approaches. Two of these were used quite fruitfully, the limitations of one method being supplemented by the advantages of the other. The positional method helped to identify the political elites and the elite political groups with which they were affiliated. The reputational method helped in the random selection of various well-known and politically active members of elite political groups, using newspapers, political networks and my own contacts in the country. Interviewing these political elites helped me to gain first-hand accounts of the political culture of Pakistani elite groups.

My second opportunity to further my research emerged when General Tikka Khan, then Chief of Staff of the Pakistan Army, visited Washington, D.C. In a short personal interview I requested permission to write a paper on the political role of the Pakistan military. He asked me to submit my research proposal and my bio-data to him in Pakistan. After a year of correspondençe, I was finally given the permission to carry out such a study and in 1975 I took another trip to Pakistan, this time as a guest of the Pakistan military. I was attached to the Research and Development Section which helped to arrange interviews with a cross-section of the Officer Corps (from the rank of a general to that of a captain).

Two factors helped me to establish a rapport with the officers interviewed. One was the direct permission of the 'Chief' (the popular name for the Chief of Staff at the G.H.Q.) and the other was my Punjabi ethnicity which created a certain degree of trust. The interviews were informal and not recorded on tape, only brief notes being made during the conversations. Many officers were embarrassed when I labelled them as 'praetorian' and some wanted to know why I had selected this term. I often asked them when the military would take over from Bhutto, being fully aware that such a question could be thought 'treasonable' by the ruling elite. Their answers were reserved in public but quite frank in private. It amused them to hear me say that the man who slept in the Prime Minister's House would always have to keep one eye open, to be focused on the military! In reply to their inquiries about why I was studying the military I replied that I was fascinated by the man in uniform. As a 'guest' of the Pakistan military, I was immune from harm and could freely discuss their political roles. The interviews were fruitful on the whole and on the basis of this study of the military elites I had predicted that under certain conditions they would take over from Bhutto. These findings were presented in a paper entitled 'The Military and Ethnic Nationalism in Pakistan' at the 30th International Congress of Human Sciences in Asia and North Africa, held in Mexico City in August 1976. Many observations made in that paper have been incorporated in chapter 8.

My observations of Pakistani politics were presented as papers at various conferences and published in academic journals. It was not until I was invited to write this book that I decided to bring together my previously published and unpublished works within one coherent framework. All the material was revised and rewritten, and new material was incorporated after another research trip to Pakistan in December 1977.

By this time, the forecast I had made earlier had come true and I was very interested in the strategies employed by the Bhutto regime and the leadership of the Pakistan National Alliance. The search for various political elites took me to the major cities of Karachi, Lahore, Rawalpindi, Islamabad and Peshawar and many small towns and villages. Most of the leadership of the Pakistan National Alliance and important party functionaries were interviewed as well as some staunch followers of the Pakistan People's Party. Labour leaders from the lesser parties like the Kissan–Mazdoor Party, old Pathan patriarchs like Khan Abdul Ghaffar Khan, and Baluchi tribal chieftains (Bugti, etc.) were also interviewed. In addition, Pakistani intellectuals from Karachi and Punjab universities, capitalists (friends and foes of Bhutto), landlords, peasants, journalists, police officers and even the man in the street (taxi drivers, rickshaw drivers, domestic servants, etc.) were interviewed. Impressions and observations from these interviews gave further insights into elite–mass relationships. Direct quotations have been avoided to keep the confidence of those interviewed but have been incorporated into the general framework of the study.

As stated earlier, the idea for writing this book was first conceived in 1971, and in the long period over which the book has taken its final shape I have incurred an intellectual debt to many persons to whom I must include a note of appreciation and thanks. The idea was first discussed with my advisor, Dr Austin van der Slice, Professor Emeritus at the American University, Washington,

D.C., who encouraged me to take the field trip in 1973. After the trip, my report was presented as a paper in the University's Sociology Departmental Seminar. Later, when I started teaching, my colleagues at Essex Community College (Maryland, U.S.A.), particularly Dr S. Verma, J. Hutchinson and S. Moskovitz, were most helpful with their discussions and comments. After arriving in England, my colleague Dr Saif-ur-Rahman Choudhri, Senior Lecturer at Salford College of Technology, was most generous with his time and in sharing his immense knowledge of the subject, despite heavy teaching work loads. My friend, Dr Frank Girling of Sheffield University, with whom I had many discussions on the politics of South Asia, read through the manuscript and offered valuable suggestions. My discussions with my colleagues Professor Khurshid Ahmad and Khurram Murad at the Islamic Foundation have helped in focusing my attention on those aspects of Pakistani politics which are often misunderstood and ignored by political scientists. Many other friends, including Mohammad Said Khan of Peshawar, Saeed Alizai of D. I. Khan, Dr Iqbal Ahmed of the International Statistical Institute (London) and Saleh Mohammad Khan, have been most helpful on my research trips. The responsibility for the conclusions drawn in this book, however, solely rests with me.

The list would not be complete without a special word of thanks to Mr Robert Seal, Sponsoring Editor of Dawson, for making this work possible and for his encouragement and help in the preparation of the manuscript. Nonetheless, I owe my sincere thanks to Ahmed and Akhter Rashid for the hospitality of their home which enabled me to concentrate on writing this book without having to worry about the mundane realities of life. Last, but not least, a special word of appreciation is due to my wife, Freda, whose counsel and constructive criticisms and typing of the manuscript could well make her the co-author of this book.

Abbreviations

AL	Awami League
BD	Basic Democracy System
BE	Bureaucratic Elite
BIA	British Indian Army
CML	Council of the Muslim League
COP	Combined Opposition Party
CSP	Civil Service of Pakistan
EBDO	Electoral Bodies Disqualification Order (1958)
EBPE	East Bengal Professional Elite
HAG	Harvard Advisory Group
ICS	Indian Civil Service
IE	Industrial Elite
JI	Jamaat-i-Islami
JUI	Jamiatul-Ulema-i-Islam
JUP	Jamiatul-Ulema-i-Pakistan
LE	Landowning Elite
ME	Military Elite
MPA	Member of Provincial Assembly
NA	National Assembly
NAP	National Awami Party
NDP	National Democratic Party
NWFP	North West Frontier Provinces
PAF	Pakistan Armed Forces
PDP	Pakistan Democratic Party
PE	Professional Elite
PFS	Pakistan Foreign Service
PIDC	Pakistan Industrial Development Corporation

PML	Pakistan Muslim League
PML (C)	Pakistan Muslim League (Convention group)
PML (Q)	Pakistan Muslim League (Qayyum group)
PNA	Pakistan National Alliance
PPP	Pakistan People's Party
PRODA	Public and Representative Offices Disqualification Act (1949)
PSC	Public Service Commission
PSP	Police Service of Pakistan
RE	Religious Elite
TI	Tehriq-i-Istaqlal
WPPDA	West Pakistan Power and Development Authority
WPPE	West Pakistan Professional Elite

1

The Ideological State

Ultimately, Pakistan owes its existence to the Arab conquest of the Indian sub-continent, and in the historical context of the birth of the state the role of Islam has been very significant. The Arabs formally entered the sub-continent in the eighth century during the Umayyad Caliphate of Walid I (705–715), by sending a young Arab general (Mohammad Ibn Qasim) to chastise some pirates off the coast of Sind. Later another Umayyad Caliph, Umar II (717–720), also extended a formal invitation to the conquered populace to accept Islam. Such overtures gradually introduced the Islamic faith to the indigenous population. Subsequently, Islam has been the strongest bond between the Arabs of the Middle East and the Muslims of India and, later, Pakistan.

Among the revealed religions of the Middle East, Islam came after Judaism and Christianity, and announced the completion of the divine message sent to mankind through Moses, Jesus and Mohammad. This kind of recognition was not accorded by Islam to the polytheistic religions such as Hinduism. Islam also gave the doctrine of 'jihad' to free man from the slavery of man. However, early Muslim conquerors used this sanction of the faith to destroy Hindu temples with fanatical zeal. The real foundation of the Muslim empire in India, however, was laid during the Sultanate period (1175–1526), and the Islamic Sharia (or code of law) had been institutionalized by the end of the fourteenth century.[1] The Muslim empire reached its zenith during the Mughal period (1526–1857). During this time the Muslims established their civilization all over India.

In Mughal times the number of Muslims in the sub-continent

increased greatly through conversions and inter-marriages. Islam offered its converts freedom from the rigid shackles of the Hindu caste system and gave them a sense of belonging to the universal Islamic community (umma). The social structure of Muslim India, at that time, could be divided into three categories: the Muslims, who were the first-class citizens; the 'dhimmis' who had not accepted Islam but had agreed to pay taxes (jizya) for protection of life and property; the 'harbis' who had rejected the faith and refused to pay the taxes and therefore left themselves open to retribution.

The Mughals and the Feudal State

The medieval Muslim state was based on a feudal system. Its most important aspect was the political and economic relationship between the ruler and the ruled, and the role of religion within this context. The essential political characteristic of feudalism was the surrender 'of one man into the hands of another, in return for which he received protection and maintenance, usually through a grant of a fief over land, in the case of king and vassal, or the direct grant of land, in the case of vassal and peasant.'[2] The political structure of such a state reflected patrimonial relations. The highest offices in the conquered territories were monopolized by the ruling dynasty, and the personal rule of the Mughal emperor was enforced by the maintenance of a large military establishment.

This military establishment was known as the Mansabdari system. Elite recruitment to it depended on the emperors who selected their mansabdars mainly from the landed aristocracy and comprised of foreigners such as Arab, Persians, Turks, Afghans and Abyssinians.[3] As a general rule the emperor bestowed a mansab (rank) on the basis of their personal loyalty rather than military prowess: the greater their loyalty, the higher the number of men (up to 10,000) under their command.[4] The Mughal feudal state was therefore centralized, militaristic and hierarchical, with power vested in the hands of the Mughal ruler and his nobility.

At the economic base of the feudal system was ownership of land. The fundamental units of production were the peasants, artisan households or the villages from whom land revenue was collected by the Mughal officials, or jagirdars.[5] Landownership was of the prebendal type where the jagirdar had no inheritable rights but only the right to collect tributes or land revenues on behalf of the Mughal ruler to whom all land legally belonged.[6] This system prevented the landlords from becoming politically powerful. In addition, they were moved to new areas after every two or three years, in order to hinder them from forming a political base in any one area. The major drawback of the system was that the peasantry was subjected to exploitation because the jagirdars, fearing a transfer, tried to expropriate as much of the agrarian surplus as they could.[7] The peasantry, however, could escape this oppression by migrating to other areas.

Most of this production surplus went to maintain the ruling dynasty as well as the large army, which at one point numbered 4.3 million infantrymen and 0.3 million horsemen.[8] Investment in agriculture (public irrigation works) was given least consideration and did not exceed five per cent of the Mughal territories.[9] The pressure on the peasant was therefore due less to economic profiteering than to the demands of the military.[10] Despite this the feudal state was self-sufficient and rich in resources, and did not have to depend on economic aid from foreign countries.

In spite of its secure political and economic basis the feudal state began to decline in the eighteenth and nineteenth centuries owing to an internal contradiction between Islam and the feudal mode of production. The Mughals used Islam to legitimate the feudal state and the faithful South Asian Muslim minority strongly supported them. But the Muslim rulers never attempted to Islamicize India, and the Islamic politico-economic system was never enforced. The reason was primarily the dependence of the imperial treasury for its surplus wealth on taxation of the Hindu majority and the collection of land revenues and tributes from conquered princely states. All this maintained the status quo of the ruling dynasty.

This accumulation of capital was not ploughed back into India's economy by the Mughal rulers. Instead, it was spent on immortalizing their own grandeur by building magnificent places, mosques, palace-cities like Fatehpur Sikri (1569) and mausoleums like the Taj Mahal (1632). This type of exploitation ultimately alienated the Hindu majority and persuaded them to collaborate with any anti-Muslim forces. The increasing concentration of wealth also made the Muslim political centre at Delhi a desirable target for political usurpation. The preceding factor, together with the lack of a system of political succession to the throne, made the feudal state vulnerable to internal rebellion (by Hindus and Muslims alike) and external agression. At that time the Mughal rulers seemed oblivious to the designs of the colonial traders and their companies which had been making inroads into the empire under the guise of providing luxury goods for the Muslim aristocracy. The Muslim rulers who opposed the inroads into the country's economy were destroyed.[11]

The internal dangers created by the feudal mode of production were, however, discerned by the ulema, or priestly class, for they did not measure the development of the Muslim empire by its wealth or the extent of the lands controlled. They looked at it in terms of its religious conformity to the ideal of Islam and the standards expected of its political leadership and economic system. As early as the sixteenth century they warned the ruling dynasties of the dangers of deviating from Islam. Sirhindi's (1562–1624) orthodox doctrines raised an alarm following the emperor Akbar's liberal experiments with synthesizing the beliefs of all faiths into one known as Din-i-Illahi—the 'divine faith' proclaimed in 1582. Shah Waliullah (1703–1762) in turn lashed out at the descendents of Aurangzeb, the great grandson of Akbar. He reasoned that if the rulers had been chosen on the basis of their ability, like the Caliphs in the early years of Islamic history, the empire would have survived. He also accused Muslim soldiers of being mercenaries and not soldiers of Islam. His logic sought to revive Islamic faith so that the Muslim community could be strengthened. Waliullah was very conscious of the breakdown of the political and economic structures of Muslim society owing to the dissipation of the Mughal elite.[12] He sought to bring Islam within the understanding of the average man by translating the Quran into Persian (the official language of the court). Muslim political leadership did not heed his advice, and in any event the feudal state was soon to disintegrate.

The British and the Colonial State

During the fifteenth century European trading companies had been penetrating Asia and Africa, establishing companies such as the Africa Company, the Vereenigde Oost-Indische and the East India Trading Company. The influx of French, Portuguese, Dutch and British in the Indian sub-continent as traders culminated in the sole trading monopoly of the latter. This was later followed by the formal military conquest of India and its recognition as a crown colony in 1857. Colonialism therefore opened the doors of the sub-continent for the penetration of the capitalist system. Indian capitalism will be examined briefly in order to identify the holders of political and economic power in the colonial state.

Although exploitation was a common feature of both feudal and colonial states, its form varied in different contexts. In the feudal state, the Muslim ruling class exploited the Hindus within the same country; in the colonial state one country was exploited by another. In spite of its shortcomings, the feudal state was not really undeveloped since the wealth had remained in the country (irrespective of who had possessed it). In the colonial state, on the other hand, the prime goal was to repatriate the profits from the periphery (colony) to the centre (Britain). This led to the reordering of the political and economic processes in the colony conducive to such exploitation, and of forced underdevelopment. The sub-continent never fully recovered from this form of exploitation and even after Independence has continued to remain dependent on developed countries under a form of domination often described as neo-colonialism.

The capitalist system could not have been transplanted without the formation of alliances by the colonial power with local elites. First, to secure the conquest of India an efficient military force was necessary, and this led to the organization of the British Indian Army (BIA). The latter's selective recruitment policies resulted in the politicization of ethnicity among various ethnic groups because of their supposed martial and non-martial characteristics.[13]

The educational policies of the colonialists initiated significant social changes in the system. They were specifically aimed at raising 'a class of persons, Indian in blood and colour, but English in taste, in opinion, in morals and in intellect.'[14] An elite group was created, the Indian Civil Service (ICS), whose members' prime qualification was their administrative skill. In addition, those who became lawyers, doctors, journalists and other professionals, were indoctrinated with Western ideas of democracy and parliamentary institutions. The BIA and the ICS, however, remained as the 'sword arm' and 'steel frame' of the colonial state and their legacies continued even after Independence.

The colonial rulers exploited the country's vast agrarian resources in collaboration with the jagirdars who were given permanent settlement rights in 1793. There was created 'a vast body of rich landed proprietors deeply interested in the continuance of the British Dominions and having complete command over the mass of the people'.[15] Land revenue was paid to the district collectors (members of the ICS) who were the crown tax agents. Such hereditary rights created vested interests in these traditional elites and led to the rigid division of labour in which the landlord lived by his permanent exploitation of the peasantry. By appropriating the surplus wealth the landlords soon developed a life-style that required the consumption of imported luxury goods, and politics became their favourite pastime.

The social, political and economic processes through which capitalism superseded feudalism in Europe were never allowed to develop in the colonial state. In Europe, rapid industrialization had absorbed the peasants, and the landlords were forced to accumulate capital through their commodity (land) by carrying out intensive agricultural production. This had resulted not only in the improvement of the peasant economy but also in increased productivity and the capitalization of agrarian processes. In the colonial state, on the other hand, the 'fortification of feudal rights, the abundance of landless proletariat with nowhere to go because of the lack of industrialization, coupled with the vagaries of the world markets and single crop production, made extensive rather than intensive agriculture a natural option for landlords.'[16] Exploitation of the peasantry reached its peak during this period.

The landlords in the Punjab province were the strongest supporters of colonialism, and in this region the British built an elaborate irrigation system to make use of its fertile soil. Similar development was also carried out in Sind. But in the North West Frontier Provinces (NWFP), and Baluchistan, owing to strong opposition, colonialism was neglected and peace was maintained through coercive methods and bought through the payment of subsidies to the tribal chieftains.

If real progress had been intended by the colonialists, capitalism would have been substituted for feudalism; instead, the important point to be made here is that both were allowed to exist side by side. The feudal landlords assured the colonialists of a steady income from land revenue, and the colony provided cheap raw materials for British manufacturers whose finished products were sold there in turn, creating a need for essential consumer goods. This system was further promoted by direct control over the means of production in the colony as well as the creation of a group of indigenous 'middle men' who readily accepted the rationale of profit-making to enrich themselves. Such control destroyed many local art and craft industries and at the same time protected British trade from competition and intrusion by other colonial powers (France, Germany and Holland). On the other hand, the market for imported luxury consumer goods meant that the newly created elite group could spend its wealth on British products and maintain life-styles that the majority could never afford. The creation of 'sterling areas' of the British Empire ensured that these goods were paid for in the currency of the colonizer.[17]

Furthermore, the gap between the elites and the masses widened owing to income inequalities.[18] The indigeneous elite groups became dependent on the technology and finance of foreign enterprise and investment, and required skilled labour and capital. This was supplied by the colonizer, and sometimes a few persons from the colony were also trained to do the job. Wide income differentials were created, and a high value was placed on the skills possessed by a few. The wealth acquired in this manner was appropriated in large measure by the colonizers and to a lesser extent by their local partners.

Modernization can properly be defined as a process for entrenching the capitalist system in another country. Colonial penetration laid the 'material foundations of Western society in Asia'.[19] The greatest impact of colonialism on the colonial state was the transplantation of the capitalist system on one hand and the creation of new elite groups in the ideological state on the other.

Islam and State Formation

The politics of independence cannot be studied without taking into consideration the political and economic context of the Muslims in India under their colonial rulers. The rise of the Pakistan movement must therefore be studied within the three-dimensional contexts of politicization, mobilization and identification, covering a long span beginning with the creation of the Muslim League in 1906, Jinnah's political leadership in the 1930s, the Pakistan Resolution in 1940 and the creation of the new state of Pakistan in 1947. The above three processes are treated separately to crystallize the forces behind state-formation, but they were not of course mutually exclusive.

The Dimension of Politicization

During the late nineteenth and early twentieth centuries many prominent Muslim leaders broke away from their historical past and began to look towards the future of the Muslim community. This resurgence of the Muslim intelligentsia was primarily due to the realization of the implications of the democratic ideology of the West. Sir Syed Ahmed Khan (1817–1898) was at the forefront of this movement and he voiced his concern at the highest levels of the colonial government, stating that the 'principles of simple elections cannot be satisfactorily worked', because 'the larger nation will dominate the smaller one completely'.[20] Sir Syed's ideas were supported by other Muslim intellectuals, a significant number of whom were from the Muslim educational institutions in Aligarh. The most important of the Muslim writers was Mohammad Iqbal (1873–1938) whose works provided the unifying concepts for the creation of Pakistan. Iqbal conceptualized a state for the Muslims and propounded a dynamic interpretation of Islamic law. He believed that the laws derived from the Quran were not static legal codes but guidelines designed to awaken man's higher consciousness in terms of his relations with God and the universe. They could be dynamically involved with legislation by staying abreast of change. This was a new approach because Muslim jurists in the past had implemented legal systems based on the Quran which had dogmatically denied avenues for change.[21]

In a speech to the All India Muslim League, Iqbal reminded them that the 'superb idealism of your faith needs emancipation from the medieval fancies of theologians'.[22] He called on the Muslims to reconstruct their political society which was buried under the debris of decadence, and added that 'a Kafir (infidel) before his idol with a useful heart is better than the religious man asleep in the harem'.[23] Iqbal also believed that the problems facing the Muslims were not only economic but also cultural.[24] He firmly argued that the Islamic order could not be established without a free Muslim state, because 'the religious ideal of Islam, therefore, is organically related to the social order which it has created. The rejection of the one will eventually involve the rejection of the other. Therefore, the construction of a policy on national lines if it means a displacement of the Islamic principle of solidarity, is simply unthinkable.'[25] Iqbal's association with the Muslim League focussed Muslim thinking on a Muslim homeland.

The democratic doctrine spread through the British form of colonialism proved to be the activating agent for the Muslims. It appealed to the Hindus as a whole because they greatly outnumbered the Muslims. The Muslim elites who had feared the British raj now began to develop fears of an impending Hindu raj. The condition of the Muslim masses had deteriorated under colonial rule while the Hindus generally had greatly benefited from it. Questions involving the fate of Islam and the economic fate of Muslims under a Hindu raj created an effective political consciousness. The most important question therefore was that of the political future of the Muslims. With a Hindu majority they would never be able to participate equally in the political system. This 'challenge from the Hindu community'[26] effectively led to the politicization of the Muslims.

The Dimension of Mobilization

In spite of their politicization the Muslim community leaders were divided among themselves because of occupational differences and vested interests. The emergence of Mohammad Ali Jinnah (1876–1948) as a leader with the political skills necessary to mobilize the Muslims filled the need of the time. He had received his education in Britain and had been impressed with the liberal ideas of Gladstone and John Morley.[27] In the beginning of his political career in India he had belief in Hindu–Muslim unity but as his attempts at attaining this goal were repeatedly thwarted by the Hindus, he became disillusioned and had almost retired from politics when he was prevailed upon to take up the leadership of the Muslim League in the 1930s. This event marked a turning point in the political mobilization of the Muslims because Jinnah had fundamentally changed his political beliefs from Hindu–Muslim unity to the political resurgence of the Muslim minority.

Under Jinnah's leadership the Muslim League became a powerful nationalist organization. It was used to rally the various sectors of the Muslim population at both mass and elite levels. The outcome of the 1937 elections was a surprise for the Muslims, the mass contact campaign of the Congress Party sweeping the polls, with the Muslim League securing only 4.6% of the votes.[28] Jinnah provided the Muslims with a goal when he decided that 'the only strong issue on which the Muslim League could mobilize was religion'.[29] Islam's driving force could be used to attract the Muslims to the Muslim League which hitherto had remained divided among themselves.[30]

The resurgence of Hinduism further prompted the nascent Pakistan movement. B. G. Tilak's aggressive Hindu nationalism, and, later, Gandhi's passive nationalism, with its symbolisms of the 'gao mata' (mother cow), the 'charka' (spinning wheel) and principles like 'satya' (truth), 'ahimsa' (non-violence) and 'tapasaya' (penance), propagated doctrines embedded in Hindu philosophy. The Muslims, alarmed by the former and unable to identify with the latter, once again turned to the Muslim League.

The Muslim League's political doctrine that Pakistan would be created for the protection of Muslims from Hindu domination provided a powerful impetus. The ulema were simple men of faith who were unable to foresee the complex political implications of the British–Muslim or the Hindu–Muslim context in the sub-continent. During the colonial period they had a negative attitude towards the politics of British–Muslim relations. Instead of preparing to fight the colonialists with their own weapons they withdrew from the scene by 1867 when the Academy for Theology was opened at Deoband and encouraged Islamic rather than Western education. This left the Muslim community backward by the standards of Western education. While the two communities drifted apart some of the ulema were still preoccupied with reconciling Islam with nationalism, while others issued a 'fatwa' (religious edict) declaring that Jinnah was 'Kafir-i-Azam' (the great heathen) and that Muslims should not join the Muslim League.[31]

Ironically, it was left to a Westernized person like Jinnah to reconcile such differences of opinion, so that the religious elite (RE) majority could work with an inspired zeal to make a success of the nationalist movement. The fastest means of political communication in the South Asian context has been through the use of political slogans, and the political mobilization of the masses was greatly aided by slogans such as 'Islam in Danger'. Such ideological reinforcement, reminding them of their past glories, transformed the nationalist Muslims into Muslim nationalists.

The Dimension of Identification

The Muslims, politicized by the negative implications for them of democracy and mobilized by the perception of the threat to Islam, now needed a concrete platform of action. In other words, they needed to identify with a Muslim homeland. A Muslim student from Cambridge coined the word 'Pakistan' in 1933, and this was adopted by the Muslim League.[32] A country's name was attached to a community, and Jinnah declared in the Lahore Resolution (1940) that the Muslim minority was a 'nation by any definition'.[33] The state was yet to exist.

Jinnah's two-nation theory, propagated in 1940, was not accepted by the Hindus who abominated the idea of a divided India. Jinnah, however, felt that 'India is not a nation, nor a country. It is a sub-continent composed of nationalities, Hindus and Muslims being the major nations.'[34] To understand Jinnah's two-nation theory one has to discern the multiple functional levels of Islam, one of which was its distinct cultural way of life. Jinnah emphasized this distinction when he stated that Islam and Hinduism

> are not religions in the strict sense of the word, but are, in fact,
> different and distinct social orders, and it is a dream that the Hindus
> and Muslims can ever evolve a common nationality, and this

conception of one Indian nation has gone far beyond the limits . . .
and will lead India to destruction if we fail to reverse our notions in
time. The Hindus and Muslims belong to two different religious
philosophies, social customs and literatures. They neither marry nor
dine together and indeed, they belong to two different civilizations
which are based mainly on conflicting ideas and conceptions. Their
aspects on life and of life are different. It is quite clear that Hindus
and Muslims derive their inspiration from different sources of history.
They have different epics, different heroes and different episodes.
Very often, the hero of one is the foe of the other and, likewise, their
victories and defeats overlap.[35]

Despite cultural diffusion over the years the Hindus and Muslims
had maintained their separate identities and had never evolved into
one nation. Jinnah's role in this situation was unique for he was not a
religious reformer like Sirhindi or Waliullah, trying to bring religion
to his followers. On the contrary, his logic was that the loss of
religion meant the loss of a way of life which would affect the
identity of a Muslim. As such, a homeland was necessary to maintain this identity which emanated from Islam.[36] Jinnah was therefore a man of revolutionary orientation whose life-work (Pakistan)
and not life-style (Westernized) was important.

Very few paid any attention to Jinnah's three-worded
motto — unity, faith and discipline — which reflected his Islamic
life-work. Many observers mistakenly believe that Jinnah was anti-
religion because he was Westernized. On the contrary, Jinnah perceived Islam as a religious system whose central beliefs identified its
adherents as Muslims (faith). Secondly, it provided a politico-
cultural system which integrated the Muslims into a nation-state
(unity). Lastly, it provided an ideological system whose principles
could politically socialize the Muslims (discipline). In other words,
the process of Islamicization was the key to the Pakistanization of
the ideological state.

Every time the slogan 'Pakistan Zindabad' was shouted, it reinforced the identity of the Muslims to the state. Muslim cultural
nationalism, with Islam as the central core of its socio-cultural
reality, had a religious and not a secular base. Jinnah used the force
of Islam to mobilize the Muslim community, and as the elites and
masses could identify with Islam, the state-to-be could not have
come into existence without it. The creation of a Muslim nation was
necessary in theory to preserve Islam, but in actuality it could only
be done through the creation of Pakistan for the Muslim minority.
Jinnah negociated Pakistan by identifying Islam with Pakistan.

Islam and the Ideological State

Islam, it should be noted, was a code of human development. It specified man's relations with God and man's relations with other human beings. The latter led to the establishment of a community of believers. Islam was therefore not a private relationship between man and God, but a set of religious, social, military, economic and political relations. It was a divine order for implementation in the community of believers and, as such, it created a criterion or standard in any Muslim society. In a society where no community is immune to the influences of other religions and cultures, it is necessary to delineate the general features of the ideological state.

In its ideal form, the ideological state was ideological not only because it was 'founded in large part of sentiments of a religion'[37] but because without religion, the existence of the state as a homeland for the Muslims was not justifiable. After all, there were just as many Muslims in India (60 million) as there were in Pakistan. What, then, did the Pakistani Muslims have that the Indian Muslims lacked? The former would have their national identity rooted in an ideological state. Such a state would have a dynamic ideology with the freedom to range from conservative to revolutionary orientations within the limits prescribed by the Quran. (See Fig. 1.)

The conservative oriented persons were blind followers of the Quran. The revolutionary orientation, on the other hand, gave a more liberal interpretation of the Quran. They emphasized the situational demands of the time period in which it was being implemented. (The term revolution is being used in the religious context and should be distinguished from political revolutions.) However, both orientations had to be legitimized by Quranic revelatory parameters and any attempt to go beyond these parameters would lead to the secularization of the political system. This in turn would create serious contradictions within the system by placing human law above divine laws.

Furthermore, in the ideological state sovereignty resided in Allah, and the laws of the Quran and Sharia were to be implemented within the territorial boundaries of the state. The political elites were to act as the agents (khalifa) of God and implement the Islamic order. Where such elites could not discharge their duties to the community (umma) satisfactorily, as judged by Islamic criteria, they could be removed from office. The relationship between the rulers and ruled was egalitarian and no one could make laws to benefit their own vested interests. In this sense the

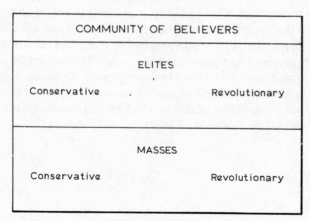

Fig 1:The Ideological State

Islamic order was democratic and its principles upheld the collective good of the community.

The concept of an ideological state, however, was incompatible with that of a secular or a communist state. A secular state guaranteed the individual's freedom of religion,[38] whereas the ideological state required that only a Muslim was eligible to be the head of state. It could therefore only operate within the framework of Islam. In a communist state, religion was completely eliminated from the political system and it was thus opposed to the concept of an ideological state. Certain similarities between Islam and communism have been observed, because they

> are concerned with life on earth. Islam and communism therefore deal with economic existence and its control by the state. Both have scorn for the rich. Both aim at a classless society and equalization of wealth, though by different methods. Both are critical of aspects of capitalism and the institution of inheritance. Both advocate certain forms of communalism and collectivism. Social reform, land reforms and economic justice are prominent tenets of Islam and favourite topics of communist propaganda . . . Muslims and communists are imbued with a pronounced sense of the righteousness of their conviction and possessed by a missionary spirit. Finally, in spite of the democratic aspects of the ideal Islamic polity, historically the Muslim world has known few liberal and many autocratic states.[39]

But the two systems, the one monotheistic and the other atheistic, are clearly fundamentally at odds with each other.

One must be careful at this stage not to confuse the ideal Islamic system with the real. As long as the former was present, as it would always be, the real would have to converge towards it to find its identity. But since human societies do not exist in isolation, old sets of human relationships (feudalism) had lingered on even when new ones (capitalism) had penetrated the society through colonialism. Those vested interests inclined towards capitalism rationalized that the Islamic system was past-oriented because it required them to give up the exploitative system in which their status quo was maintained and allow a more egalitarian system to prevail.

2

The Political System

Pakistan has presented a particularly difficult case for political analysis. Analysts have often been carried away by attempts to prove their theories rather than try and discern the political realities inherent in its political creation. Pakistan belongs to that rare category which we have named the 'ideological state', a term which does not easily lend itself to comparison with non-ideological states.

In non-ideological states, political and economic development proceed along secular lines. In the ideological state, on the other hand, political and economic development is along moral lines. Such a system, therefore, cannot be analysed according to traditional/modern dichotomies but rather by real/ideal ones. The ideal, in ideological states, exists internally and until the real coincides with it the basic contradictions of the ideological society will remain. This does not mean that other contradictions do not exist, but they can be approached from the point of 'oneness', that is, through the unification of the ideal and real.

Ideological states also present another difficulty and modernization theorists often fall into 'surface traps' in studying the politics of countries like Pakistan. On the political surface one finds many political parties, a constitution, a parliament with two houses, voting and general elections and all the visible structures of a Western democracy. By making detailed analysis of these structures it is concluded that a 'democracy' approaching Western standards is 'progressing' in a Third World country. Such attitudes, implicitly or explicitly, have an inbuilt bias because they assume that Western political structures and institutions are the highest goals that all countries must aspire for.

Such studies, therefore, either ignore or are unaware of the ideals which may exist in the internal reality. On the contrary, ideals have often been imported from Western countries and imposed on Third World countries without first inquiring whether the country may want to be Westernized or not.

Political Stratification and Political Elites

In order to understand Pakistan's political system one must first study how far the real had deviated from the ideal. The 'real' context contained the heritage of the former feudal and colonial political orders. The truth of the Pakistani proverb 'an elephant has two sets of teeth, one for eating and the other for showing' is relevant here. Political parties and other Westernized structures represent the set of teeth for showing. One would have to look beneath the surface to find the real set of teeth for biting. For such an investigation the relevant questions would be: Who were the real power-holders in Pakistan? Where did they come from? What were their vested interests? How was the political and economic power distributed among them? What strategies did they use to acquire this power? What were their political resources? The answers to these questions unravel the political stratification of Pakistani society. There is revealed a four-tier system which had political parties on the surface, followed by elites, structures and systems.

Political parties, in the Pakistani context, were organizations for the enhancement or extension of the interests of power-holders. On the second level were the power-holders themselves, the elites in the political system. These political elites are of central concern and constitute the main unit of analysis of this study. They existed within a plurality of contexts, two of which, the societal and spatial, are relevant here. In the societal context, the elites were related to the ethnic social structures of Pakistan. In the spatial context were the real modes of production (feudal and capitalist) and the ideal mode of production (Islamic) which visibly or invisibly existed in the external reality.

The general frame of reference of this study rests on two propositions which apply to all societies. The first is that every society can be divided into those who govern and those who are governed. The number of men who govern, the political organization and the political ideology may differ from state to state. Secondly, in every society political power is differentially distributed in the political system.

Political elites, as stated earlier, are the power-holders in the body politic. In the general sense, political elites refers here to all those persons who possess more power or political influence than the non-elites (the masses). Governing elites, on the other hand, specifically refers to those persons who occupy leading positions in the political arena and exercise power. The political arena, where the governing elites are concentrated and where most of the high level decision-making take place, is the Central Cabinet of the Pakistan government.

The following methodology was found to be useful for identifying these elites. A list was compiled of all the governor-generals, presidents, prime ministers, and central cabinet ministers from August 1947 to January 1978. The occupational backgrounds of those joining the central cabinets was treated as the prime indicator of the elite groups to which these men belonged. Where more than one occupation was involved, the main source of livelihood was taken as the dominant occupation. The results revealed a plural set of elite groups, summarized in Table 1.

Table 1: REPRESENTATION OF ELITE GROUPS IN THE POLITICAL ARENA 1947–1978

Elite Group	Number in each Central Government Cabinet						
	1949–1958	1958–1969	1969–1971	1971–1977	1977–1978	Total	% of Total
LE	40	10	2	6	4	62	25.2
BE	15	19	2	0	4	40	16.2
RE	0	0	0	1	0	1	0.4
IE	7	2	2	1	1	13	5.3
PE	52	27	4	10	4	97	39.5
ME	1	12	9	0	11	33	13.4
Total	115	70	19	18	24	246	100.0

Sources:
S. Mahmood, *The Deliberate Debacle* (Lahore: Sh. Md. Ashraf, 1976), pp. 144–56. A. S. Banks, *Political Handbook of the World 1977* (New York: McGraw–Hill 1977) p. 296. Circular Ministry of Foreign Affairs, External Publicity Directorate, No. 22/76 E. P. Islamabad, 9 February 1976. *Dawn* (Karachi), 5 July 1977. *Dawn* (Karachi), 15 January 1978

Note:
 (i) Only the president, prime ministers, governors-general, martial law administrators and central cabinet ministers were included in the list.
 (ii) Each list was compiled at one point in time, usually when the changes of government led to the formation of new Central Cabinets.
 (iii) The ministers and heads of state who remained in office in the reconstituted cabinets were counted again.

Two observations ought to be made to clarify this elite analysis. First, the data indicate that some elite groups (e.g. the professional elites) had a greater representation among the political elites than others. This did not necessarily mean that they exercised greater power than the other elite groups. Thus the military and religious elites, despite their insignificant representation, were powerful elite groups. Secondly, all the governing elites were not equally powerful even though their positions within the political arena gave them greater access to the use of power and political influence. Furthermore, according to the period to which their political and historical origins can be traced, each elite group was related to the others. At certain times some elite groups had common origins, though in the post-Independent stage there was conflict when one's interests were threatened by another. Thus the LE and RE issued from the traditional period and are classified as traditional elites. The ME and BE stemmed from colonial period, and the IE and PE from the post-Independent period (see Table 2).

Table 2: HISTORICAL ORIGINS OF ELITE GROUPS 1947–1978

Historical Linkage	Elite Groups
Traditional	Landowning Elites Religious Elites
Colonial	Bureaucratic Elites Military Elites
Emergent	Industrial Elites Professional Elites

The titles 'traditional', 'colonial' and 'emergent' used in the study denote time-specific relationships in the historical context. Traditional thus refers to the period of Muslim rule, colonial to the period of British rule (since their formal takeover of India in 1857) and emergent elites were those that became politically active in the post-1947 period.

Stated simply, the Pakistani political system is an elitist one in which there was a small number who rule and a majority who are ruled. Those who rule are the political elites and those who are ruled are the non-elites or the masses and the middle sectors. (The power structure of the political elites of Pakistan can be depicted as the model shown in Fig. 2).

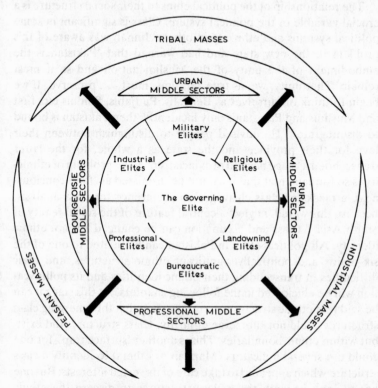

Fig. 2: The power structure of the political elites in Pakistan. Source: A. Hussain, 'Elites and Political Development in Pakistan, *The Developing Economies*, vol. xiv, no. 3 (September 1976), p. 225.

Political Alliances and Social Structure

Two types of relationship operate within the political system which are used to mobilize resources for exercising power or influence over others. Temporary relationships are formed through horizontal and vertical alliances.[1] On the other hand, permanent relationships link the political elites to the social structures to which they belong. Horizontal alliances link elite groups with one another and vertical alliances link the elites with the non-elites or masses. The political elites always try to form such alliances, but at no time has any inter-elite or elite–mass consensus been visible in the political system of Pakistan. These alliances are formed through processes such as coalitions, compromises, corruption or coercion.

The relationship of the political elites to their social structure is a crucial variable of the political system. Class is significant in some political systems and ethnicity in others. Jinnah was aware of this problem in the new state and had warned that 'Pakistan is the embodiment of the unity of the Muslim nation and so it must remain. That unity, we, as true Muslims, must . . . preserve. If we begin to think of ourselves as Bengalis, Punjabis, Sindhis etc. first and Muslims and Pakistanis only incidently, then Pakistan is bound to disintegrate.'[2] He advised people to distinguish between their love for their province and the state as a whole, for the latter transcended a 'stage beyond provincialism'.[3] The problem of ethnicity is so fundamental that it cannot be dismissed as 'false conciousness, a mask for class cleavages' in preference for class analysis, because this would 'neglect a central feature of the social reality of South Asia.'[4] Class and occupation can be changed but not ethnic identity. All political elites in Pakistan can be related to one of the six major and politically significant ethnic structures, and their difficulties in transcending their ethnic identities and its politicization will be elucidated in the following chapters. At this stage it can be said that ethnic structures were so strong that the emerging class structures could not submerge ethnicity. Class structures did exist, but within ethnic boundaries. This is another 'surface trap', for one could use several indicators (Marxian or others) to identify a class structure which appeared to take care of its vested interests. But one has to look beneath these class structures to discern the ethnic polarization of the political elites. The relationship of the political elites with their ethnic structures is briefly sketched below.

The East Bengalis

The East Bengalis were the largest ethnic group in Pakistan prior to 1971 and constituted 50.8 per cent of the total population. The province had a high degree of ethnic homogeneity with a distinct language and literature of which the Bengalis were very proud. The vast majority of the population was rural and the average population density was 920 persons per square mile. The standard of living was relatively low. The growing and processing of jute was the only important agricultural industry. Increased migration towards the urban centres of Dacca, Chittagong and Chalna had resulted in inevitable overcrowding, unemployment and the growth of unmanageable slums. The East Bengalis were involved in the civil war of 1971 which had led to the creation of Bangladesh. They were strongly represented in the PE group but not in any significant numbers in other elite groups.

The Punjabis

Before 1971 the Punjabis were the second largest ethnic group in Pakistan. After the separation of Bangladesh the Punjabis emerged as the largest ethnic group, making up 57.5 per cent of the entire population of Pakistan (1972 Census). Their political strength lay in this numerical majority, as in an electoral contest the Punjabi vote could place a candidate in the political arena. In other words, without Punjabi support a regional leader could not become a national leader.

The Punjabis had had a close association with the British and had therefore had more opportunity for further education and consequently a greater social mobility to join the military, bureaucracy and the legal and other professions. Apart from these there was a strong landed aristocracy in the Punjab. The Punjabis were therefore politically very active in the LE, ME, BE and PE groups.

The Sindhis

The Sindhis constituted 21.5 per cent of the entire population of Pakistan in the 1972 Census. The Sindhi elites had ruled the province until 1845 when the British conquered it. They were characterized as amiable, hospitable and 'less doctrinaire than their northern neighbours.'[5] Historically the province was important for two reasons. First, the ancient river Indus flowed through it and it was the site of the five thousand-year-old Mohenjodaro civilization with which some Sindhis strongly identified. Secondly, Islam had formally entered the sub-continent through the Arab conquest of Sind.

The Sindhis were well represented in the LE group, and Mr Bhutto was the first Sindhi landlord to control the political arena. Under his rule Sindhi identity began to take an ethnic nationalist trend.

Sindhi ethnicity had become politicized for two reasons. First, the Punjabi domination of the LE and PE had not given them much access to the political arena until 1967. Some Sindhis met by the author were radical advocates of the Sindhdesh movement and

strongly inclined towards ethnic nationalism. Secondly, the Muhajirs in Sind were economically powerful and this ignited ethnic
rivalry and jealousy with the Sindhis who considered themselves as
the true sons of the soil.

The Pathans

The Pathans constituted 13 per cent of the total population of
Pakistan in the 1972 Census. The tribal areas represented another 4
per cent of the population (these were known as the 'ghair ilagas', or
outside settled districts). Their feudalistic tribal structure revolved
around the tribal code of 'Paktoonwali' which embodied the principles of 'badal' (vengeance), 'melmastia' (hospitality) and 'nana-
wati' (asylum for fugitives and provision for truces). These were
widely practised and operationalized by the tribal 'jirgas' (assembly
of elders).[6]

Studies show that Pathan ethinic identity was strongly established in their belief in the kinship system and a patrilineal descent
traced to a common ancestor.[7] Pathan social organization was
divided into the 'nang' and 'qalang' categories which depicted their
life-styles in the socio-political and economic spheres.[8] The Pathans
were proud of their history and warrior-like traditions. Their anti-
colonial movement led by Khan Abdul Ghaffar Khan was known as
the 'Kudai–Khidmatgars'[9] He emphasized that Pakistan could only
become Islamic if the governing elite had the commitment and
honesty of purpose of men like Caliph Abu Bakr (632–34), Caliph
Umar (634–44), Caliph Othman (644–56) and Caliph Ali
(656–61).[10]

The Pathans were well represented in the LE and ME, but
Punjabi domination had pushed them into secondary roles. This
denial of access to the political arena had made the Pathans ethnically conscious.

The Baluchis

According to the 1972 Census, the Baluchis constituted 3.7 per
cent of the entire population of Pakistan. Some of the Baluchi
tribes, like the Bizenjos, Maaris, Bugtis and Mengals, were highly
politicized.[11]

The province was rich in mineral resources and contributed
substantial revenue to the government, but it was the least industri-
ally developed province. The Baluchis felt exploited as they were
given meagre returns for their resources.[12] The governing elites, on
the other hand, accused them of feudalism, backwardness, tribalism

and tribal chieftainism, and tried to subjugate them.[13] Ayub had used the military to suppress them in 1958 and 1963; Bhutto had done the same in 1974. Owing to such harsh policies the Baluchis became very conscious of their ethnicity.

The Baluchis had no access to the political arena and were only represented in the LE group. Within this group they formed alliances with the Pathans and political parties like the National Awami Party (NAP). This province had also shown separatist tendencies through the Baluchistan Liberation Movement. How such ethnicity became politicized will be explained later.

The Muhajirs

The Muhajirs were those people who had migrated from India to Pakistan at the time of Partition. The 1951 Census figure for all Pakistan had estimated that about 7 million people had migrated from India.[14] Large numbers came after that period and settled in Sind (particularly in Karachi), and on average were estimated to constitute fifty per cent of the Sindhi population.[15] Furthermore, the Muhajirs were of different types: some belonged to the same ethnic groups (West Bengali Muslims migrated to East Bengal and the East Punjabi Muslims migrated to West Punjab), others came from different regions, notable among whom were the Gujaratis. The Muhajirs also came from the United Provinces, and this group related to the Mughal cultural heritage of Delhi and Lucknow.

They lacked a territorial base, and their concentration in Sind created ethnic conflict with the Sindhis. They spoke Urdu and were very ethically conscious. Before 1971, although spoken by only 3.65 per cent of the Pakistani population, they wanted Urdu to be declared as the national language (inspite of the fact that Bengali was spoken by over 55.48 per cent). The proposition was strongly opposed by the Bengalis. Even in post-1971 Pakistan, Sind has been involved in language riots when the provincial government made Sindhi the medium of instruction in educational institutions. The Bhutto regime, however, upheld the Sindhi decision, and the Muhajirs were given a twelve-year period in which to learn the Sindhi language. The Muhajirs were dissatisfied with such a compromise, while the Sindhis were further frustrated since the former were well represented in the BE, ME, PE, RE and IE.

In the last tier were the systems (feudalism, capitalism) which had been generated by the historical processes. The development of the ideological state has been discussed in the previous chapter. The traditional, colonial and emergent elites constantly endeavoured to safeguard their own vested interests through maximizing political power. This resulted in a struggle for power which did not promote elite consensus but elite conflict.

Power and the Political System

Political power and political influence were the most important variables permeating the Pakistani political system. Political survival was difficult without the possession of either, that is, an elite group that did not wield power or influence would not be allowed political participation nor to derive economic benefits. It is therefore essential to examine the nature of power and influence and their distribution among the political and governing elites.

The literature on political power is extensive, and without going into any of the debates on a definition of the term the following operational definition serves the purpose of this study. Political power is the social capacity to mobilize resources for the realization of one's goals with recourse to sanctions.[16] Political influence, on the other hand, is the ability to mobilize resources.[17] The term social capacity refers to power as a relationship between individuals and groups, not a quality or an inherent characteristic possessed by them. Capacity also implies that power is potential rather than actual, that is, it can be used as an occupant of a position, but not necessarily.[18] The term resources refers to anything ranging from wealth, skills, ideologies, foreign aid, friendship, social status and religion to an ability for coercion (strikes, assassinations, etc.).

Power and influence can be placed on the opposite ends of a continuum. 'Influence' is 'power when exercised by those not having authority'.[19] Authority is the 'occupancy of a formal leadership role such as the Presidency, which is accepted by other actors in a given situation ...'[20] Political elites who may have only wielded influence (Bhutto as a member of Ayub's Cabinet) could thus become just as powerful (Bhutto as leader of the Pakistan People's Party or PPP) outside the political arena.

Power was therefore relatively distributed among the various elite groups. The greater the capacity to mobilize resources through horizontal and vertical alliances, the greater the sanctions which could be imposed. New modes of entry for elite circulation were opened up as alliances recruited new elites and aligned themselves against those to be deprived of power. The nature of the sanctions (through mobilization of resources) and their extent (vertical and horizontal alliances) were crucial in determining the outcome of the struggle for power. Some leaders like Ayub resigned, others like Bhutto had to be removed.

Power and influence structures were therefore both operating in the political system. Governing elites often resorted to the use of power through the authority vested in their positions. On the other hand, depending on what resources had been mobilized by the political elites, the legitimacy of such authority could be paralysed (e.g. Pakistan National Alliance pleas to the military to remove Bhutto after the March 1977 elections). The constant endeavours of the political and governing elites to maximize their power and the strategies employed by them will be discussed in detail below.

3

The Landowning Elites

Agriculture is the mainstay of Pakistan's economy, and its agrarian peoples comprised 86.9 per cent of the total population in 1961.[1] Furthermore, some 90 per cent of the people lived in villages and 75 per cent were engaged in the agrarian way of life.[2] The landowning elite (LE) are the product of this agrarian stratification system, and their political socialization and political ideologies have created a political style which can be labelled 'feudal'. This style is a predominant part of the political system of Pakistan and its characteristics will be elucidated in this chapter.

The LE involvement with the political system of Pakistan can be linked to their role in pre-Partition politics. But even in pre-Partition times, it is important to note that their politicization was not due to the threat posed by colonialism but from the Indian National Congress which tended towards the communalization of politics. This concern led the LE to join the All India Muslim League in 1906. Their association with the League did not turn it into a mass-oriented nationalist movement. On the contrary, by 1935 (when Jinnah took over its leadership) it had degenerated into an exclusive cartel based on 'drawing room' politics where intrigues were conducted. Under Jinnah's leadership, however, the LE's parochial political attitudes were harnessed to mobilize support for the Muslim League and make it into a nationalist movement. Their key positions in the provincial leagues (particularly in the Punjab and United Provinces), were instrumental in the creation of Pakistan.

Like the IE, the LE had found the new state ideal for their political purposes. Their predominance in the political system gave it a feudal stamp which obstructed democratic growth. In effect they treated Pakistan (in its geographical sense) as part of their personal landed estates. Since no one could question their activities, politics became a national pastime rather than a national responsibility. How the LE mobilized their resources and influenced the political system will now be discussed.

The Feudal Mode of Production

The emergence of the LE in Pakistan took place owing to the premium placed on land by the traditional structure of Indo-Pakistani society. By right of conquest the Mughal elites had extended their rule over the whole of India. In the jagirdari system, under the Mughals, the jagirdars were invested with authority from the emperor to collect revenues from a group of villages. A part of this revenue was kept by the jagirdar and the rest sent to the imperial treasury.[3] These jagirdars, as stated above, could be transferred from one jagir to another within the empire and consequently they failed to develop into a class with vested interests in the land.

The colonial government, on the other hand, was interested in creating a new class loyal to the empire. They could not develop a class structure but did succeed in forming elite groups. Such elite groups were the result of different land tenure systems implemented in different regions of the empire, based on the relationship between state and landholder.

Where the colonial state dealt directly with the landholders, different systems like the zamindari, ryotwari, mahalwari or bhaichara[4] were created as the institutional framework within which the tenure system operated. In the zamindari system, sole proprietary rights were bestowed on individuals who in turn paid a fixed revenue to the government. This class of landlord was particularly loyal to the British Empire. In the ryotwari system, the ryot was merely an occupant of the land so long as he paid land revenue to the government. In the mahalwari and bhaichara systems a group of villages formed a collective body of co-sharers who were treated as landlords, and the lambardar (headman) was responsible for the payment of land revenue to the government.

All these colonial land tenure systems were essentially political strategies for entrenching colonial power in the sub-continent so that colonial rule could be imposed without constant force. They were also intended to prevent a repetition of the mass uprising of

1857 headed by the Muslim and Hindu royalty and nobility which had revolted against the British. Besides, the Punjab and Sind, which had been annexed to the empire in 1840s were strategically important for preventing an external invasion from Afghanistan or the Czarist empire. The zamindars in these areas were feudal lords, the colonial government not interfering in the personal administration of their estates. On the contrary, the wealth and power of these elites was further strengthened by the development of vast irrigation schemes which increased the agricultural productivity of their lands. Such productivity was beneficial both to the LE and the colonial rulers. The Punjab province was also used for the recruitment of manpower for the British Indian Army (BIA), and the landlords actively assisted the British.[5] The Punjabi regiments were known for their valour and it was a Punjabi Muslim who won the first Victoria Cross to be awarded to an Indian.

The province of East Bengal, on the other hand, was characterized by a land tenure system inimical to the control of landlords. The Permanent Settlement of 1793 had allowed Hindus to become landlords, money-lenders, civil servants and businessmen while the Muslims were neglected and remained poverty-stricken peasants. In this system, which operated until 1947, it was shown that of the 2237 large landholders only 358 were Muslims.[6]

This system ultimately collapsed when the Hindu landlords had migrated to India after Partition and the Permanent Settlement was supplanted by the East Bengal State Acquisition and Tenancy Act of 1950. This Act allowed the distribution of these lands to the peasants, preventing the landowning elite from becoming entrenched in that province. Only 2 per cent of the landlords had holdings of 40 acres or over, and the average range was 18 acres.[7]

The Rural Power Structure and the Political System

The land tenure systems characteristic of the feudal mode of production were devised to suit a colonial regime that was interested not in the development of agriculture but only in its raw products and land revenues. To maximize product yield and revenue the relations of production that crystallized in the system were based on the unequal distribution of land and power. The rural power structure of Pakistan was embedded in a system in which the landlord was at one end of the continuum and the peasantry at the other. These will be discussed separately in greater detail in order to emphasize the power enjoyed by the former and the powerlessness of the latter.

The Landlords

The interests of landlords and peasants contradicted each other, the former wanting to maximize their wealth and power at the expense of the latter who had to be kept subordinated. The rural power structure was therefore based on dominant–subordinate relations which encouraged the dependence of one (the peasant) on the other (landlord).

The rural power structure can be further clarified in terms of the scope, primacy and monopoly of the services performed by the landlord.[8] The services were the control of resources available, and the greater their scarcity the more difficult it became for the peasant to acquire them. If the landlord could provide them the peasants would not seek alternative resources. The primacy of these resources was a function of their importance to the existence of the peasant and his family. If his livelihood rested upon them, the peasant would be more dependent on the landlord, and he could not risk nor afford to seek alternatives. The degree of monopoly that the landlord exercised subordinated the peasants towards him. The principal resources included land and the political power wielded by the landlord. Such power could indeed be beneficial to the peasants at times in solving their personal problems but it could also be harmful if the peasants did not obey the dictates of their masters. Thus, the scope, primacy and monopoly of the landlords strengthened their hold over the peasantry, and in many areas of Pakistan the feudal system had not changed in several centuries.

The Land Reforms Commission (1961) was aware of the power of the landlords, and stated in its report that

> Agriculture in Pakistan is not only a source of
> livelihood but a way of living with the rural masses.
> It is natural, therefore, that there should be a
> universal urge for the possession of agricultural
> land. Land, in fact, aside from its economic benefits
> (or perhaps largely because of them) has come to be
> associated with special social values. The status
> of a man on land and his right to the use of land
> also define his social status in society. The
> ownership of land has accordingly come to be regarded
> as a symbol of prestige, its management as an instrument
> of power and its possession as security against want.
> These special attributes of land invests its owner
> with a privileged position in the village (society).

Those who do not own land are relegated to a socially
inferior position with all the disabilities of that
position.[9]

Studies by other scholars have also reinforced the fact that land
was not only a source of the landlords' social status but that the
larger the landholdings the more 'power, prestige and influence'
they would enjoy because they had more tenants dependent on
them, could make more contacts with officials and thereby 'command more people and ... more respect.'[10] The influence of the
landlords was also determined by their expenditure, conspicuous
consumption and generosity being valued highly among the rural
masses.[11] This further increased the prestige of the landlord, and if
'two landlords competed for the same public goal one was more
successful because he enjoyed prestige as well'.[12] The uneven distribution of land had tended to concentrate large landholdings in
the hands of a few families.

Extensive ownership of the means of production was beneficial
to the landlords in two ways. First by appropriating the surplus
labour of the peasantry their financial gain was much greater than
they directly earned and this, in turn, strengthened their class position in their regions and ethnic groups. Secondly, their primacy and
monopoly of services enabled them to use the peasantry as a political resource in electoral contests. With the votes of the peasantry
and other resources, such as time and money, politics became a
regular political activity of the landlords. Their motives for doing so
were not necessarily the national interest, but very often for their
own personal prestige and power within the region. They dominated political parties as well as the provincial and national assemblies of Pakistan. The special type of political resource to which the
landlords had access — the peasantry — must be explored further to
understand the rural power structure.

The Peasant and Tribal Masses

The LE who inhabited the Punjab and Sind exploited the peasantry; the maliks and sardars of various tribes in the NWFP and
Baluchistan dominated the tribal masses. Landlords and tribal
chiefs had a common economic denominator, for both owned large
tracts of land and both exploited the labour of the masses and kept
them at subsistence levels. Both groups also derived their political
power and regional status through domination of the masses.

Recent peasant studies with a Marxian orientation have thrown
light on the stratification in the rural structure of Pakistan. Some of

these studies followed Mao Tse-tung's classification of the Chinese peasantry, and divided the rural society of Pakistan into five groups, using the variable of possession of land.[13] These groups were the big landlords, rich peasants, middle peasants, poor peasants, tenant sharecroppers (who have no land) and rural proletariat (who work for daily wages).[14] Other studies differentiated three sectors emanating from the rural economy.[15] These included landlords, sharecroppers and poor tenants in the first sector, small independent landholders in the second and capitalist farmers and rich peasants in the third.

Another type of study identified landlords and capitalist farmers as those 'who do not themselves work to produce and live exclusively by the exploitation of others'.[16] On the other hand, there were the rich peasants who emulated the landlords even though they could not afford the same life style.

Then come the middle peasants who owned some land but not enough to make both ends meet. The majority of peasants constituted those that depended on rented land and lived at subsistence level, and the peasant proletariat that sold its labour for daily wages.

The above-stratification can be expressed in terms of or fitted into a model of the power structure. Here, the poor peasants or the peasant proletariat come under the heading of peasantry; the rich peasants or the middle peasants are treated as the rural middle sectors, while the landlords and the capitalist farmers are labelled landowing elites. These various studies have all stressed the point made earlier—that is, the most oppressed and exploited group of people in Pakistan was the peasantry.

As early as 1947 and 1948, the condition of the peasantry was said to be such that

> whenever the hari [peasant] is in serious trouble, be it on
> account of his lack of finance, his social relations
> with his fellowmen, his implication in police cases,
> the ill-health of members of his family, the abduction
> of his women, the loss of his bullocks, the procurement
> of his home necessities in consumer goods, the
> recruitment of casual labour to aid him in harvesting
> and weeding his crops or for other reasons, it is to his
> zamindar that he first appeals for help.[17]

Such authority in the hands of unscrupulous landlords made them chart the behavioural course of the peasantry. Even the power of life and death was theirs as neither the Central Government nor the deputy commissioner considered it prudent to interfere radically with local feudal lords. It is not surprising that the writers of the First Five Year Plan stated that 'while taking stock of the conditions in the country one is struck with their similarity to feudalism.'[18]

Some legislative acts, like the Sind Tenancy Act Number XX of 1950 sought to better the lot of the peasantry, but in reality further increased the exploitation of the Sindhi hari (peasant). It stipulated that if a hari cultivated four acres of land continuously for three years for the same landlord he could not be evicted and would be conferred permanent rights.[19] Landlords, however, continued their exploitation and then evicted the peasants on some pretext before the stipulated period ended.

For the peasantry, whether tenant farmers or farm labourers, three things mattered: security of life, property and livelihood.[20] Security of life was at stake because 'villages in Pakistan are not really subject to the law of the land',[21] and as such, the peasants were vulnerable to violence from the chaudhri (village notables) or the landlords. These clashes ranged from disputes over land to those over women. For the security of property for whatever meagre possessions he owned, the peasant was more often than not in debt. The security of livelihood was almost non-existent because of the following prevailing conditions:

(a)   the name of the tenant was not recorded in any register of the patwari [revenue department functionary] so he could be evicted by the landlord without getting any share of the crop he had raised.

(b)   the landlord did not give a receipt for his share of the crops received and evicted the tenant for non-fulfilment of the contract;

(c)   peasants were often evicted by force;

(d)   landlords refused to accept their share of the crops, thus causing a wastage which the tenant could ill afford and paving the way for his eviction.[22]

The farm labourer was often paid in kind and his pay was so low that to survive he had to take some produce on loan when his stock ran out. Loans were given to him at the rate of the commodity in a season of scarcity and was taken back from him at the time when the commodity was available in plenty. In this way his debt tripled and made the farm labourer a virtual slave of the landowner. For this unfortunate citizen of Pakistan there were 'neither working hours nor a minimal wage', and he could be 'removed from service at the whim of the master.'[23]

By subjecting the peasantry to life at subsistence levels, the landlords not only exploited their labour but also used their votes to enhance their own position. According to one study, the majority of the peasants voted as they were directed by the LE or through the pressure of their friends and baradaries.[24] Simply to survive, the peasantry was forced to support the landlord of the region.

Tribal society was segmented. It was also elitist in nature and very insular as compared to the peasantry. It was thus easier to approach a peasant from the Punjab than a tribesman from the NWFP or Baluchistan. A Baluchi tribesman would listen to his tribal sardar and no one else. As such, Pehrson points out, the

> Sardar is the central and unifying leader, who by his existence creates the Marri tribe and who for formal purposes is regarded as the fount of all legitimate power in the tribe. The common attitude of respect for the Sardar, often approaching awe and ascribing magical and superhuman qualities to the person of the Sardar, is very striking.[25]

The largest tribal mass was estimated at 2.5 million in the NWFP. There were seven tribal agencies (Mohmand, Orakzai, North Waziristan, South Waziristan, Khyber, Khurram and Bajaur),[26] and these tribal areas had always been administered by the Central Government through its governors and political agents. The government also refrained from interfering with the tribal way of life. Tribal representatives had some seats reserved for them in the National Assembly and they were allowed to vote on all legislation even when it did not apply to them. The government turned a blind eye to the smuggling that went on across the borders of these regions. The smuggling centres at Bara and Landikotal flourished on this business and provided the luxury goods desired by the rich throughout Pakistan.

The prime interest of the governing elites was to secure the political co-operation of the tribal maliks and sardars, and the vicious circle was perpetuated from top (elite exploitation of the chiefs) to bottom (chiefs exploiting the masses). Tribal chiefs did not form one united class but were factionalized and, as stated above, this made it easier for the governing elites to divide and rule. Thus, on one hand, the tribal chiefs lived off the labour of their tribal masses and, on the other, they made no effort to distribute the concessions derived from the governing elites among their tribes.

The Feudal Political Order

The significance of the feudal political order cannot be analysed in a vacuum. It must be remembered that the political system of Pakistan was rooted in a context characterized by a feudal mode of production. This had not only led to the stratification of the system, as discussed earlier, but also to the evolution of the feudal political order.

This order could be compared to the law of the jungle where two animals may recognize each other as belonging to the same species, but would fight fiercely to retain control over their resources. In other words, the political socialization of the LE conflicted with the requirements of democratic processes. As elected members of the National Assemblies they were supposedly open to criticism from the opposition members and were expected to fulfil obligations towards their electorate. But once elected they found it extremely difficult to discharge their duties strictly in terms of the national interest.

The tribal and provincial areas from which the LE had originated had long-established norms consistent with ethnic loyalties. Many of the LE were often semi-literate, but some were highly educated with degrees from their own as well as foreign universities. However, despite of their sophisticated education and acculturation to urban life styles, their methods of governing remained feudal. Murders, rapes, kidnappings and threats were part of the coercive strategies employed by them to subordinate their political rivals. Horizontal and vertical alliances were only made to maximize personal power and vested interests.

The period between 1949 amd 1951 was so typified by political anarchy that provincial governments had to be suspended and placed under Governor's Rule. There was a total lack of political ethics in the struggle for political power and position. Thus, clashes between Noons and Daultanas and other elite factions were common in the Punjab.[27] As a result several top-level changes took place between 1947 and 1955. The Mamdot ministry gave way to the Daultana faction which in turn yielded to Feroz Khan Noon.

Such feudal politics also characterized the Provincial Assembly in Sind where rival elite factions led to the formation of seven ministries under the chief ministerships of Khuhro (1947–8), Pir Illahi Baksh (1948–9), Yusuf Haroon (1949–50), Kazi Fazlullah (1950–1), Khuhro (1951), Pirzada Abdus Sattar (1953–4) and Khuhro (1954–5). Between 1952 and 1953 parliamentary government was suspended by the BE. Party loyalties changed quickly in the province too, and in the struggle for political power a parallel Muslim League was created in Sind which nominated its own candidates to oppose those proposed by the Muslim League.[28] LE factions could form a ministry one day because of the backing of a majority only to be displaced by a rival faction the next. Political rewards were used to sway the loyalties of the supporters from one faction to another. Deposed leaders formed opposition parties and in their struggle for power challenged members of their previous parties. Some even made reforms that would adversely affect their landed interests, such as those introduced by the Daultana ministry in 1952 and anulled by the Noon ministry in 1953.[29]

The internecine quarrels and personal feuds of the LE factions were part of the feudal political culture which revolved around the acquisition of 'takat' (power) and 'izzat' (honour), often through 'badla' (revenge). In such a culture, individuals mattered more than organizations.

Jinnah (a Khoja) could not be accused of being ethnically conscious because he identified with Islam as a Muslim leader. But even Jinnah was bewildered by the provincial politics of the dominant LE group and was apprehensive of its ethnic impact on the future politics of Pakistan. He had therefore warned that

> the enemies of Pakistan have now turned their attention to disrupt the state by creating a split among the Muslims of Pakistan. These attempts have taken the shape principally of encouraging provincialism. As long as you do not throw off this position in our body politic, you will never be able to weld yourself, mould yourself, galvanize yourself into a real and true nation. What we want is not to talk about Bengali, Punjabi, Sindhi, Baluchi, Pathan and so on. . . . We are Muslims, Islam has taught us this, and I think you will agree with me that whatever else you may be and whatever you are, you are a Muslim. You belong to a nation now . . . it does not belong to a Sindhi, Pathan or Bengali, it is yours . . . therefore if you want to build yourself up into a nation, for God's sake give us provincialism.[30]

Liaquat lacked charisma and as such could not replace Jinnah. As a muhajir he was considered an outsider. Jinnah could command through his speeches, but Liaquat, unsure of the support of the Punjabi LE dominating the Muslim League, had to enact such political instruments as the PRODA (Public and Representative Offices Disqualification Act 1949) to control other elite groups.

It must be noted that parliaments and political parties were Western political institutions which did not evolve through indigenous conventions but were foisted on the sub-continent by colonial rulers. They were meant to align collaborators which never reached the masses. Under this the facade of 'democracy' the LE perpetuated their feudal politics within political parties which could not function. Since Jinnah's time, the head of state had also remained the head of his political party. (Jinnah had acted as governor-general as well as president of the Muslim League.) After Jinnah, Chaudhri Khaliquzzaman became the president of the Muslim League and he nominated the prime minister to head the working committee of the party. The question then arose whether a prime minister could thus participate in the Muslim League and yet refuse to abide by its decision as head of government?[31] Notwithstanding objections Liaquat, Nazimuddin and Bogra all held these dual positions. These arrangements suited the Punjabi LE who dominated the League's politics. For them, the prime minister as head of the majority party had to rely on their support in the legislature and could possibly become a political tool in their hands. Since Nazimuddin and Bogra both lacked independent political bases among the masses and elites, they were most vulnerable to such political pressures and had to toe the party line.

During the period 1951–8 the BE were in continuous conflict with the LE, who as elected representatives wielded tremendous political influence (see chapters 4 and 7). They successfully managed to safeguard their economic power in the Constitution of 1956 which incorporated a clause stating that 'No person shall be deprived of his property in accordance with the law. Compulsory acquisition only for public purposes and on payment of compensation. Existing laws and some special categories are not affected by these reconstructions.'[32]

Furthermore, all such reforms made to secure the rights of the peasantry left such loopholes which in turn preserved the privileges of the zamindars. In fact, the 'landlords subverted all attempts at a more national distribution of the land through the influence they exercised over the political parties . . .' and 'democracy could never have a chance so long as the big landlords enjoyed protected constituencies, immune to any pressure of public opinion'.[33] The LE has thus managed to keep its political power intact.

Towards the end of the decade an LE member of the Republican Party was appointed as prime minister (Feroz Khan Noon, Dec. 1957 to Oct. 1958). Noon was a staunch supporter of feudalism and openly maintained that it was a stabilizing force in Pakistan. He opposed any feudal reforms, stating that 'most advocates of land reforms were city dwellers who had no knowledge of agriculture and not many of them know what they are talking about.'[34] Noon, however, was not very efficient at the task of exerting political control over the country other than safeguarding the vested interests of the LE. The Mirza regime soon had to search for a stronger alliance, and formed one with the ME. This proved to be a danger-ous step for them since the military regime was the first to introduce land reforms in Pakistan.

The Politics of Agrarian Reforms

Agrarian reforms that would produce a just distribution of land between landlords and peasants are still a long way off in Pakistan. However, it must be said to the credit of the first military regime that it did initiate such reforms. The reforms of 1959 and 1972 will be discussed in the following sections.

The Land Reforms of 1959

The land reforms devised by the ME allowed the LE to own only 500 acres of irrigated land and 1000 acres of unirrigated land per person. Special concessions were made whereby they could retain their orchards of up to 150 acres as well as stud and livestock farms, if any, over and above the limits placed on their holdings. They could gift land to members of their family. Furthermore, these land reforms attempted to secure the livelihood of peasants. Certain provisions provided against the eviction of peasants unless they failed to pay their rent, cultivate the land, used it improperly or sub-let it. The land reforms also revealed the uneven distribution of land in the agrarian structure of Pakistan (see table 3).

Table 3:   PERCENTAGE OF LAND OWNERSHIP IN WEST PAKISTAN, 1959

Average Area Owned (in Acres)	Percentage of Landlords	Percentage of Land Owned
5 or less	64.5	15.0
5 to 25	28.5	31.7
25 to 100	5.7	22.4
100 to 500	1.0	15.9
500 and over	0.1	15.0

Source: Government of Pakistan, *Report of the Land Reforms Commission* (1959), Appendix I.

The figures in the table show that 0.1 per cent of all landowners owned 15 per cent of the private land in Pakistan. This 0.1 per cent consisted of some 6000 landlords with holdings of over 500 acres. The total acreage owned by them was estimated to be about 7.5

million. Their average holdings were 1236 acres, as compared to a national overall 'average ownership of 9.5 acres'.[35] The land reforms were therefore essentially aimed at breaking the power of the big landlords.

The implementation of these land reforms was not effectively carried out, and one study estimated that only five per cent of privately owned land was surrendered to the government.[36] One of the reasons for this failure was that since the military had been mainly recruited from the Punjab many of the officers came 'from families owning such middle-sized holdings'.[37] While this may be true to some extent, not all Punjabis belonged to the landowning families that would be affected by the land reforms. Besides, the ME's political strategy was not to destroy the LE but to curb its power.

The ME's horizontal alliance with the LE resulted in the appointment of a powerful and ruthless landlord (the Nawab of Kalabagh) as the governor of West Pakistan. His feudal politics was feared by his own group and during his six years as governor he consolidated Ayub's rule. It was not surprising, therefore, to see that the pirs (holy men) from the Punjab, Sind and Frontier, the maliks from the tribal areas, and landowing families like the Noons, Tiwanas, Talpurs, Hotis and Gardezis politically supported the military regime and were considered 'President's men'.[38] In the 1962 election to the National Assembly the LE won a majority of seats (70 out of 150),[39] and as soon as the Assembly convened they demanded political freedom which was granted (in the Political Parties Bill, 1962). In this way the LE were able to enter politics once again, and by the time of the next general elections (1964–5) the Basic Democrat of the 1964 vintage had a greater affinity with the landlord class than his 1959 predecessor.[40]

Kalabagh, however, made sure that the feudal mode of production would not be dismantled by the ME in return for LE support of the military regime. He convinced the latter that the proposed land reforms would lead to the fragmentation of land holdings and economic ruination. The land reforms were never rigidly implemented. The ME, however, used them as a threat against the LE and sought to build a political base among the rural middle sectors.

The military government did help the rural middle sectors through the mechanization of farm technology. The use of fertilizers was increased from 31,000 nutrient tons in 1960–1 to 248,000 nutrient tons in 1968–9; the number of tube-wells installed privately was increased from 6295 in 1960–1 to 75,720 in 1969–70; and the production of farm crops (rice, wheat, maize) was increased considerably between 1965 and 1970.[41] To what extent such measures extended military control over the rural middle sector is a matter of debate.

The LE, however, took full advantage of such government policies 'in improving the productivity of their land . . . through . . . mechanization of farm operations'.[42] The 'Green Revolution' was ended 'in favour of the land bourgeoisie' for the 'small farmers, due mainly to their risk-bearing ability, poor managerial skills, lack of operational capital, and poor credit worthiness have been deprived to a great degree, of the worthiness of these innovations'.[43] This factor had eluded the ME and it could do nothing about it.

Ayub's land reform had advocated the interests of the peasantry but it proved to be more helpful for the LE. This left considerable resentment among the peasantry and the rural middle sectors, who later gave their support to Bhutto.

The Land Reforms of 1972

Bhutto's land reforms appeared to be more radical than those of the ME. The 1970 Pakistan People's Party (PPP) manifesto had stated that

> West Pakistani owners of large estates, the feudal lords constitute a formidable obstacle to progress. Not only by virtue of their wealth, but on account of their hold over their tenants and the neighbouring peasantry they wield considerable power and are, even at present, a major political force . . . The breaking up of the large estates to destroy the power of the feudal landowners is a national necessity that will have to be carried through by practical measures.[44]

The land reforms announced by Bhutto in 1972 included the following features. Ownership of land was limited to 150 acres of irrigated land and 300 acres of unirrigated land. All concessions allowed by the 1959 reforms were withdrawn. State lands were reserved for tenants and resumed land was to be given to the tenants. All transfers of land made during the previous five years were to be scrutinized and those made after 20 December 1971 were declared void. Arbitrary eviction of tenants was stopped and landlords were asked to pay the cost of seeds. Lands in excess of 100 acres aquired by civil servants were to be confiscated, and all land obtained by military officers from the defence belt of the border area was cancelled. Farmers were exempted from paying the balance of their instalments and a system of 'cooperative farming' was envisaged. In this system, agricultural machinery and the irrigation water would be provided by a cooperative. 'Agrovilles' would be developed, linking the rural areas, which would contain a town hall, the offices of the cooperative, a town library, hospital, school, and a civic centre with room for 'meetings, festivities, clubs and exhibitions'. These agrovilles would also 'function as a market place for . . . agricultural produce'.[45]

These imaginative land reforms once again raised the aspirations of the peasantry and they felt that their support for Bhutto in 1970 had not been in vain. As usual, the bureaucracy soon produced statistics on how the latest land reforms were being implemented. By October 1972, it was reported that 4 million acres had been resumed from about 12,000 landlords in the provinces.[46]

In December 1976, a Peasant's Week was celebrated and it reiterated the slogan 'all power to the peasants'.[47] At the same time a 'peasant's charter' promised to distribute 25 million acres of irrigated land to approximately 2,500,000 families.[48] Two months before the elections another set of land reforms was proposed in which the ceiling of private landholdings was further reduced to 100 acres of irrigated and 200 acres of unirrigated land.

How much land was actually distributed will never be known, for the figures given are never completely accurate. Even if one accepts the Government figures for the land reforms proposed in 1972 and 1976, the percentage of land distributed amounts to a very insignificant figure (see table 4).

What is important in making any such analyses is to distinguish between the 'ideology' and the 'programme' of land reforms.[49] The ideology articulated by the governing elites may be anti-land and in favour of the interests of the peasantry, but the programme may seem to serve the landlords.

Bhutto himself was a member of the LE and he could not be expected to reduce his own landholdings to a mere 100 acres. When questioned on how he could distribute land when he was a land-owner himself, he threw his jacket to the audience who scrambled to it and it was soon torn to shreds. He then asked his audience that if he gave away land like his jacket no one would get a share. He added that when 'he introduces land reforms, he would be the first to offer his land for distribution'.[50]

Academic assessments of Bhutto's land reforms regarded the innovations as political strategies for rural poverty had not been touched and the PPP pledges were considered 'political rhetoric'.[51] One assessment states that the 1972 land reforms resulted in the

ALL PAKISTAN

	Cultivatable Area Available for Redistribution (000 acres)	Number of Tenants Benefited* (000)		Beneficiaries** as a % of Poor Tenants		Beneficiaries*** as a % of total Agrarian holdings	
		Assumption A	Assumption B	A	B	A	B
1. 1972 Government Figures							
a) if 100% cultivable	850	68	136	6	11	2	4
b) if 75% cultivable	612	49	98	4	8	1	3
c) if 50% cultivable	425	34	69	3	6	1	2
2. 1976 Government Figures							
a) if 100% cultivable	1140	91	175	8	15	2	5
b) if 75% cultivable	855	68	132	6	11	1	4
c) if 50% cultivable	570	46	88	4	7	1	2

Source: These figures were compiled by an Agricultural Economist in Pakistan (private communication)

* Assumption A = each tenant receives 12.5 acres
   Assumption B = each tenant receives 6.5 acres

** Poor tenants = tenants operating less than 25 acres = 1,200,009 holdings (1972)
   This definition ignores the small owner-cum-tenant holdings.

*** Total agricultural holdings = 3,761,688 (1972)

distribution of only one per cent of cultivable land among 130,000 tenants.[52] Most of the land had been sub-divided among family members. The ideology and programme of the 1976 land reforms did not supplement each other. It retained loopholes in 'defining ownership by individuals rather than by the family.'[53] In any case, the political networks had tipped off the landlords about the impending land reforms and they had had time to revise their limits.

For the land reforms to be really radical and free from vested interests even the latest ceiling placed on landholdings was considered too high. A small number of people would remain with large holdings and 'contain the ever-increasing disparities of incomes between the large owners and tenants'[54] which these elites could manipulate to their own advantage.

Conclusion

It does not appear that the feudal system in Pakistan will end in the near future. The land reforms introduced since 1958 are indicative of the concern for an equitable distribution of wealth. So far, none of the land reforms, however, have been radical enough to change land tenure systems.

Major changes will be introduced into the system as capitalism makes further inroads in the country. Ayub was not successful in the implementation of his land reforms but the 'green revolution' had a considerable impact on the agrarian sector. Modernization introduced new ideas through seed and soil technology and mechanization. Greater crop yields increased the wealth of the landlords and strengthened the feudal power structure.

On the other hand, it also encouraged progressive feudalists to make capital investments in industry. Thus groups such as the Noons, Qureshis and Qizilbashs from the Punjab, the Talpurs, Soomros and Jatois from Sind, and the Hotis from the NWFP have become feudal industrialists. Their power over the agricultural and industrial sectors not only increases the power of capitalism but creates class structures which could lead to stronger horizontal alliances with the IE. In other words, there would be a unification of the two modes of production as the country comes more under the domination of the capitalist system.

4

The Bureaucratic Elites

A central concern of successive conquerors of the Indian subcontinent was to construct an administrative system sufficient for the necessities of state-functioning. The Mughals had developed a mansabdari system which was bureaucratic–military in style. The British used two separate systems, the Indian Civil Service (ICS) and the British Indian Army. After Independence, the ICS was renamed the Indian Administrative Service in India and the Civil Service of Pakistan (CSP) in Pakistan. The rise of this higher bureaucracy and its role in the political system of Pakistan have left an indelible mark on the politics of the new state.

This chapter will focus on the bureaucracy in general and on the bureaucratic elite (BE) in particular. The BE were those members of the bureaucracy (including the CSP) whose political and economic decision-making powers were instrumental in the political and economic development of Pakistan since its inception. The BE belonged to various bureaucratic institutions, but the term bureaucracy will be used to refer to the whole bureaucratic apparatus.

Historically, the rise of the BE cannot be directly linked to the Mughal mansabdari system. The latter was geared to the needs of the medieval feudal state, with its extensive revenue-collecting apparatus and ability to recruit manpower in times of war. The British concentrated power in the hands of the ICS to such an extent that it became known as the 'steel frame'. Through it, a handful of men governed the colonial state with an iron grip.

The Colonial Heritage

The bureaucracy was a colonial infrastructure between the rulers and the ruled. During the course of its administrative rule, the institution developed its own political culture and traditions which were not only inherited by the CSP but were internalized by them. This resulted in the CSP acquiring a self-image as the most-suited-to-rule which was reinforced by efficiency in administration. However, it must be remembered that their training and traditions of service had geared them to fulfil the needs of the colonial state. To understand their role one must examine the colonial traditions.

First, the members of the ICS belonged to an elite which enjoyed the highest prestige in British India. This was due in part to the kind of examinations that prospective members were required to pass. These were so difficult that only those with a superior education could get through. Secondly, the natives who were accepted into the ICS were marginal men, for although they belonged to their traditional society their outlook was westernized. They identified not only with the institution they belonged to but also with the colonial political system. Thirdly, their relatively high salaries, tenureship and the power vested in their bureaucratic positions were factors which reinforced their alienation from the masses.[1] Their authority in decision-making and policy formation was supreme since they were in control of all central planning bodies of the state. Fourthly, the ICS developed a paternalistic attitude to the masses and an approach that was often 'authoritarian in tone and content'.[2] They tolerated no outside interference and exercised absolute power over the public. As a consequence, the civil servant in British India had 'no experience of working with the politician as an equal partner let alone of accepting him as a superior'.[3] This was also a characteristic of the attitude of the bureaucratic elites in the post-Independence period. Fifthly, the administrative powers of the ICS were generalized to cover a variety of areas, from supervising land revenue collection, to the maintenance of law and order and enjoying judicial powers. All other service cadres of the state machinery were secondary to the ICS, and even the lowest-ranking position in its hierarchy, the deputy commissioner, was regarded as the 'government in the field'.[4] Sixthly, over a period of almost a hundred years, bureaucratic sophistication in administration and rigid role-behaviour had reached the point of institutionalization. This structure transposed itself within the bureaucracy in Pakistan and operated as a self-contained system opposed to fundamental internal changes.

This colonial instrument helped the CSP in the new state to play an 'even more powerful role than that of their imperial predecessors'.[5] Before looking into the political roles of the BE, however, a brief survey of the structure and method of recruitment to the institution will help to make the significance of its role become clearer.

Elite Recruitment

At the time of the Partition of India, it was estimated that there were 1157 ICS officers of which 608 were British, 448 Hindus and 101 Muslims. Of the latter, 83 decided to choose Pakistan as their homeland. None had a rank equivalent to that of a secretary and, since higher-ranking posts in the new state lacked personnel, vacancies were filled by quick promotion into the CSP. This was done by ad hoc appointments from other services and also by the retention of some British officers until as late as 1957.[6]

The bureaucratic structure of the services had four classes. In hierarchical order, classes I and II were gazetted officers while III and IV were non-gazetted. The gazetted officers were allocated their positions through the Central Superior Services of which there were three main categories. First, there was the general administrative category from which the CSP were recruited. Secondly, there was functional recruitment for services such as the Pakistan Foreign Service (PFS), the Police Service of Pakistan (PSP), Income Tax Service, Customs, Central Excise and Audits and Accounts. Thirdly, there were the specialist and technical services such as engineering and health. Among these, although the CSP, PFS and PSP were considered the most prestigious, real power lay in the hands of the highly politicized CSP.

As the most prestigious group within the country's bureaucracy, the CSP was very conscious of its importance and had designed stringent measures to exclude the unwanted. The Public Service Commission (PSC) was in charge of the recruitment of new members and through it only those with the best education could gain entry. Since a high-level formal education was available only to a few, this system excluded the masses from entry. The minimum qualification was a good bachelors degree and satisfactory completion of an entrance examination. The first part of this examination was a written test designed to test the candidate's verbal ability. The second part was an oral examination to evaluate his general knowledge, intelligence and personality. The third part was a physical and psychological stability test. Of those finally selected, 20 per cent were chosen on merit and the remainder according to a biased quota system applied to each of the provinces.

After selection, the recruit was sent to the Civil Service Academy where indoctrination into his role began. The prime values he was taught were group consciousness, prestige of position, utilization of power and officership. The director of the Academy from 1951 to 1960 was a retired ICS Officer (Geoffrey Burgess) who, along with a few other British officers, supervised training. By the time the recruits had completed training they were well aware of their elite status. The CSP academy was thus an institution which instilled in the recruit 'a sense of belonging to a privileged group which had a major responsibility for the future governing of Pakistan'.[7] This training produced a 'literary–generalist' officer 'steeped in the ethos of British colonial administration'.[8] Critics of the academy in Parliament likened it to a 'manufacturing laboratory' which created 'Anglicized officers', and some pointed out that if that was what the government wanted they could bring 'some from England' for 'they would be better people with better integrity'.[9] The BE paid no heed to these criticisms from elected political leaders and regarded them with contempt.

By the mid-1950s ethnic biases which had crept into recruitment policies became more obvious. The East Bengalis, who were out-numbered by other ethnic groups by five to one, accused the BE of ethnic group discrimination.[10] The service since its inception had been dominated by a Punjabi and Muhajir bureaucratic elite who in turn had used the PSC for recruiting favoured candidates. Table 5 gives figures for the representation of East Bengalis in the CSP.

As Punjabi and Muhajir representation increased in the higher ranks of the bureaucracy, the officers gradually abandoned their national role and began to show increasing involvement in regional and ethnic politics. Table 5 reflects the developing significance of ethnic attitudes through the growing representation of East Bengalis in the higher bureaucratic orders. The resulting ethnic conflict split the higher bureaucracy into two elite factions: the East Bengalis and the West Pakistanis (mainly Punjabis and Muhajirs). Some of the former joined the EBPE in their struggle for the political separation of East Bengal, and were persecuted by Ayub Khan in the Agarthala Conspiracy case brought against them in 1968.

Ethnicity was therefore not a myth. Other studies also reinforce this ethnic bias of the BE. A recent survey revealed that some 49.1 percent of the bureaucrats agreed that they were subject to regional

Table 5:   REPRESENTATION OF THE CIVIL SERVICE OF PAKISTAN IN EAST
BENGAL AND WEST PAKISTAN 1948–1967

Year	Total No. of Officers	East Bengal		West Pakistan	
		No.	% of total	No.	% of total
1948	18	2	11.1	16	88.9
1949	20	9	45.0	16	55.0
1950	20	6	30.0	11	70.0
1951	11	4	36.4	7	63.6
1952	17	5	29.4	12	70.6
1953	13	3	23.1	10	77.9
1954	25	7	28.0	18	72.0
1955	17	5	29.4	12	70.6
1956	21	11	52.4	10	47.6
1957	20	7	35.0	12	65.0
1958	24	10	41.7	14	58.3
1959	24	12	50.0	12	50.0
1960	31	10	32.3	19	67.7
1961	27	10	37.0	17	63.0
1962	27	12	44.5	15	55.5
1963	31	13	41.9	18	58.1
1964	33	14	42.2	19	57.8
1965	30	15	50.0	15	50.0
1966	30	14	46.6	16	53.4
1967	30	13	43.3	17	56.7

Sources: Raunaq Jahan, *Pakistan: Failure in National integration* (New York: Columbia
Univeristy Press, 1972), pp. 26, 107. Compiled from: Pakistan Establishment Division, *Civil List of Class I Officers Serving under the Government of Pakistan,* 1 January
1965 and 1966; *Graduation List of the Civil Service of Pakistan,* 1 July 1967 and 1
January 1968.

biases in their decision-making, 14.4. percent indicated that it had
some influence and only 22.9 percent denied that there was any
such bias.[11]

The Emergence of the Administrative State

The colonial bureaucratic system had operated under a viceregal
system in which the viceroy was the representative of the British
Government. The latter's role was to act as 'an instrument for the
execution of imperialist policies'.[12] In the post-Independent period
the BE's role surpassed that of their predecessors for they became
the executors as well as the makers of policy. The BE claimed that it
knew what was 'good for the nation',[13] monopolized decision-

making at economic and political levels, and participated in the creation of an administrative state completely under their control.

The BE's organizational expertise had given them access into strategic positions from where they could exert considerable political influence. By manning the planning boards and planning commissions they controlled the economic funds for development. As will be shown in the last chapter, such strong concentration of the bureaucracy in these bodies, coupled with their strong ethnic biases, led to disastrous consequences for national economic development. Besides, Jinnah had set certain precedents which later determined this role of the BE. He had appointed British bureaucrats as governors of provinces, believing that their experience and bureaucratic acumen were necessary for Pakistan's survival in its early stages.[14] These governors enjoyed power over the elected representatives of the people, and often dispatched secret reports on the political activities of chief ministers to Jinnah.[15] This background also meant that there should be a strong centre which would keep the provincial governments in check. Jinnah's personal decision to become governor-general and not prime minister—a precedent that the head of state should be all powerful—reinforced this tendency. Liaquat, on the other hand, wanted the position of prime minister to be strong, and after Jinnah's death he remained in that office and appointed Khawaja Nazimuddin as governor-general.

Jinnah had advised Pakistani bureaucrats that they constituted the 'backbone of the state' and that 'governments are defeated, Prime Ministers come and go, but you stay on, and therefore, there is very great responsibility on your shoulders.'[16] Yet, on another occasion, as if apprehensive of their political strength he warned them to stay away from politics, dispel their 'past reputation' of belonging to the 'ruling class' and discharge their duty by being 'servants of Pakistan'.[17]

Furthermore, the colonial instrument, the Government of India Act (1935), facilitated the entrenchment of the BE in the political arena. The act was an authoritarian and elitist vehicle which was unresponsive to the needs of the masses. It was used to spell out the parameters of the administrative state.

Although Jinnah had initiated the task of preparing a constitution which would replace the Government of India Act, Liaquat was too weak to complete the task in the face of opposition from the professional and landowning elite groups. The act thus continued in force and benefited the BE who willingly took up the political leadership of the new state.

The governor-general could also dismiss the whole provincial administration and impose Governors' Rule under Section 92A of the 1935 Act. This clause was frequently applied in the Punjab, NWFP, Sind and East Bengal and became an instrument of enforcing BE rule rather to restore democracy.

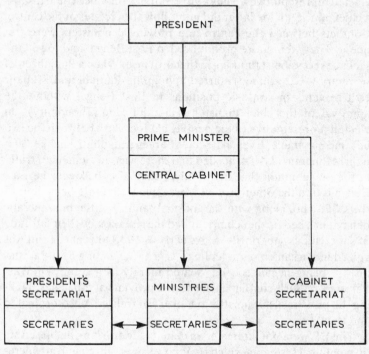

Fig. 3: The Central Secretariat

Within the administrative state, the stronghold of decision-making was the Cabinet Secretariat (see Fig. 3). The most important part of the Secretariat was known as the Cabinet Secretariat. It was directly under the control of the prime minister and all Central Government directives had to be channelled through it. It was manned by the bureaucracy and 'acted as a communication and co-ordination agency between the Cabinet and the Ministers.'[18] Each of the ministers headed a department or ministry assisted by a CSP secretary and a joint secretary, a deputy secretary and a host of lower-level functionaries. These secretaries in the ministries and Cabinet Secretariat wielded tremendous power and influence, particularly when ministers or the prime minister were weak and depended on their advice.

At the provincial level, control of the administrative state was exercised through a governor or CSP officers who were directly appointed by the Central Government, and were again bound by the directives of the Cabinet Secretariat. As stated above, here again they were politically more powerful in the provinces than the elected representatives. Thus a governor of a province could dismiss a chief minister if the latter did not follow the dictates of the centre. Conflicts between the centre and provinical ministers were frequent. They were more pronounced in East Bengal and sowed the seeds of secessionist thinking in that province. When a Punjabi chief secretary (Aziz Ahmed) started appointing Punjabi and Muhajir civil servants in strategic positions in East Bengal without the approval of the chief minister (Hamidul Huq Choudhury), an elected representative of the people, a direct clash between the two became inevitable. Even a die-hard bureaucrat–politician like Chaudhri Mohammad Ali conceded that there was 'an element of truth' in the presumption that the political alienation between the East Bengalis and the other provinces was due to the role-behaviour of the CSP, who, along with the 'normal failings of the bureaucratic behaviour', had further compounded the situation by their 'attitude of supercilious superiority'.[19] As early as 1948, this alienation was voiced in Parliament as a 'feeling . . . growing among East Pakistanis . . . being neglected and treated merely as a colony of West Pakistan'.[20] Such conflict also affected provinicial efficiency, making the provinical administration 'over-centralized, unco-ordinated and slow'.[21]

The BE were not interested in democracy or Islam, but in setting up a political system in which their power was supreme. Bureaucratic rule in Pakistan was not the result of organizational superiority but had stemmed from 'the pre-emption and monopolization of key government offices'[22] in the political system. Certain aspects of the administrative state need to be discussed to bring out the issues and conflicts which preoccupied the political elites.

Political Rule by the non-elected Leadership

When Ghulam Mohammad (1951–5) became governor-general and Khawaja Nazimuddin (1951–3) was prime minister, the political system of Pakistan was under complete bureaucratic control. Nazimuddin was an old member of the Muslim League and belonged to the landed aristocracy of East Bengal. Even though he was not ambitious, Ghulam Mohammad feared Nazimuddin because he was a member of the largest East Bengali ethnic group and would inevitably triumph in an electoral contest. In order to secure the interests of the bureaucracy, Ghulam Mohammad began to look for ways of getting rid of him.

He did not have to wait long. The language riots (East Bengal 1952), the Ahmadiya riots (Punjab 1953) and the food situation in Pakistan provided him with the excuse to dismiss Nazimuddin on 17 April 1953. Nazimuddin, however, had enjoyed the confidence of the Constituent Assembly and refused to submit, maintaining that the 'Governor-General was the only constitutional head while his own Ministry had the real support of the public and legislature'.[23] Ghulam Mohammad, on the other hand, had drawn his authority from the colonial instrument, the Government of India Act 1935.[24]

The personal conflicts of these two men brought to the surface important underlying issues which had afflicted the political system. First, the political system was strained because the non-elected leadership had triumphed over the elected leadership indicating the supremacy of elitist political control rather than democratic political cal order. Secondly, among the non-elected leadership, Ghulam Mohammad, a bureaucrat, institutionalized bureaucratic rule rather than that of the political parties. Thirdly, the animosity between Ghulam Mohammad and Nazimuddin was more than personal—it was indicative of the basic distrust which existed between the two most powerful ethnic groups. Fourthly, it also established that the office of the governor-general, by Jinnah's precedent, was vested with more political power than that of the prime minister of Pakistan.

Nazimuddin was replaced by Mohammad Ali Bogra, an East Bengali, who was then the Ambassador of Pakistan to the United States. He was not a member of the Constituent Assembly and had no political support, but his appointment gave Ghulam Mohammad a weak prime minister and at the same time placated the Bengalis. Bogra's course of action was politically defensive, and some of his efforts in suppressing various elite groups met with little success. An examination of some features of his administration gives an indication of how the BE were ready to go to any extremes to maintain control of the political arena.

Bogra took steps to please both Punjabis and Bengalis. He cleverly defused the language problem in May 1954 by getting the Constituent Assembly to accept Urdu and Bengali as the national languages. To please the Punjabis he produced what popularly came to be known as the 'Mohammad Ali Formula' which spelled out a framework for the future constitution of Pakistan (see chapter

7). He remained under tremendous pressure, however, from LE domination in the Constituent Assemby and the EBPE in East Bengal.

Political Participation During Bureaucratic Rule

The Bogra regime is significant in Pakistan's politics because during this period the BE attempted to maintain their power in an administrative state. In doing so they committed the worst political blunders in the country's history which resulted in the provinces becoming ethnically conscious, the growth of nationalist tendencies and the destruction of political institutions. Some of the important events that crystallized during the Bogra period are discussed below to show how elite politics operated in Pakistan.

The Myth of National Parties

The EBPE had lost faith in the East Bengali premiers (Nazimuddin and Bogra), both of whom had succumbed to the political influence of the BE and LE. The former were in control of the political arena while the latter (mainly Punjabis) dominated the Constituent Assembly through the Muslim League, which sought to transform Pakistan into a one-party state. This was resented by the EBPE, which challenged the power of the Muslim League in East Bengal in the elections of 1954. Their democratic ideas were articulated by H. S. Suhrawardy who stated that:

> In the very first place we do not believe in identifying the state with the party, the ministry and the administration, i.e. we believe in democracy as opposed to fascism. Next, we believe that an opposition is necessary for the proper functioning of democracy, this is the only influence that can keep the rulers in check and at work, and can create public opinion. The Muslim League, on the other hand, labels opposition as disruption, demands that there shall be no parties other than itself and that all parties must be crushed out of existence.[25]

In 1953 Suhrawardy, A. K. Fazlul Huq and Maulana Bashani formed a coalition of their parties (the Awami League, the Krishak Sramik Party, the Ganatantri Dal and the Nizam-i-Islam Party). This was known as the United Front and it was able to mobilize the East Bengali masses and elites with its 21-point manifesto. The result was that in the elections in 1954 the Muslim League could only secure 10 out of a total of 309 seats. This election was significant because it 'marked the rejection of the national elite by the Bengali electorate.'[26] It was the death of the Muslim League which never regained its footing in that province.

If East Bengal was elated at its victory, the feudal LE and the bureaucrats were deeply upset by their defeat. The LE had sought to extend their sphere of influence through the Muslim League in East Bengal; its defeat not only showed the strength of the EPBE but had reduced the status of the Muslim League to that of a regional party. For many staunch supporters of the Muslim League it was the only party which could consolidate Pakistan and its destruction implied the destruction of the state.[27]

The outcome of these elections also posed a threat to the Punjabi governing elites (the BE). Thus when there were riots in East Bengal, following a split in the United Front after the election, Ghulam Mohammad imposed Governor's Rule in the province. Iskander Mirza, another bureaucrat, was sent as governor of the province, and Fazlul Huq was accused of treasonable activities and placed under house arrest. The Provincial Assembly was dismissed on 30 May 1954, the press was censored and the Army was kept on alert. Mirza even threatened that, if necessary, martial law would be declared and troops used to prevent political disturbances.[28] Such actions did not help in nation-building or in the integration of the new state.

The One-Unit Plan

Domination of the East Bengalis through the imposition of Governor's Rule was a temporary measure to keep the Bengali PE from immediately threatening the position of the BE. The Bengali PE had also developed ties with the political elites in the NWFP, Baluchistan and Sind. The Punjabi governing elites therefore coalesced with the Punjabi LE in the Muslim League and put forward a proposal for the unification of the NWFP, Punjab, Sind and Baluchistan into a single zonal subfederation.[29] This was known as the One-Unit Plan and it was devised for three important reasons: first, to confront the East Bengalis who had taken a united stand to oust the Muslim League in the 1954 elections; secondly, to integrate the four provinces into a large unit so that no one of the three could collaborate with the East Bengalis; thirdly, within the one unit, Punjab would be the largest province and would thus be able to override any political issues raised by the other three provinces on the strength of sheer numbers.

That this plan would ultimately be implemented was a foregone conclusion, but the role of the Bengali Prime Minister, Bogra, and the methods by which the plan was forged into the Provincial Assemblies were significant. The strategies used by the governing elites further exposed the bureaucratic skill and feudal power of these elites and how their position strained the political system.

Bogra was expected to support the One-Unit Plan but the non-Punjabi provinces strongly resisted it. The governing elite threatened to use PRODA to cruch any political opposition, thus denying them any political freedom. Although Bogra had failed to undermine the power of the Secretariat, he attempted to curb the BE through legislative acts. With the help of the political elites threatened with PRODA, Bogra was able to pass a motion in the Constituent Assembly for its repeal while the governor-general was not in the capital. Amendments to Sections 9, 10, 10A and 10B of the Government of India Act 1935 were also passed. These curbed the power of the governor-general to dismiss the prime minister and his cabinet.[30] Ghulam Mohammad's reaction was to dissolve the entire Constituent Assembly in 24 October 1954 on the pretext that it had failed to produce a constitution for the country.

The country was again governed for ten months without a Constituent Assembly until an election in 1955. During this period (24 October 1954 to 7 July 1955) Bogra was allowed to continue as a prime minister with power only after he had obtained 'his master's pardon'.[31] Even his ministers in the so-called 'Cabinet of Talents' were selected for him by the governor-general. The Ministry of Talents became more of a governor-general's council and its prime objective was to crush all opposition to the One-Unit Plan. Thus, when the chief minister of Sind (Pirzada Abdus Satter) dissented from supporting the One Unit, his ministry was dissolved on charges of 'maladministration' and a favourite of the governor-general was installed as chief minister of the province. The opposition in the Provincial Assembly (the Speaker, three former chief Ministers, five Provincial Assembly members and one ex-minister) was arrested and held in police custody.[32] Similarly in the NWFP, Sardar Abdur Rashid's ministry was dismissed because of his opposition to the One-Unit Plan.[33] Such actions destroyed the credibility of the centre and it came to be perceived as a force of oppression.

When the second Constituent Assembly convened in July 1955, the Ghulam Mohammad era was at an end for he was very ill. Political power, however, remained with the BE for he handed over his office, like a legacy, to his protégé, Iskander Mirza. During the Mirza reign, another strong East Bengali premier emerged who was also dismissed from his post (see chapter 7). Mirza's bureaucratic prime minister, Chaudhri Mohammad Ali, did, however, give the country its first constitution.

The Constitution of 1956

This constitution was modelled after the colonial instrument of 1935. Discussion occupied seventeen sittings of the second Constituent Assembly. On one occasion, when some of the dissidents walked out, the Government passed fifty clauses without opposition.[34]

The constitution upheld the parity principle and stated that the Constituent Assembly was to be composed of 310 members, 150 of whom had to be elected from East Bengal and 150 from West Pakistan. In addition, 10 seats were reserved for women. Two other Provincial Assemblies of East Bengal and West Pakistan were also to have 310 seats.

The president was to be elected by the consensus of the 930 members of the three houses. He could be impeached if three-quarters of the Constituent Assembly consented. He was to choose a prime minister who commanded the confidence of the National Assembly and would 'hold office during the pleasure of the President', but 'the President shall not exercise his powers under this clause unless he is satisfied that the Prime Minister does not command the confidence of the majority of the National Assembly'.[35]

The most important point was that the constitution entrenched the power of the BE. The CSP could not be dismissed unless the president, as the appointing authority, himself authorized it. Such tenureship further enhanced the power of the BE. The first constitution of the ideological state thus set a precedent, that those who possessed political power could also make the laws to maximize it. It did not reflect the aspirations of the masses and did not mean anything to them, nor to those elite groups whose interests were not represented.

Elite Conflict and Decentralization

The BE ruled Pakistan for a decade 'through a highly centralized administration' in which they were the powerful actors.[36] This autocratic rule had resulted in such strains within the political system that there was widespread evidence of political anarchy.

During its rule the BE had capitalized on the disorganization of other elite groups by using the colonial political philosophy of divide and rule. It made no effort to develop political institutions but through its generalist role-expansion kept other elite groups (except the military) dependent upon itself. This concentration of political power escalated the conflict of the BE with other elite groups and led to the ethnicization of politics through the polarization of national identities.

The major opponents of the BE had been the RE, LE and the EBPE. The BE had believed in separating religion from politics and in maintaining law and order. By making superficial concessions they were able to compromise the RE and convince them that the needs of Pakistan as an Islamic state were at least being minimally served.

The bureaucrats' conflict with the LE was inevitable, for not only was the latter oriented towards a feudalistic state but were also in competition with the BE for positions of power. The BE's administrative state machinery extended right through to district and tehsil (subdivision of a district) levels and the assistant and deputy commissioners were tangible symbols of government authority in rural areas.[37] Such officials frequently came into contact with the landowning elite, and apart from their administrative tasks they often tried to harness the power of the landlords into the federal designs of the government.

Where the LE were active in the political arena they would commonly use their influence to secure the transfer of government officers from one district to another or from one province to another.[38] On the other hand, official interference was encouraged by the government, and 'government servants were actively participating in party and factional politics through their wives, children, fathers and brothers.'[39]

The conflict with the EBPE had led to the dismissal of two East Bengali prime ministers as well as the dismissal of a whole body of elected representatives of the people, the first Constituent Assembly. The EBPE were also the first to launch an attack on bureaucratic institutions by inviting an American expert (Prof. R. Eggar) to evaluate the system. The Eggar report found fault with the Secretariat system which had been functioning as a policy-making directorate under CSP officers and had dominated the political system. The Eggar report clearly stated that the 'deficiencies in the public administration of Pakistan are not deficiencies of intelligence or understanding but are the deficiencies inherent in an administrative system designed for a day that has gone by. Both the political leaders and civil service are fully aware of these defects . . .'[40] But with the domination of the BE it was not possible for Bogra to implement these recommendations and the report was filed.

Later, another expert (Prof. B. Gladieux) was invited to undertake a study of the administration. The BE did not cooperate with him, stating bluntly that the system worked perfectly. However, the Gladieux report backed Eggar in finding that the administrative system, a legacy of colonial policy, was unfit as a vehicle for democracy. Gladieux pointed out that 'the major weakness of the present administrative system with respect to national development stems largely from the fact that the Government is still substantially directed to the law and order function in its organizational, procedural, personnel and fiscal aspects'.[41] He advocated that the bureaucracy should be decentralized. The central and provincial services should be unified into one administrative service which would eradicate social differences within the bureaucratic elite group. Needless to say, this report met with the same fate as its predecessor.

These reports, however, had crystallized the defects of the administrative system, and the BE began to feel the pressure of criticism not only from political elites but also from their own less powerful factions. In order to defuse this situation without relinquishing their role supremacy the CSP began to devise various job schemes such as the 'Economic Pool' to share their power and status with selected officers from other cadres. They also introduced a Section Officers' scheme for people with suitable education and experience who could not otherwise enter the CSP. In order to counteract the pressures of economic development, many semi-government organizations, such as the Pakistan Industrial Development Corporation (PIDC) and the West Pakistan Power and Development Authority (WPPDA), were set up. These were under generalist supervision but were staffed by specialist officers. The BE's political position therefore remained intact.

The rise of the military regime precipitated the downfall of the BE in 1958. The military regime (see chapter 8) used them for their own purposes but the BE managed to salvage their position to some extent by making compromises. The real purge of the bureaucracy was carried out by the LE who came to power under Bhutto.

When Bhutto took over the government of Pakistan in 1971 he was well aware of the political role of the bureaucracy in the political system. His own departure from the Ayub Cabinet had rapidly been filled by a civil servant through whom the bureaucracy continued to exercise influence over Ayub's regime.[42] His own bitter experiences with the BE after his exit from the Ayub regime made him determined to strenghten his own political position by subordinating all forces of power or influence which may have posed a threat to him.

Bhutto's attitude towards the bureaucracy was clearly articulated in many of his speeches. First, he believed that the bureaucracy was a class by itself who were so insulated from the masses that they could not identify with them. Secondly, the neutrality of this class was therefore a myth, for it had always been more concerned with its own welfare than that of those whom it claimed to serve. He advised civil servants to change their attitudes in accordance with altered conditions in the country. His government would not give constitutional guarantees of tenureship, and security lay in their hard work and integrity. The era of what he termed as 'naukar–shahi' (servant–kings) was over.[43] Thirdly, he believed that piecemeal reforms would not change the bureaucratic apparatus which required radical reform. Only then could the system be made more responsive to the needs of the masses. Fourthly, the bureaucracy was to be under the control of the political party in power, the PPP. The latter could not tolerate 'a government within a government, which is what the CSP represented. Furthermore, the CSP represented vested interest, and given the PPP's emphasis on socialist reconstruction, the CSP was judged expendable.'[44] The bureaucrats thus would not be so powerful as to be able to dictate to the politicians.

The Administrative Reforms Committee proposed a set of recommendations in August 1973. The old structure of the bureaucratic system was reformed. All services and cadres were integrated into one unified service. Within this there were twenty-two gradations, giving equal opportunity to all. This grade structure replaced the class system which had been like a caste system in restricting vertical mobility. The services were further divided into separate functional groups, such as the Foreign Affairs Group, Federal Revenues (direct taxes), Federal Revenues (indirect taxes), Commerce, Information, Secretariat, Postal, Cantonments Management, Railway, Tribal Areas group, District Management and Office Management. Horizontal mobility within the services was assured and personnel from technical and generalist cadres could be interchanged. Furthermore, there were provisions for lateral entry into the bureaucracy and opportunities were given to talented and qualified individuals from the private sector. By this means the government hoped to attract a wide range of talents including scientists, engineers, doctors, economists, accountants and other 'professionals and specialists in policy-making, management and administration'.[45]

Although these reforms appeared radical and progressive, they changed the structure but not the men holding strategic positions. In an attempt to salvage their position, old bureaucrats rigidly maintained their 'naukar–shahi' categories within the unified grading system. Thus, the CSP and PSP were renamed the All-Pakistan Unified Grade while the other services were renamed the Federal Unified Grades.

Three new acts were also introduced in the Constitution. These were the Civil Service Act 1973, the Service Tribunals Act 1973 and the Federal Service Commission Act 1973. Through the use of these acts new rules and regulations were issued by the establishment division in the name of the president. These acts thus helped to concentrate power in Bhutto's hands, especially with regard to controlling the bureaucracy through appointments, dismissals, retirements, recruitment and promotions. The Civil Services Act 1973 ensured that civil servants could hold office only at the pleasure of the president.

The lateral entry system for ad hoc recruitment into the services was used as a political bribe to win over dissatisfied ethnic groups (the Sindhis in particular) and for staffing the bureaucracy with persons personally loyal to Bhutto. This process was accelerated during the March 1977 elections in order to get support for Bhutto from various factions. The lateral entry system and other malpractices of the PPP leadership made 'a mockery of the Administrative Reforms and brought about complete chaos in the bureaucratic set-up of Pakistan. Today every group of service Ministry or Department stands divided into various groups of interests, each indulging in intrigues to secure advantages and benefits of seniority, promotion and prize postings and, of course, each airing its own grievances.'[46]

Despite the reform, the BE remained non-cooperative and inefficient. Having lost their former power and prestige, they showed little enthusiasm for Bhutto's programmes nor submitted any creative schemes themselves (as they had done for the Ayub regime). The emergence of the party as a powerful instrument in the state made the bureaucracy withdraw into the background where they merely followed the government's directives. In a country with a scarcity of skills and expertise, such an attitude sabotaged Bhutto's programmes. The BE were not a spent force for they remained busy with their personal rather than national interests. They were known to tout for illicit gain and in some cases became CIA agents to sell information from countries like China.

Conclusion

The role of the BE as a governing elite cannot be underrated. Scholars have noted that a strong bureaucracy in a new state inhibits the growth of political institutions necessary for the establishment of a democratic government. Pakistan's bureaucracy, as seen in this chapter, was not different in this respect. It was a self-serving autocracy. To centralize its own power it brought in extensive changes in the scope and jurisdiction of governmental operations while ignoring changes in its procedures and mechanisms. Even when they ceased be the ruling elite after 1958, their skilful manipulation, resilience and patience in slowly rendering the ruling elite impotent and dependent upon itself were notable.

The administrative reforms of 1973 were constructive but they were utilized to fulfil the personal goals of the governing elites. One can argue that the future development of Pakistan will need a trained bureaucracy but such a bureaucracy must undergo two radical changes—decolonization and Islamization. Most reform committees have looked at macro rather than micro aspects of bureaucratic change. As an income tax officer in the 1960s, the author had two lower-division clerks, two upper-division clerks, one stenotypist, one inspector, one peon and one notice server working under him. Such a surplus of staff is reminiscent of colonial times where each official could hold his 'darbar' (court) at his own leisure. The process of decolonization will have to keep up with the changed times and introduce structural changes from filing systems to the dismissal of the die-hard bureaucrats. Bhutto could not implement such changes because his own office was staffed by people trained in the colonial tradition. The bureaucracy could not therefore make a complete transition towards decolonization. Along with decolonization, the process of Islamization must also be implemented. This would mean a change in the BE's thinking from an individualist to a collectivist level. Furthermore, it also means a transevaluation of all values in practice and internalization of the social ethics of Islam. Such a task is easier said than done for it can only be implemented through the institutionalization of the Islamic order in society. How far vested interests would allow this remains to be seen.

5

The Religious Elites

The role of Islam in the Muslim and British empires of the subcontinent has been outlined earlier. The focus of this chapter will be the roles of the religious elites in the post-Partition period and their influence on the political system of the ideological state. Although the RE did not have a significant representation in the political arena, their indirect political influence should not be underrated since they identified strongly with Islam and thus with the very basis of the ideological state.

Islam does not have an ecclesiastical system for the training of its religious leaders, and three distinct types of authority could be identified in Pakistan. These were the local Maulvis, the learned Maulanas (Ulema) and the Pirs (spiritual leaders). They operated through their mosques, political organizations or group of followers in the various provinces.

The local Maulvis were conservative and had a limited knowledge of theology. They approved of democracy in principle, but any social changes that reflected a bias towards Western culture were thought of as 'immoral, materialistic or unspiritual'.[1] Many of this group came from small towns or villages and could not comprehend the economic or political problems of an ideological state. Their strongholds were the mosques and their personal influence extended into many aspects of their local community life (solemnizing marriages, teaching the Quran, etc.). One estimate indicated that they controlled about 40,000 mosques in West Pakistan and a similar number in East Bengal.[2] Their political influence was exerted through the Friday sermons which were powerful instruments for the mass mobilization of the industrial, tribal and peasant masses. They could not however influence the urban (government officers, etc.) bourgeois (businessmen, etc.) and professional (lawyers, doctors, etc.) middle sectors who tended to consider the local Maulvis illiterate fanatics.

The Ulema were also conservative in outlook but their vast knowledge of Islam made them national authorities on the various schools of Islamic thought. Some, like Maulana Maudoodi, had a world-wide reputation for Islamic scholarship.[3] The latter was feared by some political elite groups (BE, IE) and respected by others (ME, PE). None could deny his religio-political influence on the political system.

In the provinces the Pirs were a powerful group which exerted considerable influence over their ethnic followers. Some, like the Aga Khans (spiritual head of the Ismaili sect), had been strong supporters of the British Raj, while others such as the late Pir of Pagaro (head of the Hur tribe in Sind) and the late Faqir of Ipi (of the NWFP) had fiercely resisted colonialism.[4] In the early years following Independence the Muslim League had many Pirs among its supporters and, as such, was able to exert grass-roots influence in the provinces. Political elites seeking bases for political support often bargained for the consolidated blocks of votes of the fanatical followers of the Pirs. Thus Ayub's position was strengthened in the NWFP by the Pir of Manki Sharif and Bhutto was supported by Pir Makhdoom Shah of Hala in Sind. When the Pir of Pagaro did not support Bhutto he considerably undermined Bhutto's political position in Sind by joining the Pakistan National Alliance (PNA) in March 1977.

In general, the RE subscribed to the establishment of an Islamic state in which their power would be unrivalled. They exerted pressure on the governing elites through political organizations such as the Jamiatul-Ulema-i-Pakistan (JUP) and the Jamiatul-Ulema-i-Islam (JUI) which were powerful in the regions. The latter was influential in the NWFP, and its candidates in the southern districts made subtle use of religio-political slogans to induce voters to choose between RE candidates and others. Such slogans would ask questions like 'Will you vote for Abdul Majid or the Quran Majid?' The vote would decidedly be in favour of the RE.[5]

The most important political organization was the Jamaat-i-Islami (JI) which had been founded in 1941 by Maulana Maudoodi. Its well-knit internal organization consisted of members, workers and associate members. Its membership had increased from 75 in 1941 to 3,500 in 1978, and its associate members numbered close to half a million in Pakistan by the latter date. The head of the organization, known as the Amir, was elected by secret ballot and its power structure was decentralized from the centre to provincial, division and district branches within a wide-ranging organizational network.[6] According to Maudoodi, 90 per cent of Pakistani Muslims were illiterate, with a sound but blind faith in their religion. They were particularly open to exploitation by other political elites. Of the remaining ten per cent, he considered that 5 per cent had been corrupted by Westernization, and only 5 per cent were enlightened about Islam.[7] It was this group which constituted the most dedicated JI followers. Upon gaining admission to the JI, members had to adhere to stringent rules and live a life in accordance with the Quran and Sunnah.

The appeal of the JI was founded on three factors. First, its well organized publicity expounded Islamic formulae as solutions to all political, social and economic problems confronting the nation. Most JI publications were in Urdu and reached a mass readership. Secondly, party members exemplified the ideal Islamic man, free of corruption and other worldly evils. The perfection of Islam was shown to be their source of power, in marked contrast to the corruption rampant among other elite groups. Thirdly, Maudoodi's Islamic dialectics presented keen logical arguments to support Islamic orthodoxy.[8]

The JI's basic demand was the fundamental transformation of society to an Islamic model of development. It had constantly acted as a strong pressure group on the governing elites and although the RE never gained complete political power, their political influence often placed constraints on the political actions of the governing elites.[9] The latter therefore often paid lip-service to the RE in an effort to accommodate them.

Among the RE, there was elite factionalism between the Sunnis and Shias. The main reason for this conflict was historical, that is, the Shias believe that after the death of Prophet Mohammad, Caliph Ali (656–661) should have been installed as the first Caliph instead of Caliph Abu Bakr (632–634). The Sunnis hold that their differences could be settled by 'ijma' (consensus). This idea is rejected by the Shias who would lose to the Sunni majority. Shia Ulema are extremely powerful within their close-knit community and their support of the political elites is significant. However, despite such differences both sects approved the Islamization of the state. They differed rather on how it should be achieved, not on whether it should be done at all.

Islamization of the Ideological State

Until 1956 Pakistan was a state in political limbo. It did not have a constitution and there was a continual struggle between the traditional and colonial elites as to the role of Islam in the ideological state. In his address to the first Constituent Assembly on 11 August 1947 Jinnah had stated that religion, caste or creed would have 'nothing to do with the business of the state'.[10] In another speech to the nation, he had declared that although the majority of the people followed the teachings of Prophet Mohammad and enjoyed equal rights, self-respect and a sense of unity, Pakistan would not be a 'theocracy or any thing like it'.[11] He wanted a democratic constitution incorporating 'the essential principles of Islam', but Pakistan should not be a theocratic state, 'to be ruled by priests with a divine mission'.[12] Jinnah, as stated earlier, was a man of revolutionary orientation, but he did not live long enough to implement his ideology.

Liaquat Ali found himself under considerable pressure from the RE, apprehensive of their political future in the state. But the LE, BE and PE tried to influence the RE not to push for the institutionalization of Islam. They succeeded to some extent with the help of Maulana Shabbir Ahmed Usmani (a member of the Muslim League) who exerted his political influence on other members of the RE into accepting a compromise, the Objectives Resolution of 1949.

The following extract from the Resolution is quoted at length because of its far-reaching implications for the future of Islam. It stated that:

> Whereas sovereignty over the entire Universe belongs to Allah Almighty alone, and the authority which he has delegated to the State of Pakistan through its people for being exercised within the limits prescribed is a sacred trust;
>
> Whereas the founder of Pakistan, Quaid-i-Azam Mohammad Ali Jinnah, declared that Pakistan would be a democratic state based on Islamic principles of social justice;
>
> And whereas the Constituent Assembly, representing the people of Pakistan, have resolved to frame for the sovereign independent State of Pakistan a Constitution; wherein the State should exercise its powers and authority through the chosen representatives of the people;
>
> Wherein the principles of democracy, freedom, equality,

tolerance and social justice as enunciated by Islam, should
be fully observed;
    Wherein the Muslims of Pakistan would be enabled
individually and collectively to order their
lives in accordance with the teachings and
requirements of Islam, as set out in the Holy
Quran and Sunnah.[13]

The importance of the Objectives Resolution was such that it was
incorporated with minor changes in the Constitutions of 1956 and
1962. Many observers who endorsed it failed to see the contradictions thereby created, for the Resolution had integrated 'traditional' with 'Western' ideas and 'political democracy'. The country
was well on its way towards modernization.[14]

The truth of the matter was that the institutionalization of Islam
in the ideological state would have jeopardized the vested interests
of the feudal and capitalist forces as well as those of the BE and
PE.[15] It was interesting to note why the Objectives Resolution
'enabled' the Muslims of Pakistan and not 'compelled' them to
follow Islam. The Resolution actually avoided calling Pakistan an
'Islamic' or an 'ideological' state, which again indicated the triumph
of vested interests. Furthermore, it stated that 'sovereignty over the
entire universe belongs to Allah Almighty alone', and that He had
delegated authority to the people 'within the limits prescribed' by
Him' as a 'sacred trust'. Again, there were vital questions that were
not asked: through what media had God delegated this authority to
the people? Had He spoken to the then Prime Minister? If so, did
the limits prescribed by Him refer to the Quran and Shariah? How
could they be implemented if Pakistan was already a sovereign
independent state? Such contradictions in the Objectives Resolution destroyed rather than helped to build a national identity based
on Islam.

The PE viewed the Islamic teachings 'merely as a set of general
principles' on which they could not base the constitution of the
country.[16] Islamization was never attempted as it would have dis-
turbed too many political arrangements necessary for modernization. Their most important political gain was that by transferring the
authority from the Quran to the people of Pakistan, the governing
elites managed to keep their political authority intact.

The RE, as stated earlier, were generally distrustful of the Western educated political elites, and Maudoodi believed that only men
with intensely religious personal lives could be trusted to lead the
country. Otherwise, he questioned

Who will build up the required Islamic atmosphere? Can an
irreligious state with westernized persons at its helm do the job? Will
the architects who are all versed only in building bars and cinemas
spend their energies in erecting a Mosque? If the answer is
affirmative, it will indeed be a unique experiment in human history.
Godlessness fostering Godliness to dethrone itself.[17]

To Maudoodi the Muslim Shariah (Law) had three aspects: the
mandatory, recommendatory and the permissible. Mandatory laws
were fixed for eternity and had to form a major part of the Islamic
state. Recommendatory laws were those which were expected to be
followed but not formally enforced. Permissible laws were ones
where changes relative to the times could be instituted. To those
who considered that the mandatory Shariah, if applied, would leave
the ideological state unalterable, Maudoodi replied that these laws
had been operative in Indo-Pakistan until 1857 (when the British
assumed control), and with the creation of Pakistan the application
of Islamic laws should have been resumed.[18]

In 1948 Maudoodi proposed four conditions necessary for an
Islamic state. These were:
(1) That Pakistanis believe in the supreme sovereignty of God and
     the state will govern as His agent.
(2) That the basic law of the land is the Shariah which was rendered
     by Prophet Mohammad.
(3) That all such existing laws in conflict with the Shariah will be
     gradually repealed and no such conflicting laws may be framed
     in the future.
(4) That the state in exercising its powers shall have no authority to
     transgress the limits proposed by Islam.[19]

He further proposed that the Islamic state would have an elected
leader (like the Caliphs), there would be no political opposition,
and non-Muslims would be excluded from decision-making roles.

Maudoodi was one of those Ulemas who in the pre-Partition
times had found it difficult to compromise Islam with nationalism.
His political opponents, unable to match his scholarship, resorted to
stigmatizing him as anti-Pakistan. His views were held to reflect
traditional thinking because, 'shorn of their modern trappings and
the jargon of social sciences', they were 'similar to those of Ulemas
whom he criticized for being out of date and reactionary'.[20]
Maudoodi's opponents used every available political strategy to
separate Islam from Pakistani politics, but as suggested above, his
influence on the political system could not be ignored.

Despite the Objectives Resolution the RE were able to exert sufficient pressure to get the following concessions in the 1956 Constitution.

(1) The preamble stated that Pakistan would be a democratic state founded on Islamic principles.
(2) The name of the new state would be the Islamic Republic of Pakistan.
(3) The Head of State would be a Muslim.
(4) The specific Islamic provisions were that an Islamic research and instruction organization would be opened to give guidance to the President as well as assist in reconstructing a Muslim society. No anti-Quranic laws would be enacted and an Islamic Commission would redefine Islamic laws so that they could be integrated in an Islamic framework over a period of five years.
(5) Directive principles of state policy would be issued which would eliminate gambling, drinking, alcohol, prostitution, and parochial, racial, tribal, sectarian and provincial prejudices while implementing Zakat (alms-tax) and Islamic moral standards.[21]

In spite of the preceding clauses the 1956 Constitution in its entirety reflected the exploitation of Islam. The governing elites knew that religion was a link between them and the masses and that it acted as 'a foil to provide provincial and parochial loyalties'.[22] At the same time, they did not want the political participation of the Ulemas at the highest levels of decision-making. The RE were therefore consulted when needed and ridiculed at other times.[23]

In 1958, when the ME came into power, they were well aware of the political influence of the RE which had led to the imposition of the first martial law in the Punjab in 1953. On that occasion, the RE had forcefully confronted Nazimuddin's government with the anti-Ahmadiya movement. Maudoodi compared the Ahmadis to a 'cancer eating up and gradually consuming Muslim society'.[24] The movement demanded that the Ahmadis be declared a non-Muslim minority and that Foreign Minister Zafrullah Khan and all other Ahmadis be removed from governmental positions.[25] They threatened to resort to direct action unless their demands were met. Although the government rejected these demands if failed to take action to curtail the activities of the orthodox RE. Daultana (the Chief Minister of Punjab) delayed action because he believed it would damage the basis of his political support in the Punjab. Nazimuddin did not want to accede to the Jamaat's demands lest

Pakistan be accused of being a medieval theocratic state.[26] The outcome was that the RE incited the masses and encouraged religious fanaticism and violence which left murdered Ahmadis, riots and looting in its wake. Martial law had to be imposed to crush this revolt.

The ME therefore publicly professed the importance of Islam as a basis for national cohesion and solidarity. According to Ayub, the principles of Islam were eternal and were beacons for the faithful—for guidance and not stagnation. Hence the 'real secret of progress' was to 'comprehend the basic principles of Islam, hold fast to them, and under the searchlight of the past, discover fresh avenues for their application in the present and the future'.[27] In reality, the ME were not in favour of maintaining 'a medievally based religious state'.[28] The RE, too, had learned the futility of force when faced with the power of the military institution and began to resort to constitutional methods to achieve a place in the ideological state.

The 1962 Constitution introduced by the ME had included the Objectives Resolution in its Preamble. It also contained provisions to open an Advisory Council of Islamic Ideology whose twelve members would advise the governing elite on any questions for 'enabling and encouraging the Muslims of Pakistan to order their lives in all respects in accordance with the principles and concepts of Islam'.[29] Furthermore, in its amended principles of policy in 1963, the Constitution stated that 'no law shall be repugnant to the teachings and requirements of Islam as set out in the Holy Quran and Sunnah and all existing laws shall be brought in conformity with the Holy Quran and Sunnah'.[30]

Such clauses were not very meaningful and raised a number of questions. For example, who would decide whether a law was repugnant to the Quran and Sunnah? If it was to be a board of Ulemas, who would select and appoint them? If, on the other hand, the 'question was to be left to a court or law . . . whether the present courts of law were competent to decide the issue? Whether such courts or a board of Ulema be given legislative powers or should they be only recommendatory bodies?'[31] Such questions were left unanswered.

In 1961 the ME had enacted a Family Laws Ordinance which placed restrictions on polygamy and divorce practices. This was strongly opposed by the RE. The latter also opposed the military regime's foreign policy towards Communist China and accused it of being authoritarian, badly administered and attempting to undermine the Islamic basis of the country.[32] The ME responded by banning the party in January 1964 and imprisoning Maudoodi and 43 other leaders on charges of 'subversive activities against the state' and of becoming a 'danger to the public peace'.[33] This punishment was declared illegal by the judges of the High Court as the PE were also becoming more anti-Ayub.

In desperation, the RE then gave their political support to the Combined Opposition Party candidate, Miss Fatima Jinnah, in the elections of 1965. They rationalized her political candidacy by stating that in the 'unusual situation' that existed in the country the 'candidature of women as Head of State is not against the Shariah'.[34] This gamble, however, was unsuccessful.

The ME realized that they could not risk losing the support of the masses by being anti-Islamic. The military institution itself used the concept of 'Jihad' to reinforce the morale of their soldiers. Ayub, therefore, 'shrewdly used Islam to support the kind of authoritarian system that he envisioned for Pakistan.'[35] He did this in two ways: through religious training and the establishment of a Central Islamic Research Institute.

A Bureau of National Reconstruction organized religious training by holding three-day seminars for the Ulemas and two-month seminars for the Mullahs in charge of the Mosques. It also developed 'Khutbas' (sermons) for Friday prayers in Bengali and Urdu.[36] At Ayub's request, Javaid Iqbal (son of the philosopher Iqbal) wrote a book providing a national interpretation of Islam.[37] He proposed that the National Assembly could be given the power to interpret the law of Islam and that the government should establish a Ministry of Religious Affairs. In addition, all the mosques should employ Mullahs and Imams at fixed salaries. In this way, thought Ayub, the RE, with their tangential Islamic doctrines, could be state-controlled and supervised.[38]

The Central Islamic Research Institute was established by the ME to justify their political policies. The most sensitive of these were birth control, family laws and banking interests. It purported to 'interpret the teachings of Islam in such a way as to bring out its dynamic characteristics in the context of the intellectual and scientific progress of the modern world'.[39] The director of the Institute, Fazlur Rahman, wrote a book in 1966 assessing the religious dilemma of Pakistan. He stated that it lacked a 'positive formulation of Islam, of exactly spelling out what Islam has to say to the modern individual and society', for, 'should these societies fail to find an adequate answer, the only alternative left to them will be some form of secularism, and there is little doubt that this solution is tantamount to changing the very nature of Islam'.[40] The RE protested against the secularist trends evident in the interpretation of Islam, and, under their pressure, the director had to resign.

Ayub was a political pragmatist who claimed that without 'centralization, unity, and solidarity, no system can claim to be an Islamic system'.[41] His government therefore went so far as to set a date for the appearance of the moon, on which depended the celebration of the Muslim religious festivals. This date clashed with that set by the Ulemas and there was a great deal of public dissatisfaction. The Ulema subsequently attempted to discredit the use of scientific methods and Ayub was forced to relent. Later, when the state capital was moved from Karachi to Rawalpindi in 1960 and the new capital was named Islamabad, after the Islamic religion, even the city's architectural design showed that 'the main influence had been the teachings of the Koran, in which it was fobidden to represent certain shapes and forms'.[42] Thus, although government policies often toned down 'the religious issues in internal affairs',[43] this had to be done very carefully.

The RE survived all attacks, and during Yahya's regime (1968-71) put out a manifesto for contesting the 1970 elections. This manifesto included the following points:

(1) to consolidate the ideological basis of Pakistan;
(2) to ban usury and interest, stock exchanges, gambling, illegal sales and hoarding. In fact all forms of exploitation were to be ended by breaking monopolies and cartels in industry;
(3) national languages to replace English as the medium of instruction so that the dual system of education in Urdu and English could end;
(4) family planning schemes to be disbanded and the challenge from the growing population to be met by improving the resources of the country;
(5) social environment to be moulded in accordance with the tenets of Islam, and opposition to imperialism.[44]

The RE's policies were not supported in the 1970 elections because their manifesto proposed a religious solution to the problems confronting the country. They could not, and did not make claims that could not be legitimized by Islam. The PPP, on the other hand, made exaggerated promises which it had no intention of keeping.[45] Furthermore, the LE had supported the PPP in these elections, despite the fact that the PPP's socialist ideology was anti-Islamic. After the PPP victory, Bhutto's role in manipulating elite politics soon involved the Yahya government in a civil war.

The creation of Bangladesh shocked the whole Pakistani nation but it registered very strongly with the RE, particularly the JI. They knew that failure to institutionalize Islam had divided the nation. East Bengali scholars rationalized the separation by stating that they had supported the Pakistan movement, not because of the two-nation theory, but because it promised protection from economic exploitation by Hindus.[46] It can be argued, however, that the threat from the Hindu landowning and commercial classes was not only economic but religious as well, that is, the Muslims were primarily a target for exploitation because they *were* Muslims. The East Bengalis were as sensitive to the issue of religion as other Muslims,[47] and the 1946 communal riots had been the worst of their kind in the history of Indo-Pakistan. In the post-1971 period, the Bangladeshi do not have a significant ethnic problem but their attempts to secularize Bangladesh have not succeeded.

The role of Islam as a unifying political base in terms of consolidating a national identity had been completely ignored by the governing elites. The confusion over a national identity and the conflicts between various elite groups had made the governing elites insensitive to the real needs of the East Bengalis. This led to the emergence of ethnic nationalism (see chapter 10).

The State Religion and Islam

Bhutto's mandate for a socialist state, based upon the economic problems of Pakistan, had yet to be tested. His prime concern was to attract the masses to strengthen his political organization. The Ulema were distrustful of Bhutto's socialist ideology and called upon the military to assume power. The Jamaat's leader was arrested for this action.[48]

In April 1973, Bhutto tried to appease the RE by making Islam the 'state religion'—a status not given to religion by the previous Constitutions of 1956 and 1962. He also promised that 'all existing laws shall be brought in conformity with the injunctions of Islam as laid down in the Holy Quran and Sunnah'.[49] Like Ayub's Advisory Council of Islamic Ideology, Bhutto also made provisions for an Islamic Council which would give advice on Islamic matters. It made the teaching of 'Koran and Islamiat' compulsory and encouraged the teaching of Arabic and the inculcation of Islamic moral standards. Bhutto also set about to 'reorganize and nationalize religious affairs and institutions so that they are enabled to play their dual role in national affairs'.[50] His government wanted to 'integrate the Mosque and the Pesh Imam [the local Maulvi] into the progressive forces now being generated to revolutionize the society'.[51] A Ministry of Religious Affairs was opened, headed by a Maulana whose religious credentials were not accepted by the RE.

In time it became clear to the RE that the more Bhutto implemented socialist measures to justify his policies through economic rather than religious legitimation, the more it led to the secularization of the state. He even sought to replace the fundamental pillar of Pakistan, Islam, by following the Bengalis' rationalization that it was the economic advantages for the Muslims that had led to its creation and not religion. Bhutto's socialism, therefore, was never able to reconcile the RE, most of whom issued 'fatwas' (religious decrees) condemning his regime's policies.[52]

Bhutto's final strategy was to win RE support by attempting to resolve the problem of the religious status of the Ahmadiya sect which had remained in abeyance since 1953. Through an Act of Parliament in 1974 he declared the Ahmadiyas a 'non-Muslim minority'. In 1976 he invited Imams from the mosque in Medina (Saudi Arabia) and the Ka'aba to lead the faithful in prayer in cities all over Pakistan and also ordered copies of the Holy Quran to be placed in every room of 'all first-class hotels in the country'.[53] His manifesto for the 1977 elections also promised to 'hold high the banner of Islam', declare Friday a holiday, establish a Federal Ulema Academy, and make Quranic instruction compulsory.[54] Despite all these measures his credibility, like that of his Maulanas (Kauser Niazi), remained dubious.

The RE led the nine-party coalition, the Pakistan National Alliance. Bhutto's success in the 1977 elections led to post-election conflicts where the conservative elites and masses totally refused to accept secular political leadership. They demanded his resignation and asked for new elections under the supervision of the ME and PE (i.e. the judges). As a last bid to win the support of his rivals and the masses, Bhutto constituted an Islamic Ideological Council to submit a report containing proposals for the implementation of the Islamic Shariah in the state within six months.

The Future of the Nizam-I-Mustafa

Since the third military regime took over the political arena, there has been a tremendous resurgence of the demand for the Islamization of Pakistan. This has meant the ushering in of a new political order: the Nizam-i-Mustafa (the Islamic system). The lack of a national identity has been recognized by the military regime and some practical steps are being taken to resolve the problem. In January 1978 the Supreme and High Courts were empowered to redefine any laws considered repugnant to the Quran and Shariah.[55] In addition, a high-powered Council of Islamic Ideology was set up in 1977 to recommend to the government the measures necessary for the imposition of the Nizam-i-Mustafa in the state. This council had representatives from the PE, RE and BE.[56]

The receptivity of the governing elites to ideas about the implementation of the Nizam-i-Mustafa has further encouraged the RE to articulate their demands. The All Pakistan Khatim-i-Nabuwat Conference held in Chiniot (Punjab) in December 1977 condemmed socialism and the Ahmadiya sect, and demanded that only Islamic ideology be propagated in the ideological state.[57] They also wanted any anti-Islamic forces to be eliminated. The RE belonging to the JUP (Maulana Noorani, Maulana Niazi and Maulana Okarvi) issued a joint statement to the Chief Martial Law Administrator, urging him to make the future Constitution of Pakistan subservient to the Nizam-i-Shariah and to impose the civil, criminal and social laws incorporated the medieval Islamic codes (the Fiqh-i-Hanafia, Hadaya Shariah, and Fatawa-Alamgiri).[58] The new Constitution of the PNA also reiterated that the solidarity and integrity of the ideology of Pakistan must be safeguarded and preserved, and all steps necessary should be taken to organize national life in accordance with the Nizam-i-Mustafa.

The Council of Islamic Ideology has brought out an ambitious programme for the Islamization of Pakistan, and some of the Islamic criminal codes have already been put to practice (e.g. public hanging and flogging). How far these measures will succeed will depend on the sincerity of the governing elites and their ability to maintain their position against vested interests.

The history of Pakistan has shown that its political elites have used Islam as a tool to generate acceptance and to reinforce their elite doctrines and policies. Ayub's Constitution Commission had stated that

> this state cannot be, in the nature of things, secular, as Islam pervades the life of a Muslim in all its aspects and does not allow politics to be kept apart from ethics, as in the case of countries with secular constitutions. The moment it is stated that Pakistan is an ideological, and not secular, State, our critics at once think of a theocracy which, in its widely accepted sense, is ruled by the priests in the name of God; but there is no priesthood in Islam and we are . . . therefore

theocratic only to the extent that we hold that real sovereignty belongs to God.[59]

Ayub had believed that the Islamic social order was interchangeable with a welfare state,[60] but his alliance with the IE created antagonistic class structures incompatible with the egalitarianism explicit in Islam.

For the implementation of an Islamic system, a radical change in Pakistan's feudal and capitalist system will be necessary. In an interview with the Chairman of the Council of Islamic Ideology, the author did not get the impression that such radical changes within the conservative or revolutionary Islamic contexts were likely to be forthcoming. What seemed to emerge was a mixture of compromises with the previous corrupt system. An Islamic system cannot be introduced by forcing people to say prayers, propagating Islam through posters and media, or by cutting off hands for theft. A start should be made by focusing on the systems operating in Pakistani society and not on the people. The infrastructures created by the feudal and capitalist systems to safeguard vested interests will offer the greatest resistance to the Islamic order. Furthermore, the hierarchical judicial system will have to be dismantled if justice is to be brought within the reach of both rich and poor. Before cutting off the hand of a poor thief, the important question that must be asked is what factors led him to commit the crime? If it turns out that he stole, not out of compulsive habit but out of a need or necessity, then the whole economic system needs to be questioned. This cannot be done without reconstructing the social realities of the prevailing capitalist system which has generated the class structure within each ethnic group.

A radical reconstruction within the conservative or revolutionary prescriptions of Islam would narrow social disparities by the redistribution of wealth. Other infrastructures that maintain the status quo of the rich will also have to be closely examined. For example, the educational system which imparts differential education in the country on the basis of wealth and not ability will need to be completely changed. At present there are institutions where the medium of instruction is English, others where it is Urdu—while the poor child can neither afford nor get the opportunity for any education. The class structure corrodes the egalitarian principles of Islam, and no Nizam-i-Mustafa can be implemented without first removing the disparities caused by the feudal and capitalist systems operating in the country.

6

The Industrial Elites

The industrial elites were the ultimate product of the capitalist system which had been introduced into the sub-continent in the eighteenth century. Before the Partition of India the economic roles of the IE were basically unpolitical since they were content to be politically dependent upon the colonialists.

The Hindus had established themselves at the top of the business hierarchy in India. In the areas of India which later became Pakistan, the Hindus owned banks, insurance companies, manufacturing plants and commercial firms. Partition precipitated their mass exodus to India from these regions, leaving the capitalist system 'leaderless' in Pakistan.[1]

Pakistan's industrial elites can therefore be categorized as emergent, for the history of their rise to both economic and political power can be traced from 1947 onwards. Some of the big business families, like the Adamjees, Isphanis, Wazir Alis and Habibs, had funded the Pakistan Movement, but apart from this their political activity was of minimal significance.[2]

Since British rule had been opposed by some Muslim-dominated regions, the colonial reward system had been differential. Thus, the NWFP and Baluchistan had only been developed to facilitate colonial military operations in these areas. In the Punjab and Sind, the feudal system was promoted and the development of these states was more pronounced than the tribal regions. East Bengal was undeveloped and it remained as a hinterland for Hindu Bengali landlords and businessmen from Calcutta. It was estimated that out of a total of 921 factories in British India, only 34 came within Pakistan's territorial domain.[3] According to another estimate, of the 14,569 industrial units only 1,406 were located in Pakistan.[4]

The Muslim trading communities that migrated from India emerged as the new business leaders in Pakistan. At the time of Partition, the new state had very little business capital but an enormous business potential. The new entrepreneurial group came primarily from Bombay, Kathiawar and Gujrat; some arrived from Burma and East Africa as well. They brought their capital with them, some of which was smuggled by concealment in personal effects.[5] They did not face business competition with other elite groups, and gradually began to construct a major role for themselves in the country's industrial development.

Ethnic Structures and Economic Power

As ethnicity permeated Pakistani society, its peculiar imprint, by accident or design, was also characteristic of the business structure. Muslims in general had not been inclined towards entrepreneurial activities, and West Pakistan had a feudal structure with a history of domination by the military, landowning and religious elite groups. A sample of twelve business families gives an idea of the predominant ethnic structure of the IE (see Table 6). Three significant observations can be made from this sample. First, there was a lack of East Bengali entrepreneurs among the IE. Secondly, the IE were mainly from the Punjabi and Muhajir groups. Among the Punjabis, the Chiniotis predominated, while among the Muhajirs, the Memons, Bohras and Khojas (from Gujrat, Kathiawar and Surat in India) were the dominant group. Thirdly, the headquarters of their business concerns were located in Lahore (Punjab) or Karachi (Sind). The political and economic impact of these factors was important for its reinforced elitist rule and led to uneven economic development of other regions in the country.

The range of the manufacturing assets of these business concerns was rather limited, as indicated by the following table based on a study of 43 businesses (see Table 7). From this table it is evident that over 40 per cent of the manufacturing assets were concentrated in cotton textiles and jute, followed by chemical and sugar industries, with over 20 per cent of assets. Jute was grown only in East Pakistan, and the EBPE were not wrong when they accused the IE capitalists of treating their province as a colony of Pakistan to be exploited for its raw materials and resources.

The speed with which the IE built their industrial empires surprised outside observers who noted how this 'small but active

Table 6: SOCIAL AND BUSINESS BACKGROUNDS OF THE TWELVE
BIG HOUSES

Name	Community	Family Origin	Business Location pre-1947	Head-quarters Location* post-1947
Dawood	Memon	Kathiawar (Bantua)	Bombay	Karachi
Habib	Khoja Ishnasheri	Bombay	Bombay	Karachi
Admajees	Memon	Kathiawar (Jetpur)	Calcutta	Karachi
Crescent	Punjabi Sheikh	Western Punjab (Chiniot)	Delhi	Lahore
Saigol	Punjabi Sheikh	Western Punjab (Chakwal)	Calcutta	Lahore
Valika	Dawoodi Bohra	Bombay	Bombay	Karachi
Hyesons	(None)	Madras	Madras	Karachi
Bawany	Memon	Kathiawar (Jetpur)	Rangoon	Karachi
Amin	Punjabi Sheikh	Western Punjab	Calcutta	Lahore
Wazirali	Punjabi (Syed)	Western Punjab (Lahore)	Lahore	Lahore
Fancy	Khoja Ismaili	Kathiawar	East Africa	Karachi
Colony	Punjabi Sheikh	Western Punjab (Chiniot)	Lahore	Lahore

Source: Adapted from: Hanna Papanek, 'Pakistan's Big Businessmen: Muslim Separatism, Entrepreneurship, and Partial Modernization', in *Economic Development and Cultural Change*, Vol. 21, No. 1 (October 1972), p. 27.
*Note** This portion of the table has been added by the author.

entrepreneurial class'[6] had taken 'the busy bee route to development'.[7] The ruthlessness of their capitalist exploitation was not learnt through academic institutions, but through family socialization. One study indicated that 46.5 per cent of the industrialists from leading families had never finished high school education. Only 19.0 per cent had done so and 27.5 per cent had had some kind of college education, while 6.5 per cent had received no formal education at all.[8] Socialization within the family provided them with all the skills necessary to appropriate surplus value through others' labour and their own investment. This ensured that the business remained under family control or within the ethnic community.

When business empires expanded and became too complex for the family to handle, corporations were formed. Actual control, however, was still retained by members of the family. A number of families was sometimes interlocked in corporate organizations, with representatives of each family forming the board of directors. Very few, if any, outsiders were allowed into decision-making positions. In the ultimate analysis, these groups were very ethnically oriented.

Table 7: CONTROL OF MANUFACTURING ASSETS BY INDUSTRY, 1968 (RS. MILLION)

	Assets controlled	% of total holdings by 43 families
Cotton Textiles	Rs. 1,707.8	27.0
Jute Textiles	1,004.1	15.9
Chemicals	763.2	12.1
Sugar	696.6	11.0
Petroleum	464.9	7.4
Cement	360.5	5.7
Steel and Metal Manufacturing	271.6	4.3
Paper	263.8	4.2
Wood and Artificial Silk-textiles	169.8	2.7
Vehicle Assembly	133.1	2.1
Vegetable Ghee	119.2	1.9
Miscellaneous Food	53.8	0.9
Miscellaneous	306.2	4.8
Total	6,314.6	100.0

Source: L. J. White, *Industrial Concentration and Economic Power in Pakistan* (Princeton, N.J. Princeton University Press, 1974), p. 68.

Most business families preferred to employ management personnel from within their own ethnic groups. They also showed a great deal of concern for their own communities and provided trust funds for orphans and employment for members of the community. Some, like the Bohras and Khojas, had very close-knit communities with a deep distrust of members of other ethnic groups.

Economic Power and the Political System

Political scientists have recognized that there are some cases where new states were autonomous and political power shaped economic power.[9] In Pakistan, the state was not ruled by a permanent oligarchy but at any point in time was under the control of an elite group, who, by horizontal or vertical alliances, could keep others from dominating it.

Economic wealth was only one means of acquiring political power, but coercion (ME), administrative skills (BE) and ideology (RE) were all equally, if not more, powerful channels. Above all, apart from capitalism, feudalism was entrenched in the countryside and the political influence of the LE was predominant, concerned as they were with their own landed interests. The latter considered the IE 'upstarts', as money could not be equated with a good family background. Thus the IE had to forge alliances with the governing elites to secure their vested interests and extend their business ventures into other provinces.

In their new environment the IE were quick to learn certain political strategies to maximize their economic power. They did not enjoy any political power in the early years, and commercial legislation seemed to have been conceived 'almost independently of the interests of the IE'.[10] The BE were in control of the political arena and the IE soon formed a horizontal alliance with them, establishing some formal channels of interest articulation. Trade associations had begun to emerge but they were not forceful enough to secure their demands. During the first decade of Pakistan's independence there were as many as 1300 chambers of commerce and trade associations, each of whose vested interests competed for priority in the government's economic policies.[11] With a proliferation of interest groups there was little organizational cohesion, and competition against other groups often served to diffuse their political influence.

Such organizational weakness and factionalism within the IE served the interests of the governing BE. The latter were facing a threat to their political power from the LE at provincial and national levels. The underdevelopment of the agricultural sector and the development of the industrial sector during this period was not by accident, and was related to the forces operating within the political system. In the 1950s the surplus value earned from agricultural exports such as cotton and jute was siphoned off and used for industrial development.

One commentator suggests that the 'major impact of economic policy in the 1950s was to transfer income away from agricultural and from urban consumers and to the new and rapidly growing manufacturing sector'.[12] This was achieved by setting low prices for agricultural output and high prices for consumer goods produced by industry. Investment in the agricultural sector was no longer a profitable proposition. Bureaucrats rationalized that 'government policy . . . did not adequately emphasize agricultural development, perhaps because everyone unconsciously took food surpluses for granted and [also because] a mistaken belief seemed to gain ground that economic development was synonymous with industrial development'.[13]

Despite their struggle with the LE the BE had continued to exercise strong and rigid control over the industrial sector because they did not want the IE to become a threat to their political power. They controlled imports, exports, investments and production.[14] The IE did not try to oppose the BE by forming an alliance with the LE. On the contrary, they attempted to open new channels for exerting political influence on the BE. They advertised appeals to the governing elites through the media and reported their demands in business journals. They invited governing elites to business meetings and annual dinners as guests of honour. Lobbying in the legislatures was done 'armed with their cheque books . . . without having to go to the trouble of becoming members of the House'.[15] Their strongest strategy, and one of mutual benefit to the BE and IE, was the use of corruption. Such private transactions became the accepted mode of operation whenever the IE faced obstacles with government departments whose decisions could directly or indirectly affect their vested interests.[16]

The corruption of the bureaucracy was not a random occurrence. The author's close observations gave him an insight of how it operated, at what levels and with what benefits. It was the IE's strongest alliance-forming linkage with the political system. Although the Ayub, Yahya and Bhutto regimes dismissed a number of corrupt officials, those replacing them often continued the same practices.

During the second decade of Pakistan's existence, the power of IE increased, but not before the ME had chastised the BE for their corruption and the IE for deriving illegal benefits from them. Under Martial Law regulations, some industrialists were arrested (e.g. A. A. Karim, M.A. Rangoonwala and A. K. Sumar) but later released as a gesture of goodwill. Others were prosecuted for filing incorrect income tax returns, black marketeering, dealing with illegal foreign exchange and hoarding wealth abroad. Through these measures the military government recovered about 50 million dollars from tax evaders, and 281,400,000 dollars were declared as hidden wealth.[17] In fact, one of the reasons for moving the old capital from Karachi to Islamabad was to maintain a check on the alliance between the BE and IE.

Economic development was the first priority of the ME. They organized the Federation of the Chambers of Commerce and

Industry by uniting all previously isolated chapters. This became the principal channel of communication 'between business and the government'.[18] The private sector was assisted in increasing its industrial output and expansion. However, as wealth alone was not a guarantee of their security in an elitist system the IE sought further alliances with the bureaucrats, military and landlords through inter-marriages and offering partnerships or employment in industry.[19] They also assumed control of some newspapers. The ultimate ambition of young Pakistanis changed from joining the CSP to wanting to become industrial magnates.

The IE's financing of political parties has been mentioned earlier. This strategy safeguarded their vested interests whichever party came to power. One industrial family (Haroon Group) had retained Mujibur Rahman on their payroll as the director of an insurance company for fifteen years. They also donated 300,000 dollars to his 1970 election campaign.[20] Other industrialists (e.g. the Dawoods) were loyal supporters of the Ayub regime, and one of them (Siddiq Dawood) even became the treasurer of the Pakistan Muslim League and funded Ayub's election campaign. The 'Basic Democracy' system of the ME further encouraged them to consolidate their position and political power. The National and Provincial Assemblies of 1962 and 1965 had a considerable representation of businessmen.[21] Ayub's government was accordingly labelled a 'businessman's government'.[22] The progress of the 'Robber Barons' along with the 'Gentleman at Work' did succeed in 'confounding the prophets'.[23]

The IE had thus succeeded in forming alliances with the BE during the 1951–8 period and with the ME during the 1958–71 period. These alliances were clearly influenced by the fact that the BE and ME were also dominated by the Punjabi and Muhajir groups.

The Capitalist Mode of Production

The ideology of the capitalist system is based on the essential dogma that 'the function of economic enterprise is the pursuit of profit'.[24] The goal of profit maximization has many aspects, three of which were particularly relevant in the case of Pakistan. First was the creation of a class structure in which the IE emerged as a product of the system. Secondly, with no limits on their possession of wealth, the IE expanded in all directions irrespective of the social or political cost to the nation. Those who prospered called it economic freedom while those who suffered called it exploitation. Thirdly, the capitalist system necessarily involves imperialism. Such imperialism (under U.S. hegemony) was easily accessible. The USA was not interested in disturbing internal political arrangements so long as their foreign policy interests were served. How their influence related to the political system has been discussed elsewhere. Suffice it to say here that these factors all contributed to the uneven economic development of the country.

The capitalist system also created an inequality of income because incomes were distributed 'to each according to what he and the instrument he owns produces'.[25] This was another dogma of the capitalist system which succeeded in adding to the ranks of the industrial masses and appropriating the surplus value of their labour power.[26] With the maximization of profits as their main goal, the capitalists controlled the industrial masses through the payment of low wages. Such inequality did not help to integrate a nation like Pakistan, especially in view of the ethnic nature of the exploitation.

Pakistan's capitalist system had been described as the 'most primitive system in the world ... a system in which economic feudalism prevails', and 'a handful of people . . .' made 'all the basic decisions and the system often worked' simply because there 'was an alliance between various vested interests'.[27] The most appalling aspect of the system was that nothing was done to diffuse the gross inequalities it created. The imperialists were aware of the 'problems of inequality' but dismissed them by stating that such inequalities contributed to 'the growth of the economy which makes possible a real improvement for the lower income groups'.[28] These attitudes towards income differentials were typical of capitalist thinking for they justified the existence of 'lower income groups' as an essential incentive for 'improvement'. The rationale was that if the wealth was distributed, who would have the motivation to work? Pakistani economists indoctrinated with Western academic theories reasoned that 'social surplus' was not exploitation but a form of savings or capital formation. To them the important thing was 'maximizing the creation of this surplus' because 'its justification was economic growth'.[29] How such imperialist influences penetrated the central economic planning bodies has been discussed in the last chapter. It led later, by their own confessions, to the enrichment of the few families who controlled 66 per cent of Pakistan's industrial assets and 80 per cent of its insurance funds.[30]

Income inequalities were reflected in the different life styles of the people. The elites had life styles that involved the conspicuous consumption of imported goods. For example, during the development decade (1958–68) over 300 million dollars were spent on the import of private cars while 20 million dollars were spent on public transport. At the same time, private luxury housing accounted for 80–90 per cent of the construction that took place in the country.[31]

Since capitalism is not the main theme of this book it will be treated in the Pakistani context in terms of its ethnic implications for the political system. The two main areas of impact were uneven economic development in the provinces and inequalities in income differentials, both of which politically mobilized the elite/mass.

Uneven Economic Development

The uneven economic development of Pakistan was not a coincidence. The IE had wanted to transform Pakistan into a capitalist state in which their vested interests were given priority and they in turn could control political power. Their ideology of profit maximization was not concerned with the social, political and economic

Table 8:   DEVELOPMENT EXPENDITURE OF PAKISTAN: 1947–1970
(crores of rupees)

Period	East Bengal	West Pakistan	East Bengal as a % of total
Pre-Plan period 1947–55	240	618	28
First Five Year Plan, 1955–60	336	722	32
Second Five Year Plan, 1960–65	970	1860	34**
Third Five Year Plan, 1965–70	1680	2610*	39
Total for 23 years, 1947–1970	3266	5810	35.7

*A crore is ten million

**Excluding Indus Basin expenditure in West Pakistan of Rupees 290 crores and 360 crores in the Second and Third Plans respectively. Including Indus Basin expenditure in West Pakistan, the proportion for East Bengal would be 33.5 per cent of total expenditure.

Source: Adapted from: M. A. Mannan, *Economic Problems and Planning in Pakistan* (Lahore: Ferozesons, 1970), pp. 253, 256 and 258.

Table 9:   TRADE BALANCES FOR EAST AND WEST PAKISTAN 1948–1967
(crores of rupees)

Period	Foreign Balance		Inter-wing Balance	Overall Balance	
	East	West	East(−) West(+)	East	West
1948–49	14.68	−64.83	12.05	2.63	−52.78
1949–50	24.41	−34.70	18.51	5.90	−16.19
1950–51	75.82	−17.54	20.85	74.97	+38.39
1951–52	32.31	−15.20	18.77	13.54	−36.43
1952–53	27.61	−14.99	6.92	20.69	−8.07
1953–54	35.19	−18.33	23.50	11.69	+5.17
1954–55	41.14	−29.16	10.68	30.46	−18.48
1955–56	68.08	−22.21	9.55	58.51	−12.16
1956–57	9.09	−81.78	19.77	−10.68	−52.01
1957–58	25.25	−88.07	43.29	−18.04	−44.78
1958–59	32.72	− 58.02	39.71	−6.99	−18.31
1959–60	42.43	−104.26	20.10	22.33	−84.16
1960–61	24.48	−163.30	45.54	−21.06	−117.76
1961–62	42.78	−169.30	45.09	−21.31	−124.25
1962–63	23.06	−180.20	48.44	−25.38	−131.76
1963–64	−22.44	−190.66	38.40	−60.84	−152.26
1964–65	−43.37	−252.63	33.74	−77.11	−218.87
1965–66	18.61	−167.67	—	—	—
1966–67	10.04	−126.76	—	—	—

Source: Mohammad Anisur Rahman, 'East and West Pakistan: A Problem in the Political
Economy of Regional Planning' (Cambridge: Center for International Affairs, Harvard University Press, 1968), pp. 8, 12.

costs incurred in the process of national development. Their wealth
was more important than their loyalty to the country. Since such
wealth was easily transferrable, whenever political upheavals
threatened the country they were the first to flee with their riches.
During the civil war of 1971, many of the industrial families were in
London looking for new sources of investment. One London bank
even started advertising for deposits at $7\frac{1}{2}$ per cent interest for such
purposes.[32]

The alliance of the IE with the governing elites and subsequent
political strategies have been mentioned earlier. These alliances
were used to influence economic policies in the IE's favour. The
most blatant of these was the much greater industrialization of West
Pakistan as compared to East Bengal.[33] Table 8 outlines clearly the
allocation of development expenditures. The frustration and dis-

content of the people in East Bengal were further aggravated by the low wages in both its urban and rural areas. The cost of living index was also lower than that of West Pakistan.[34] The situation was not improved by the transfer of resources from East Bengal to West Pakistan. In East Bengal there was a surplus of foreign exchange from international trade but a deficit in the balance of their inter-wing trade with West Pakistan. The foreign exchange earnings of the East Bengalis were used to make up this inter-wing deficit, primarily incurred by West Pakistan (see Table 9).

A further example of this uneven economic development can be seen in the case of one city in West Pakistan, Karachi, which had a population of less than 4 per cent of the national total. Of a total of 1940 million dollars invested in 1958, 1146 million went to Karachi.[35] Private investment on the whole was much greater in West Pakistan (see Table 10). Industrialization of the provinces of Punjab and Karachi was much faster than that of East Bengal, NWFP, Sind and Baluchistan.[36] A widening of the disparities between West Pakistan and East Bengal led to an increase in the per capita income of the former from 17 per cent in 1949–50 to 32 per cent in 1959–60 and 60 per cent in 1969–70.[37]

Table 10:   PRIVATE INVESTMENT IN EAST BENGAL AND WEST PAKISTAN
1963–1968

| | Million rupees | | Percentage of total | |
	East Bengal	West Pakistan	East Bengal	West Pakistan
1963–64	547	2,091	21	79
1964–65	817	2,614	24	76
1965–66	681	2,397	22	78
1966–67	819	2.918	22	78
1967–68	1,038	3,647	22	78
Total	3,903	13,667	22	78

Source: Pakistan Planning Commission, *The Mid-plan Review of the Third Five Year Plan, 1965–1970*, p. 39.

The Fourth Five-year Plan (1970–75) realized that the concentration of wealth in the hands of a few family groups had led to 'pre-emption of new sanctions and bank credit by big industrial families, resulting in denial of fair opportunities to late comers'.[38] It had therefore stated that a 'determined effort' would be made to spread industrialization to East Pakistan[39] and some measures would be adopted to redress the economic disparity (such as the redistribution of resources between centre and province, regional economic planning, and rural economic development through works programmes).[40] All these measures proved to be insufficient.

The Pakistan Industrial Development Corporation (PIDC), established in 1951, was primarily responsible for industrial investment by industrial families (particularly the Adamjees, Dawoods, Amin, Crescent, Isphani and Karim) in East Bengal, but their head offices were all in West Pakistan. The PIDC even had many industrialists on its board of directors (e.g. Isphani, Naseer A. Sheikh, Adamjee and Syed Amjad Ali). The main objective of the PIDC was the 'promotion and not state ownership of the industries'.[41] As individuals tended to be concerned with the welfare of their own region, the ethnic factor in uneven economic development becomes evident.[42]

The influence of Western economic models of development, foreign advisors (notably the Harvard Advisory Group) in the Planning Commission, foreign aid and some governing elites helped to perpetuate such uneven economic development. One economist apologised for the 'seven deadly sins' they had committed, which had sown the seeds of vehement distrust between the ethnic groups.[43] Their policies led neither to structural integration of the two wings of Pakistan (by giving the East Bengalis numerical representation) nor to functional integration (by giving the East Bengalis a united identity through political participation). In order to defend their economic policies the West Pakistanis had propounded the 'one-economy' thesis, which rationalized that economic development of any part (where its demand and absorption capacity could be utilized) would automatically result in the 'development' of the less developed areas. The Bengalis therefore put forward a 'two-economy' theory because they realized that investment in one wing of the country had been to their disadvantage and had not had a 'spread effect' on their province.[44] Bengali investors faced unyielding competition from well-established Punjabi and Muhajir business families which hindered the economic development of East Bengal.[45]

Bengali political elites had warned the West Pakistanis that if they wanted 'national integration', they should 'treat us equally in the economic life of the country'.[46] It was not surprising, therefore, that the Awami League's Six Point Programme was fanatically supported by the EBPE, the middle sector bourgeoisie and Bengali industrial masses.

The Plight of the Industrial Masses

While the rich capitalists became richer the poor became poorer in Pakistan owing to the inequalities of income inherent in the primitive capitalist system. Who were these masses? This section will focus on the masses who had only one commodity—their labour—to sell and no power.

The industrial masses were composed of two main groups, the Muhajirs and the people who had migrated from rural areas. The Muhajirs were mainly resident in Karachi, and in 1950 they made up 14 per cent of the total labour force in Pakistan's manufacturing sector. By 1961 this figure had reached 29 per cent.[47] The others had come from the rural areas of NWFP and the Punjab. The industrial masses were somewhat more organized than the peasantry, and worked in close cooperation with political parties which could promise them concessions.

In 1964 there were 844 trade unions, most of which were affiliated to the All Pakistan Confederation of Labour. A majority of the union membership was from establishments employing from 1000 to over 20,000 workers. Despite this apparent strength, 'most unions were largely paper organizations'.[48] The labour leaders developed a 'middleman' role to bargain for the interests of the industrial masses with the industrialists. They were essentially 'gherao organizers' who could incite the industrial masses into taking industrial action.

The industrial masses lived at a subsistence level, owing to their low wages and high prices in the country. They worked long hours under unsatisfactory conditions and no security of service. Their unions demanded better pay scales, bonuses, pension schemes, housing, medical and transport allowances, the right to form trade unions and strike for negotiation of better conditions.

Ayub had promised to give a better deal to the industrial masses, and some laws were enacted (e.g. the West Pakistan Industrial Relations Ordinance 1960, Minimum Wages Ordinance 1961 and Industrial Relations Ordinance 1969) to that effect. These were essentially half-measures, as Ayub depended on the IE to provide jobs, and the question that arose was 'how could the system permit more benefit to workers . . . when [its] policy was to increase the income of the industrialists'.[49] The Joint Labour Council, formed in 1969, joined the anti-Ayub movement and helped to paralyse his government.[50] During the Yahya regime, a new labour policy was formulated by Air Marshall Nur Khan—but it was never implemented.

The industrial masses had supported Bhutto in the 1970 elections. In 1972, he sought to protect the rights of the workers by providing increased participation in management, bonuses, housing and job security. He also created organizations like the People's Public Works Department, the National Development Volunteer Corps and National Development Corporation which helped unskilled, semi-skilled and skilled workers to exploit job opportunities in the private and public sectors. The government also facilitated the migration of Pakistani labour into Middle Eastern countries.[51]

Bhutto's labour policy of 1972 brought relative benefits to the industrial masses, but could neither meet their increasing demands nor stem the rising inflation in the country. The industrial masses continued to suffer hardship and, in April 1977, 'leadership of the anti-Bhutto movement in the principal cities was also assumed by the industrial workers'.[52]

The Industrial Elites Under Bhutto

The IE feared Bhutto for two reasons. First, Bhutto was a product of the feudal political culture and his horizontal alliances were with the LE. Secondly, Bhutto was popular with the masses, particularly the peasantry and workers. Bhutto had promised them 'roti, kapra and makan' (food, clothing and shelter), and this could not be achieved without an equitable distribution of wealth.

Bhutto's first action on assuming power was to purge the IE by impounding the passports of leading capitalists.[53] One of them (Ahmed Dawood) immediately made a plea for the political survival of his elite group by stating that 'If you kill [a] cow, you have meat for one day only. But if you keep [the] cow, you have milk everyday. Pakistan needs milk now.'[54]

As part of his socialist programme, Bhutto's next step (in January 1972) was to nationalize 31 industrial units in ten basic categories. These were iron, steel and heavy engineering, heavy electrical, basic metals, assembly and manufacture of motor vehicles, heavy and basic chemicals, petrochemicals, cement, utilities, electricity, gas and oil. In March 1972, 32 life insurance companies were nationalized, and in January 1974 the private banks followed suit. Some industrial units lost all their assets in the process of nationalization, while others lost up to 50 per cent of them.[55] Despite these measures, however, they still held considerable economic power through other investments.

Bhutto's initial enthusiasm for nationalization did not last long, as his bureaucratic appointees could not adequately control the industrial units nor could they produce the same profits as before.[56] In this instance, Bhutto's lack of faith in the bureaucracy was not misplaced. To stop the panic among the IE he had to assure them that the 'government had no intention to take over any more industries'.[57] These measures had a profound impact on the economy of the country and the IE retained its distrust of Bhutto.

To consolidate his control over the business families, Bhutto's Managing Agency and Election Directors Orders (1972) abolished the Managing Agency System. This was a system the IE had learnt from the colonialists,[58] whereby 'promotion, finance, and administration of a vast agglomeration of miscellaneous and unrelated enterprises' were 'controlled by a single firm'.[59] By a combination of underpricing and overpricing inputs and outputs these agencies appropriated profits that were neither shared by non-family stockholders nor paid in taxes to the government. One such example was the group that owned the controlling stock of the Steel Corporation of Pakistan, Ltd.[60] Its purchasing agents were Pakistan Industries Ltd., and the selling agents Steel Sales Ltd. It was managed by another company Industrial Managements Ltd. All these were owned by the Fancy family group. The Managing Agencies were criticized as the 'worst institutions of loot and plunder through which the cream of profit was skimmed off by a handful of people' and they exercised a 'complete stronghold over the industry'.[61]

Bhutto, as mentioned earlier, was a feudalist and not really a socialist and, as such, his measures were not very effective. Only a political leader without vested interests could accomplish his declared purpose. But, even so, Bhutto had to yield to some of the demands of his electorate. His economic strategy was therefore to keep the IE in control through the industrial workers. Nationalization was a political weapon to control industrial wages, which were 60 per cent higher than under the Ayub regime.[62]

Bhutto's labour reforms had helped to improve labour–management relations to some extent. But his attempts to maintain a stable price policy 'brought the private sector into direct conflict with the administration', because it 'eroded industrial profits'.[63] To prevent the IE from sabotaging his economic policies he assured them that 'private enterprise has a role to play in the progress of Pakistan'.[64] Later, he also affirmed his belief in 'the concept of a mixed economy in which both private and public sectors play their due share' and not in 'absolute state power manifesting itself in a totally nationalized, centralized economy'.[65]

Such dual policies raised serious differences of opinion within the PPP on the mode of action to be taken towards the industrial sector. The party's left wing was in favour of a command economy whilst Bhutto and others favoured more moderate policies. This led to the removal of the left-wing Dr Mubasher Hassan on 22 October 1974 to be replaced by Mohammad Hanif, who was more moderate.

The IE remained suspicious of Bhutto, and investment in the private sector suffered due to fluctuations in the regime's socialist facade. As Table 11 points out, there was a decrease in the large investments of the private sector and an increase in the public sector.

Table 11: INDUSTRIAL INVESTMENT 1970/71–1976/77
(MILLIONS OF RUPEES, CONSTANT 1969/70 PRICES)

Year	Private Sector			Public Sector	Total Industrial Investment
	Large and Medium Scale	Small Scale	Total		
1970–71	1,166	192	1,368	65	1,423
1971–72	876	189	1,065	85	1,150
1972–73	468	157	625	68	693
1973–74	335	157	492	188	680
1974–75	414	187	601	446	1,047
1975–76	503	196	701	1,224	1,924
1976–77	438	213	650	1,563	2,213

Source: S. J. Burki, 'Employment Strategy for Economic Stability in Pakistan: New Initiatives', unpublished paper delivered at the Jinnah–Iqbal International Seminar on Pakistan, Columbia University, New York, 9–11 March 1978.

Note: Investment in current prices deflated by using price indices of investment goods for the manufacturing sector calculated by the Central Statistical Office.

On the other hand there was an increase in total investment during the Bhutto period (1971–7), but most of it was in the public sector. The objective of this investment was to make Pakistan self-sufficient in the production of certain commodities (steel, cement and fertilizers). Bhutto's economic policies failed primarily because of his regime's inability to implement socialist policies and tightly harness the uncooperative IE into its programmes. The PPP had envisaged that the private and public sectors could coexist, but this did not happen and wealth remained concentrated in a few family groups.

The 'mixed economy' policies of the PPP incorporated partial nationalization and a growing dependence on the inefficient bureaucracy or inexperienced party functionaries to make a success of its economic strategies. Since neither of the latter had any commitment to socialism, implementation of the mixed economy programme the contradictions into the open and created imbalances within the economy. One of these was the imbalance between exports (which had declined) and imports (which had gone up).[66] The reason for this was the large market for luxury consumer goods that only the elites could afford. The IE could get foreign investment or even loans for financing the demands of this market.

As stated earlier, the resulting inflation and recession in the economy turned the industrial workers against Bhutto as their wages had not kept pace with prices. The IE were already dissatisfied with the regime's policies. Both groups found an outlet in the PNA challenge to the PPP after the March 1977 elections.

Conclusion

The class structure that existed within ethnic boundaries was never strong enough to cut across them. This did not mean that there were no inter-ethnic horizontal and vertical alliances but that these were only used for the maximization of a group's own power. Where ethnic domination of one group by another had led to the politicization of ethnicity, the resulting ethnic solidarity did cut across class barriers. This happened in 1971 when East Bengali solidarity led to ethnic violence against all non-Bengalis, the Biharis and Punjabis in particular.

If ethnic nationalism is not allowed to grow to the same extent again, the break-up of the state will cease to be a problem. The danger will then lie in the rise of capitalism and the domination of one class by another. In this case, the exploited peasants and workers can form horizontal alliances to strengthen their revolutionary potential and combine against the dominant class. This revolutionary potential is at its strongest in a new working class, the urban peasant worker. This group has demonstrated its force in urban strikes, processions and violent demonstrations in the cities. However, only ethnic leaders have been successful in mobilizing the revolutionary potential of this group and utilizing it. Thus, Pathan leaders could effectively call the Pathan urban peasant workers to go on strike wherever they happened to be working.

The urban peasant workers lack organization and leadership at the present time but with the spread of capitalism this mass will become stronger and at some stage will be able to demand political responsiveness for its survival.

7

The Professional Elites

In Pakistan the PE were composed of people from various professions, such as the law, medicine, engineering, journalism, and education. Of these, members of the legal profession played the most important role in national politics and in constitution-making.[1] Although they made the most significant impact on the political system in the post-colonial period, it is worthwhile examining briefly the development of the legal system during the traditional and colonial periods.

In the Mughal judicial system, there were legal functionaries (wakils) who could represent their clients' interests in the courts (adalat), which were mainly located in urban areas.[2] There was, however, no institutionalization of the legal profession through law schools or other outlets. The only law which guided the qazis (judges) was the Shariah, and that too depended upon the individual qazi's interpretation and understanding of it. But no man was above the law for it derived its sanctions from the revelation prescribed in the Holy Quran.

During the colonial period, the traditional Muslim legal system was replaced by Western penal systems. These established new civil and criminal codes and an infrastructure with a hierarchy of judges and courts. The new laws claimed to be secular although they were based upon Judeo–Christian precepts of social justice. This new system was tendentious, because although it claimed to safeguard the rights of the individual and provide equality in justice, a white person could not be tried in a court by a native judge. However, this legal system did create a new occupational structure which opened job opportunities for educated persons. Some of them came to

Britain for their legal training, became receptive to Western ideals and started advocating Western democracy and British-style political institutions. The legal profession became a 'fertile field' where 'much political activity grew'[3] as the lawyers saw themselves as guardians of the fundamental rights of the masses and as experts in constitutional matters. One of the most distinguished members of this profession was M. A. Jinnah.

In the post-Independence period, the legal profession was highly respected and attracted people from all sectors of society. Over a period of time the profession came to be considered the 'most powerful elite group'[4] in politics apart from the bureaucracy, and were well represented in the Constituent and National Assemblies (see Table 12).

The PE had a direct link to the political arena since every Central Cabinet carried the post of law minister. The governing elites made this appointment to maximize their political power. Thus the PE were represented in the Central Cabinet as well as the legislatures, and their political influence outside these institutions should not be underrated.

Table 12:   PERCENTAGE OF PROFESSIONAL ELITES IN THE LEGISLATIVE
ASSEMBLIES OF PAKISTAN
1947–1969

Assemblies	Professional Elites (Lawyers) %	Other Elites %
First Constituent Assembly 1947–54	39	61
Second Constituent Assembly 1954–5	28	72
First National Assembly 1962–5	26	74
Second National Assembly 1965–9	21	79

Source: Adapted from: Mushtaq Ahmed, *Government and Politics in Pakistan* (Karachi: Space Publishers, 1970), pp. 89, 106, 236, 247.

Note: Other elites includes the landowning, industrial, bureaucratic, military and professional elites other than lawyers.

The Democratic State and Elite Factionalism

Although the PE were committed to being the 'custodians of Westernized secular legal systems'[5] their political experience was limited to the parliamentary system operating on the sub-continent and not the one in Britain. The latter had developed over a long period and had resulted in the institutionalization of political parties, with an opposition forming an essential part of the system. Political parties had not developed in the Western democratic sense, that is, they did not serve individual but national interests. On the contrary, the political parties, as stated earlier, were organizations for the maximization of the power of the political elites, and in some cases they disappeared as soon as they had served this purpose (e.g. the Muslim League and the Republican Party).

The PE advocated a parliamentary form of government with a strong legislature and a House with two chambers. Their concept of a democratic state was based on an 'electoral competition democracy' in which the masses could choose their leaders from the candidates contesting the elections.[6] This was not representative democracy nor was it participant democracy, for the electorate could neither pressure nor lobby their leaders, and political participation was a privilege granted to some and denied to others.[7] Elections were not a regular process of the political system, and if the governing elites agreed to hold them they made sure that the state machinery ensured their victory and the mass media projected only their views. So many obstacles were created for the political opposition that the spirit of the contest was rendered meaningless. In spite of these obstacles, however, the PE encouraged a multi-party system in which the governing elites could be kept in check by political elites in the parties.

The PE also wanted a constitution which would guarantee the fundamental rights of all individuals and a clear definition of the distribution of political power between the centre and provinces. The PE thus appeared to have some notion of majority rule, parliament, political parties, elections and an opposition, but they found it extremely difficult to operate these institutions in a manner conducive to democratic growth.

One does not have to look far to discern why such political institutions did not function in Pakistan. Within the feudal and capitalist vested interests considerable restraints were placed on the ideas of the PE. This was the main reason for their division into two powerful factions, the East Bengali professional elites (EBPE) and the West Pakistani professional elites (WPPE). The distinctive features of these elite factions are listed in Table 13.

The table requires no explanation as it is evident that the EBPE were a cohesive group that grew quite strong because of the policies of other elite groups (BE, LE ME) who had excluded them from political participation or power-sharing. Besides, their influence extended to the grass roots and they were able to demonstrate this unity as early as 1954 when during the elections they successfully eliminated the Muslim League in East Bengal. Similarly, in the elections of 1970 under the Yahya regime they once again demonstrated their solidarity. Their unity and identity were embedded in a distinct linguistic nationalism of middle class culture which politicized ethnicity and later, in 1971, erupted in ethnic nationalism.[8]

Table 13:   MAIN CHARACTERISTICS OF WEST AND EAST PAKISTANI
PROFESSIONAL ELITES

West Pakistani Professional Elites	East Pakistani Professional Elites
Minority group	Minority group
Regionally fragmented	Integrated
One of several elite groups in W. Pakistan	The dominant elite group of E. Pakistan
Conservative views and values	Radical views and values
Co-operative with other elite groups	Very independent
Mainly urban	Urban and rural
Belonging to the upper and middle classes	Belonging mainly to the middle classes
Advocated strong centre	Advocated provincial autonomy

The WPPE belonged to different provinces and had always struggled for power against the other elite groups. They had therefore very little chance of 'capturing the allegiance of the rural masses for any length of time'.[9] The landlords had almost complete control over the political allegiance of the peasants occupying their lands. The WPPE thus had their power base mainly in urban areas, but even here there were limitations on their influence. When the Basic Democracy Scheme was introduced during Ayub's regime the IE could easily manipulate political support by 'purchasing' votes which the PE could not afford.

For the post of law minister the governing elite always sought men who would rationalize, justify or legalize the political policies of the regime as democratic. The PE who occupied such posts often compromised their political views with the roles prescribed for them, and the more they became involved with the policies of the governing elites the less they identified with their own group. The esprit de corps found among members of the ME and the BE was missing among the PE because they were lacking in strong organizational development.

Constitution–making and Ethnicity

The Constituent Assembly which had been convened four days prior to Independence on 10 August 1947 was given the task of making a constitution for the new state. Until such a constitution could be produced, the Government of India Act of 1935 would remain in force. This had already been used by the BE for enhancing their power and for dominating the political arena, as we have seen. As such, the country was run without a real constitution. The PE, on the other hand, relentlessly pursued the task of constitution-making. The debates and controversies that raged during this period centred on two main points, the role of Islam in the political system and the distribution of political power among the ethnic groups. Each ethnic group endeavoured to impose its own ideas through the political elites.

The issues relating to religion have been dealt with elsewhere, but ethnicity will be described here. The implications of ethnic matters impeded the harmonious running of the political system. This meant not only the implementation of democracy but also the political participation of various ethnic groups and the distribution of power between the centre and provincial administrations. The trends underlying these important issues in the early years of Pakistan's history could be seen in documents such as the Objectives Resolution of 1949, the Interim Report of the Basic Principles Committee (1950) and the Report of the Basic Principles Committee (1952).

The Objectives Resolution was devised as a framework for the future constitution of the country, and it had clearly stated that

the territories now included in or in accession with Pakistan and such other territories as may hereinafter be included in or accede to Pakistan should form a Federation, wherein the provinces would be autonomous with such limitations on their power and authority as might be described . . .[10]

The 'limitations' of the provinces were exercised by those who held political power. This left the door open for the struggle for power between the LE and the EBPE. The latter's hopes for a democratic state were short-lived, and the Interim Report of the Basic Principles Committee presented clearly indicated the power of feudalism. The LE wanted to concentrate all political power into their own hands and would not subscribe to the principle of majority rule. By giving equal representation to both the upper and lower Houses of Parliament, the East Bengali majority was deprived not only of its proportional representation in Parliament, but also political domination through their numerical majority.

In 1952, the Basic Principles Committee Report further reinforced feudal power by proposing that there should be two Houses of Parliament, the House of Union with 120 members and the House of the People with 400 members. It also proposed that 200 members should be from East Bengal and 200 from the four provinces of West Pakistan. Once again the East Bengalis did not get proportional representation, and considerable strain was imposed on the political system from the conflicts that followed. The EBPE did not support the 'parity principle'[11] which contravened the principle of federations proposed by the Objectives Resolution.

Prime Minister Mohammad Ali Bogra (1953–5) devised a formula which sought to compromise the political conflict between the EBPE and the LE. It proposed that if the prime minister was an East Bengali, the governor-general would be West Pakistani, and vice versa. Furthermore, it suggested that of the 300 seats in the Lower House and 50 seats in the Upper House, the East Bengalis would have 165 seats in the Lower and 10 seats in the Upper House while the Punjabis would have 75 seats in the Lower and 10 seats in the Upper House. The remaining seats would be equally divided between Sind (29), NWFP (34), and Baluchistan (27) in the Lower House, with 10 seats for each province in the Upper House.[12] Although this division would give the East Bengalis a slight majority in the Lower House, it limited their power by stipulating that the 'parity principle' would operate at joint sessions of both houses for the discussion of controversial issues.[13]

The EBPE's demand for a 'one man, one vote' principle was never conceded because it would have destroyed the 'parity principle' which the LE supported. The Basic Principles Report was thus aptly labelled the 'Bengali–Punjabi Crisis Report'.[14] The Punjabis in particular feared that on a numerical basis they would be faced with Bengali domination of the political arena. In general, the political elites were so blinded by their struggle to remain in the political arena that they did not realize the impact of their actions on the national political system. Ironically, the fear of Hindu domination that had led them to struggle for the creation of a homeland had now changed into a fear of ethnic domination of one group over others. None of the political elites believed in political sacrifice in order to maintain the integration of the ideological state, and ethnic distrust resulted in serious cleavages in the political system.

The Parity Principle and Economic Development

Iskander Mirza's reign as governor-general and later as president of Pakistan (1955–8) ushered in another era of political intrigue for the strengthening of administrative control over the state. His political ideology clearly stated that 'some underdeveloped countries have to learn democracy, and until they do so they have to be controlled. With so many illiterate people, politicians could make a mess of things'.[15] Mirza's political actions were not so crude as those of Ghulam Mohammad's, however, and as a bureaucrat he selected another bureaucrat (Chaudhry Mohammad Ali) as his prime minister. The political control of the Assembly still remained a problem since it was dominated by the LE, and the minority provinces remained opposed to the One-Unit Plan. Mirza used a new strategy of appointing the governor as the temporary presiding officer of the Legislative Assembly for more than a month in an attempt to quell opposition to the One-Unit Plan.[16]

To control the LE Mirza appointed his friend, Dr Khan Sahib, as chief minister of the Constituent Assembly in 1955. Khan Sahib was not affiliated to any political party and his mission was to weaken the power structure of the LE. He did this by forming his own political party—the Republican Party[17]—weaning one of the feuding factions of the LE to his side. In this way, Mirza gained the support of the rival LE faction, and the 'balance of power was in the hands of the BE and LE'.[18]

The East Bengalis, disillusioned at the non-implementation of the 'majority' principle, found a strong defender of their rights in the powerful leader H. S. Suhrawardy. The latter's political organization, the Awami League (established 1949), had initially proposed the implementation of the Islamic political order in Pakistan.[19] However, the political blunders of the BE and LE soon pushed the League to change its stand from religion to ethnicity. Suhrawardy was appointed by Mirza in an attempt to defuse the political situation in East Bengal. Suhrawardy soon decided to test the 'parity principle' which had been favoured by the LE.

Suhrawardhy reviewed the poor concession of import-export licences granted to East Bengali's in a cabinet meeting (10 November 1956) and decided that such concessions should be granted to newcomers into the private sector from East Bengal and the underdeveloped provinces of West Pakistan. He further implemented the parity principle by allocating U.S. aid of 10 million dollars to be distributed among industrial development projects in East Bengal. He also proposed the establishment of a Public Shipping Corporation which would break the monopoly of coastal trade enjoyed by West Pakistani shipping companies. While the IE loudly protested in the Constituent Assembly, the East Bengalis welcomed these steps.[20] Suhrawardhy justified his actions by maintaining that one wing should not develop at the expense of another as Pakistani was essentially one country.[21]

The IE exerted tremendous political influence on Mirza and accused the Prime Minister of 'provincialism' and 'party politics'.[22] Later, they convinced the President that Suhrawardhy's political policies would have a serious impact on the economic development of the country because, they reasoned, 'parity in the political sphere may be a workable compromise but its application to economic planning without considering other economic factors may lead us into blind alleys from which there may not be a way out'.[23]

A deputation of the Shipowners Association met the President to register their complaints, and full-page advertisements repeatedly appeared in the newspapers protesting that the government was establishing a 'monopolistic National Shipping Corporation'.[24] Apart from the tensions between the Bengali premier and the IE, Suhrawardhy further exacerbated the situation when he threatened the LE with agrarian reforms. At this provocation the Republican Party withdrew its support, and the Suhrawardhy Ministry, formed by the coalition of the Republican Party and the Awami League, collapsed in the summer of 1957.

The new Premier (I. I. Chundrigar, 18 October 1957—15 December 1957) quickly acceded to the demands of the LE and IE. He did not pursue agrarian reforms and assured the IE that his political and economic policies would not damage their interests.[25] The plans for the Public Shipping Corporation were shelved and the import–export licences granted under the U.S. aid programme were cancelled.[26] The failure of the parity principle now left the Bengalis with very little hope of political participation in the national arena.

Political Legitimation and Political Opposition

The political role of the WPPE and the EBPE had become rigidly aligned along ethnic lines by the time the military took power in 1958. The WPPE strongly supported the political rule of the governing elites while the EBPE strongly opposed it. Constitution-making depended heavily upon the skills of the WPPE. The ME considered the Constitution of 1956 an 'unholy wedlock of the executive, legislative and judicial functions of the state in which the ultimate power for good government remains divisive, undefined and therefore, inoperative'.[27] The Constitution Commission (1961), set up for formulating proposals for the constitution of the ME (many of which were finally rejected),[28] identified three areas in which past governments had failed:

(1) Lack of proper elections and defects in the late Constitution.
(2) Undue interference by Heads of State with the Ministries and political parties, and by the Central Government with the functioning of the governments in the provinces.
(3) Lack of leadership resulting in lack of well-organized and disciplined parties, the general lack of character in politicians and their undue interference in the administration.[29]

The second clause was directed at the BE but it exonerated them from causing the disruption of the 'parliamentary form of government'.[30] The Commission failed to identify the power-holders in the body politic of Pakistan, a deliberate omission for many judges who had headed such commissions had been members of the bureaucracy and in the past the judiciary had justified the actions of the BE.[31]

In the Constitution of 1962, the provincial governors were made direct agents of the president and were to be appointed by him. Power was thus centralized in the position of the president. Not even a two-thirds majority in the National Assembly could override non-financial legislation proposed by the president because he could subject it to a referendum of the 80,000-strong electoral college of the Basic Democracy System.

The position of law minister, as stated earlier, had always been important for the political legitimation of a regime's policies. In Ayub's Cabinet, Law Minister Manzur Qadir was the prime architect of the 1962 Constitution. His skills had made it possible for the ME to impose their will on the masses without seeking their legitimation.[32] His collaboration with the ME had also made the 'Constitution democratic in name rather than in fact',[33] as it aimed to 'perpetuate the present regime for a long time to come'.[34] For his services Qadir was elevated to the position of a High Court judge. The Bar Associations of both wings of the country protested at this appointment.

The ME's attempts to transform Pakistan into a praetorian state through authoritarian directives antagonized the PE which had hoped for a democratic system. This made them the foremost opponents of the military regime. The situation was further compounded by Ayub's towards the legal profession, which he considered to be overstaffed, with 'all sorts of abuses' going on, including 'fabrication of false evidence to support the case of their clients'.[35] Furthermore, the Law Reform Commission recommended that specialist courts should be established to streamline judicial processes. Ayub responded by enacting the Conciliation Courts Ordinance of 1961 which imposed specific restrictions on the legal community.[36] In addition, the Code of Criminal Procedure (Amendment) Act of 1963 made it possible for cases to be referred to jirgas (tribal assemblies of elders) rather than to lawyers. As a result the small-town lawyers lost a large number of clients.

Under so much pressure from the ME both individual lawyers and the Bar Associations began to register their dissent more and more frequently. The lawyers mobilized public opinion in seeking to repeal the Constitution of 1962. The ME responded by attempting to 'reduce their influence by increasing the use of special tribunals from which lawyers were banned and by eliminating justifiable fundamental rights'.[37] The safeguarding of fundamental rights became an important national issue with the PE for opposing the military regime.

Bar Associations were the centres of political activity for the PE and were considered to be 'uncommonly vigorous in taking stands on political issues'.[38] The WPPE used their political influence to mobilize their resources in favour of the Combined Opposition Party to displace Ayub's regime.[39] They were unsuccessful. On the other hand, the EBPE organized themselves along ethnic lines.

The Rise of the Awami League

When the Awami League sought to oppose the military regime, Suhrawardy was detained without trial for eight months under the Security of Pakistan Act in January 1962.[40] His arrest led to political disturbances in the province and another wave of arrests of members of the Awami League, including Mujibur Rahman. On his release in August 1962, Suhrawardy did not try to reorganize the Awami League but joined the stronger organization, the National Democratic Front (a loose coalition of all opposition parties) to bring down the Ayub government. The credo of this party was that 'Pakistan belongs to its people and not to any persons, a group, or a party, and that no one has the authority to deprive the people of their inalienable rights of freedom and the democratic exercise of the supreme authority of the State'.[41]

The ME, anticipating opposition from other political elites, had earlier enacted the Political Parties Act which disqualified politicians like Suhrawardy from holding office in any political party. They had not accounted for organizations like the National Democratic Front which were neither political parties nor had any office-bearers. Ayub stated that he would not feel threatened if fifty organizations like the National Democratic Front were formed by Suhrawardy.[42] But when the NDF started to attract support from the RE, WPPE and some factions of the LE,[43] the Political Parties (Amendment) Ordinance was enacted in January 1963. This prohibited 'a group or combination of persons who are operating for the purpose of propagating any political opinion or indulging in any other political activity'.[44]

The death of Suhrawardy in December 1963 removed Ayub's greatest opponent from the political scene. A year later, Mujibur Rahman announced the re-emergence of the Awami League as a mass organization to 'fight constitutionally for the rights of the people'.[45] Suhrawardy's policies had put the parity principle to test and had failed. Mujib's approach was to stress provincial autonomy, but when in 1966 he found that the ME were too strongly influenced by the vested interests of the IE to allow them provincial autonomy he brought out his Six Point Programme. This programme was perceived by some as a demand for provincial autonomy and by others as a design for political secession. According to the 'six points', the Federal Government would control only defence and foreign affairs, while foreign trade, taxation, a separate currency and _a provincial parliamentary force would be under provincial control.

The Six Point Programme of 1966 was the most radical demand yet put forward by any political party in Pakistan. It gained widespread support among East Bengali masses and elites—the latter particularly derived from East Bengalis in the bureaucracy and the armed forces. From 1966 to 1969 the EBPE were in constant conflict with the military regime, a situation which ultimately resulted in a confrontation in what came to be known 'Agarthala Conspiracy Case'. In 1967 thirty-eight Bengalis were charged with conspiring to incite ethnic nationalism for East Bengali to secede from Pakistan in collusion with India. Along with Mujibur Rahman, those charged included of the Awami League, the bureaucracy and the military. The political outcome of the case was that Mujibur Rahman emerged as an ethnic nationalist hero who had reinforced 'his grip on the increasingly potent symbols of Bengali nationalism'.[46]

The new military regime under General Yahya Khan (1969–71) tried to remove the sting from the EBPE programme by a Legal Framework Order. It did not succeed because the PPP continued to grow in strength in West Pakistan with its socialist ideology and the Awami League in East Bengal with its ethnic nationalist ideology. The Mujib–Bhutto–Yahya strategies have been discussed elsewhere in the book. Suffice it to state here that the EBPE of the Awami League were forced into a position by the LE whereby they had to declare their politically separate state of Bangladesh.

Regime Oppression and Political Accountability

PE opposition to the Bhutto regime started as early as 1972. As the task of constitution-making began the strong LE faction heading the NAP wanted measures to safeguard the rights of the minorities and a constitution which would ensure political participation, provincial autonomy and the economic development of their provinces. Bhutto had agreed to make such concessions (in his March 1972 Accord) but with little intention of keeping these promises. The law minister (M.A. Kasuri) resigned because he did not want to be party to such underhand dealings. Bhutto, therefore, appointed another law minister (Hafiz Pirzada—from his own ethnic group), who in the tradition of Manzoor Qadir was interested in rationalizing, legalizing or justifying the policies of the regime.

The resignation of Kasuri was a political loss for the Bhutto regime. With Kasuri's political support the ranks of the political opposition grew from 1972 to 1976, especially among the PE. In January 1976 Kasuri called an All Pakistan Lawyers Conference which was attended by lawyers from all over the country. The conference sounded the alarm that constitutional amendments were leading to 'serious erosion of the rule of law by Executive and Legislative measures'.[47] They were also endangering the fundamental rights of the people and parliamentary sovereignty.

These constitutional amendments gave the regime greater power for imposing political oppression, for example in extending the period of preventative detention of persons suspected for anti-state activities from one month to three (Art. 10:4). Another amendment extended the six-month limit on the period of Emergency Powers to an indefinite period, and Emergency Powers could only be ended by a majority of the two Houses of Parliament. In addition to these measures, strict restrictions were imposed on the freedom of movement, speech or assembly. Special tribunals were created to try cases which hitherto would have been heard in ordinary courts. Such measures not only excluded lawyers from taking up the cases of their clients but the justice meted out was widely regarded as 'the denial of justice', as the 'nomination of executive functionaries as members of such special courts . . . renders proceedings before such a forum farcical'.[48] Above all, parliamentary sovereignty was rendered superfluous by limiting the working days of Parliament from 130 to 45 a year, which amounted to a mere fulfilment of constitutional obligation.[49]

The judiciary had never taken a strong stand on issues in Pakistani politics. Their judgements often reflected their support of the actions of the governing elites, and very few judges could be said to be free from political pressures. In earlier years most of them had been selected by the governing elites from the BE (for example, Justice M. R. Kayani, Justice S. A. Huq and Justice M. Shahabuddin). Those taking up such positions were loyal to their political benefactors and were interested in perpetuating a penal system made by the colonizers for the colonized.

Over the years it became a practice that judges could only retain their positions if they legitimized the actions of the governing elites rather than taking an impartial stand for the rights of the people. Justice Munir's judgement upholding Ghulam Mohammad's dissolution of the Constituent Assembly was an example of such a judgement and it reinforced elitism in the political system, Justice Hamoodur Rahman absolved Bhutto of playing a major role in the secession of East Bengal and, later, his banning of the NAP in 1975 for the establishment of the One-Party State was another instance of how the judiciary served the governing elites.

After Bhutto's fall from power, the disclosures about detentions, tortures, unlawful arrest, bullying of the judiciary, abductions, and political murders further indicated how the judiciary could become an instrument of the governing elite. A chief justice of the Supreme Court publicly stated that 'frequent and uncalled-for amendments in the Constitution, coupled with an aggressive attitude on the part of the Executive, had the effect not only of curtailing the powers and jurisdiction of the superior courts to the detriment of private citizens but also of creating an unhealthy sense of insecurity in the minds of the judges, thus impairing their ability to do justice without fear or favour'.[50]

Some Chief Justices (e.g. Mr Yaqub Ali) had obtained an extension of their terms through constitutional amendments to remain in office for an additional three years, but in doing so they damaged the credibility of justice in a political system which came to have two sets of justice—one for the elites and another for the masses.

It must be said to the credit of the present military regime that they have taken up two issues whose implications on the political system will be crucial if they lead to the establishment of an independent judiciary and bring about political accountability of the governing elites.

On the first issue, the independence of the judiciary can only be achieved through the Islamization of the laws of the country. This will take away the power of manipulating justice to suit the political ends of the governing elites. In the ideological state, the political corruption of justice had made vested interests stronger. Islamization of the laws would not mean public hangings and flogging of the poor and helpless but also of the wealthy and powerful—that is, it would establish the principle that nobody should be above the law. Such a law, by its nature would have to be Quranic for this would eliminate the possibility of its being changed by the political elites to suit their own needs.

The second issue relates political accountability to the political system. Can a ruler commit any crime and be exonerated from it because of his position? This refers to the Bhutto case. Bhutto was convicted in March 1978 of aiding and abetting the murder of a political opponent and of using the state machinery (Federal Security Force) to eliminate him. In the attempt, the opponent's father was assassinated, and for this action the High Court of Pakistan has sentenced to death Bhutto and others implicated. Hitherto the governing elites have all enjoyed the power not only of doing what they pleased, but also of avoiding accountability. Corruption in the political system was thus fostered. The Islamic system demands political accountability, a fact made clear by the judges (appointed by Bhutto when he was in power) who referred to the example set by the first Caliph (Hazrat Abu Bakr) in their judgement. The latter had told the believers that had elected him to the Caliphate that he was no better than them. He further warned them to support him for his upright actions, criticize him for any wrong ones and obey him only if they found that he himself was following the laws of the Quran. The judge in the Bhutto case further stated that

> Islam does not believe in the creation of privileged classes. It believes in the equality before law of all—ruler and governed alike . . . Even the Caliph, the King, the Prime Minister or the President, by whatever name the ruler may be called, is as much subject to the law of the land as any ordinary citizen. Islam is opposed to the establishment of church or priesthood. It does not recognise any distinction between divine laws governed by priests and secular laws administered by a secular government.[51]

The important point to be noted is that Islam has once again inspired accountability in the political system of the ideological state. The General (Zia-ul-Haq) who initiated it, also made it clear that he could be in the same position if he was found guilty of political wrongs. For the type of political system which currently operates in Pakistan, political accountability of its governing elites is necessary to restrain them from violating the rights of the masses. As yet, as stated earlier, politics has been the way to riches but with the precedent of political accountability at the end of a hangman's noose, such riches in the future might not be so tempting after all.

8

The Military Elites

The ideal of civilian supremacy over the military is a distinctive aspect of Western political theory. This theory, however, does not hold for many developing countries where the military's direct or indirect control of the political system has given rise to considerable debate on civil–military relations. Many of the theories put forward apply to Third World countries, but one has to exercise caution in applying them to ideological states like Pakistan and Israel. In the latter case, the military was found by one observer to be the 'only thing that made the state a reality . . . the beginning and end of political existence.'[1] In the case of Pakistan, military supremacy has dominated the political scene, although its influence has oscillated. From 1947 to 1958 it exercised indirect political influence and from 1958 to 1971 direct political control. In the post-1971 period the military reverted to indirect influence, until July 1977 when it once again took over control of the government through popular public consent. The recurrence of military rule has established the military as a powerful political force within Pakistan. Before the military's political role can be understood, however, it is imperative to examine three contextual linkages which bound it to the state. These were the identity, colonial and structural linkages which entrenched the military within the political system of Pakistan.

The Contextual Linkages

Pakistan was all that remained of the Muslim empire in the Indian sub-continent. The military's identification with Islam linked it to the pre-colonial Muslim state. For the Muslim units of the British

Indian Army, the transfer of loyalties from the colonial to the ideological state did not present a problem. They could relate to a new role of protecting Pakistan as an extension of the role of the Mughal armies in being the defenders of the faith and state.

The Identity Linkage

Identification with Islam reinforced the military commitment to the state, for historically Islam had had a special relationship with the Muslim armies. Islam was considered to be 'the most martial of major world religions'.[2] On the other hand,

> Islam's attitude towards political and military power is not one of negation, disassociation or suspicion, but of complete affirmation. A religious value is attached to power, success and victory as such. Islam endows the army with the prestige and authority of an institution meriting divine blessing and its heritage paves the way for military intervention which is to be regarded as most fitting and proper in the eyes of God and man.[3]

The role of the military in the ideological state was to defend Islam, and a Muslim soldier who 'turned his back on the enemy, except for tactical and strategic reasons, did not remain a Muslim any longer'.[4] Religious attitudes, understandably, were found to be quite strong among the soldiers and the officers of the Pakistan military. The use of Islamic concepts such as 'jihad' (holy war), 'ghazi' (victorious warrior) and 'shaheed' (martyred warrior in the name of Islam) evoked strong sentiments and were utilized for morale-building. The 'izzat' (honour) and 'ghairat' (self-respect) of the nation were of prime concern to the Pakistan military.[5] Islam was considered a powerful motivating force 'for soldiers during peace and war'.[6] Military officers were advised not only to 'seriously study Islam' but to display visible 'signs of religiousness'.[7] The officer corps were thus found to be religious, and well versed in Islamic history and the Muslim history of India. They also had a great deal of admiration for the South Asian and Arab Muslim generals whose example they tried to emulate. Two trends of religiosity appeared to be significant: first, the higher the age structure of the officer corps the stronger were their religious convictions, and, second, the greater their combat experiences the stronger were their religious convictions.

In the ideological states, the relevance of political legitimacy is rather different from its role in other states. The military's political relationship insofar as it related to the integration of Pakistan could be legitimated by Islam. The military's regard for the constitution indicated its allegiance to the government in power. When such allegiance was withdrawn the constitution was abrogated (Ayub abrogated the Constitution of 1956 and Yahya that of 1962). Such political actions indicated that the military's allegiance to religion and the state normally took precedence over that to the government in power.

The Colonial Linkage

In an effort to consolidate their empire the British had raised an army of native soldiers in India which was known as the British Indian Army (BIA), based on the pattern of their own armies. Because of its changeover from Mughal to colonial institutions the military's internal organization and skill structure was very receptive to modernization.

Colonial policies within the given political context politicized the native officer corps in spite of its professionalization. Thus the BIA's 'apolitical behaviour' was a legitimizing myth serving colonial interests and was only true of the British officers who identified with the colonial state. In the sub-continent centuries of Muslim rule had been interrupted by British rule (1857–1947), and Hindu and Muslim officers were indifferent neither to their political history nor to their political future. Muslim officers were concerned because they could identify neither with the colonial state nor with a Hindu majority state. So intense was the animosity between the Hindu and Muslim officers that one year after the creation of Pakistan the Pakistani and Indian armies were engaged in battle over Kashmir despite having shared the same mess or regimental affiliations in the BIA.

The impact of the British ethnic recruitment policies and their 'martial race' theories had created inter-ethnic animosity. The Gurkhas, Pathans, Sikhs, Rajputs, Dogras and Punjabi Muslims were among the groups labelled as 'martial'.[8] One ethnic group had been used to suppress internal insurgencies by other ethnic groups within the empire. The indoctrination of 'martial race' not only helped to reinforce the self-images of the officer corps but made the military profession the principal means of social mobility. Inter-ethnic group relations in the post-Independent period thus came to be judged along such martial and non-martial group dimensions and this in turn affected their own recruitment policies.

Thus, before 1964 the Bengalis were seldom recruited into the Pakistan military as it was thought that since they had not been 'infantry soldiers for well over a century', their 'physical and professional aptitude could not reach such high standards' as were required of the average enlisted soldier.[9] They also exhibited a certain degree of ethnic distrust towards the East Bengalis, and it was argued that even if they were recruited and trained their loyalty would still be in doubt. The best military training institutions were concentrated in West Pakistan. To conceal such recruitment disparities, concessions were made from time to time, such as lowering of the height requirements from 5' 6" to 5' 4" to allow for the shorter stature of the Bengalis.[10] At the present time, the Sindhis and Baluchis, although possessing the physical attributes necessary for recruitment into the military, are not adequately represented.

The Structural Linkage

The province of Punjab, as stated earlier, had been a major recruitment ground for the soldiers of the BIA, and this practice was continued in the post-Independent period. The Punjabi commitment to a military career never left the voluntarily recruited army short of manpower.

Most of the recruitment of the Pakistan Army took place from the Punjab districts of Jehlum, Gujrat and Campbellpur. In the North West Frontier Province, Pathans were recruited from Peshawar and Kohat, and from the Yusufzai, Khattak Afridi and Bangash tribes.[11] Although exact figures were not available from the General Headquarters of the Pakistan military, Table 14 is based on estimates given by the officers interviewed and it indicates the ethnic strength of the officer corps.

Table 14: APPROXIMATE ETHNIC GROUP STRENGTH OF THE PAKISTAN MILITARY OFFICER CORPS

Ethnic Group	Percentage
Punjabis	70
Pathans	15
Muhajirs	10
Baluchis and Sindhis	5
Total	100

Source: Based on subjective estimates made by a number of Pakistani military officers interviewed by the author.

Social scientists have often made civil–military distinctions, and while these may be true of Western societies it is futile to make them in societies with strong ethnic and tribal relationships. As recruitment in Pakistan became biased towards a particular group, it necessarily assumed a political dimension. The military's structural linkage with the Punjab province gave the Punjabis direct access into this powerful elite group. The military's institutional boundaries were also penetrated by other elite groups, and, for example, one member of a family may have been a general in the army, another a senior civil servant and a third could be in control of the family's landed interests. Such close relationships placed high expectations on individuals from their families and ethnic groups. In the political arena these ranged from delivering collective benefits to the group in materialistic terms (such as economic development of one's own region) to non-materialistic gains (power, prestige or position).[12]

The military was aware of ethnic-group majority, and General Tikka Khan assured the author in 1975 that they were trying to encourage recruitment from other ethnic groups, but as it was a volunteer army they could not recruit by forced induction.

The Officer Corps and Military Ideology

The officer corps of the Pakistan military can be divided into two stratarchies: a political military stratum and a military professional stratum. Officers within these strata could be of the same rank, except that one would be concerned with the political role of the military and the other with the military aspects of the state. These roles were not mutually exclusive.

Officers belonging to the military–professional stratum were committed to managerial responsibilities and the professionalization of the internal organization and skill structure of the force; while those in the political–military stratum were committed to the security role of the military within the state.

In military–state relations the military through its commitment to religious ideology was its guardian in the state. Just as religion could not be separated from politics, so too the military could not be separated from the political system. Military ideology was therefore a coherent body of doctrines, beliefs and values emanating from Islam and the Pakistan movement.

The military had made special arrangements to make its officers aware of the political problems of the country. The ideological state was the responsibility of every Muslim in the state and not of a particular class or elite group, and at the time of a political crisis they could not shirk their political role. For this purpose the military trained the political military stratum for the future. Selected senior officers (of the rank of brigadier and above) were instructed in various aspects of national security to 'prepare them for planning national strategy and for assignment at policy-making levels'.[13] This instruction focused on the following factors:

(1) Study and analysis of Pakistan's national aims and their implementation, particularly in the military field.
(2) Study of the particular situation which needed to be controlled in order to achieve Pakistan's national aims.
(3) Study of elements which constituted national power and their relation with military power.
(4) Study of comprehension, direction and control of national power including military power, leading to planning of national strategy.[14]

Both the conservative and the revolutionary oriented officer corps believed firmly that 'Islam was the basis of the creation of Pakistan'. Its perception of socio-political realities pointed out in 1975 that

> since Pakistan is a rich mosaic of ethnic groups, therefore circumstances have gradually led to a stage where these groups have little sympathy for each other and less participation in common ideals. There has developed much suspicion and even hostility among these groups. Ethnic, caste, regional and kinship alignments are now predominant in our rural areas and also in our urban centres. The religious cleavages have also been inducted through uneducated Mullahs, between various Muslim sects. Over and above the internal dividing forces working against our ideology, there is a wily enemy who has chalked out a plan to obliterate Islam and in turn the existence of Pakistan . . . therefore in any training or guidance towards our ideology, it is essential to first define the Muslim ideology and then suggest ways and means of introducing it as part of the regular training of the Armed Forces.[15]

This ideology envisaged the 'establishment of an Islamic and truly welfare state' where exploitation would cease 'to exist and where all human affairs' would be 'conducted in accordance with the norms of justice and fraternal co-operation', facilitating the 'establishment of a truly democratic order' which would give 'freedom and opportunities to all members of the society to conduct their affairs through consultation and mutual consent'.[16] Such an ideology, it was stated, would result in the 'desired will to fight and defend this soil', for the strength of the Pakistan Armed Forces 'lies in quality and not in quantity'.[17] The failure to establish such a state was due to the abandonment of this ideology in the multi-ethnic state.

Praetorianism and the Political System

Many political scientists have put forward theories of military interventions which derive either from the nature of particular military organizations or the nature of a particular society.[18] Those who subscribe to the former view state that the colonial heritage equips an army with professionalization, discipline and in-group solidarity, and that it acts as a modernizing agent.[19] In such a situation, military intervention becomes inevitable if the politicians create chaos in the country. On the other hand, if societal conditions are such that there is class dominance or if elite factions fight for political power without legitimation,[20] the military may resort to intervention into the political arena.

Without underestimating the merits and demerits as well as the applicability of these theories, it must be stated that they do not adequately explain military intervention in Pakistan. In fact, the word 'intervention' is a misnomer in the case of Pakistan. Many political scientists, influenced by Western civil–military distinctions and eager to extend the generality of their theories to all Third World countries where the military has taken over political power, fail to give adequate consideration to the extent to which political and military roles are diffused in their political systems.

The Pakistani military was praetorian in that it patrolled its own society. The definition of praetorianism, however, has varied from casting the military in the role of the king-maker to one which intervened to maximize its own power.[21] In Pakistan the military was neither the 'king-maker' nor was it seeking 'role-expansion' to maximize its position. If it had been a 'king-maker' it would not have removed its own generals (Ayub Khan and Yahya Khan) from positions of power, nor would it have returned to the barracks when not needed.

To understand the role of the military in Pakistan it is imperative to understand the military–state relationship. As mentioned earlier, Western models of civil–military relations operationalize Western conceptualizations and as such cannot discern relationships in the ideological state. The military–state relation conceptualizes a dialectical relationship between Islam, Pakistan and the military. Without Islam, Pakistan would not have come into existence; without Pakistan the military would not be able to exist; and without the military, Islam and Pakistan would be threatened. In perpetuating such a state, the military was perpetuating Islam. Such perceptions of the officer corps were well articulated when one senior officer stated to the author that 'the military was Pakistan and Pakistan was the military'.[22] The military's relationship with the ideological state had a dual basis. First, it was a *part* of the political system, and, as such, its takeover of the political arena could not be termed 'intervention' as such. Secondly, apart from Islam the military was the only other pillar of the ideological state and it provided alternative political leadership whenever there was a crisis.

The first coup d'état (popularly known as the Rawalpindi Conspiracy Case) occurred as early as 1948. It was led by the Commander-in-Chief (Major-General Akbar Khan) who felt strongly about the political arrangements made by the governing elites (through Liaquat Ali Khan) with the Indians over the Kashmir dispute. The coup failed because it was exposed in time (supposedly by Ayub Khan), and the officers were imprisoned. The army, hardly a year old, was still in the process of internal reorganization, but the national political arena was always accessible to their direct or indirect political influence.

Another important observation must be made here, that the Pakistan military, after internally organizing itself, never had to usurp power as it always held sufficient political power in its own right. In fact, it was often invited to involve itself directly in the politics of the country by the elites and masses. In 1954, the BE (Ghulam Mohammed) had invited the military to take control of the government, but it declined. In 1958, the elites and masses both welcomed it. In 1972, the RE (Mian Mohammed Tufail) appealed to them to remove the Bhutto regime, but they did not respond. Later, in 1977, when the PPP and PNA had reached political deadlock they responded to the appeals of the elites and masses and took over the government. All these cases uphold the contention that whenever the military had decided to involve itself directly in the politics of the country it did not have to make a particular effort as it always had the consent of the masses. The fact that some alliances exposed the ME to political corruption was due to deflection from their original goal. In such cases, the military often withdrew its support from its own ex-members (as from Ayub in 1969).

The multiple roles of the Pakistan military, involving social, political and professional skills, were therefore accepted by other elites and masses. In its professional role it maintained a large military establishment that was well trained to ward off any external threats. A large part of the military's expenditure was derived from the military aid supplied by countries like the United States.

The nation-building role of the military was well documented for its activities ranged from giving help for flood control to catching smugglers, from building roads, bridges and dams to fighting off locust swarms.[23] It was also the largest single employer of man-power not only in its military establishment but also in its business ventures for the benefit of servicemen. The Army Welfare Trust[24] and the Fauji Foundation[25] were examples of such ventures.

The internal security role of the military was also very important as there had been a greater threat to the disintegration of Pakistan from within (East Bengalis and Bangladesh) than from external sources (notably India).[26] It was most sensitive to internal threats by its very nature as the military–state relationship was an interdependent one. That is, the military could not exist without the state nor the state without the military.

The military was well aware of the problems facing the country, the most important of which was the lack of a 'solid and cohesive nationhood'.[27] Many of the officers interviewed believed that the military had become the only 'stabilizing force' in the new state and that it was looked up to by other political elites as a 'saviour' because they had no 'axes to grind'.[28] The military's nationalistic socialization was strong, and as long as the political system remained integrated it took no action over changes of government. Over a period of time the inter-elite conflict had become transformed into an inter-ethnic conflict. The military perceived such ethnic cleavages and conflicts as an internal threat to the integrity and ideology of the state. It was therefore with the fullest 'conviction that there was no alternative' that the ME had to take control of the political arena in October 1958 to save the country from 'disintegration and complete ruination'.[29] Their mission had a single direction—to maintain the territorial integration of the Muslim homeland.

The Ayub Regime (1958–69)

When General Ayub Khan formed his military government he was aware of the internal political forces operating in the country. His objective was to liberate the country from those centrifugal forces that threatened to disintegrate it. As the first powerholder of a military regime, he had to prove to other elite groups that he was more powerful than them. To this end he enacted the Electoral Bodies Disqualification Order (EBDO) to eliminate all opposition. Those who suffered most under EBDO were the East Bengali PE[30] and to a lesser extent the LE. The latter, however, disappeared from the political area for only a short time and wielded influence through 'front men', like their sons, or through backdoor political intrigues.[31]

Ayub's main aim was to subdue the BE and LE in order to push through his development schemes and legitimize his political position. The ME were aware of the political role of the BE which had brought 'Pakistan of the edge of total disaster'.[32] They had not faced the political realities of an ideological state and had continued to act as 'denationalized rulers' who maintained a social distance from the masses, whereas the 'demands of an independent society' required the 'growing involvement of the government in many new spheres of social life'.[33]

The ME initially endeavoured to bring down the BE from their invincible position by purging the bureaucracy, removing corrupt senior officers and ordering them to declare their assets or suffer fines, confiscation of property and imprisonment. (This set a precedent which was to be followed by the Yahya, Bhutto and Zia regimes.) Such measures effectively brought the BE under control as they could not resist the coercive power of the ME. They assumed a secondary role and promised that 'under honest and inspiring leadership the Civil Service was fully competent to deliver the goods'.[34]

The BE, however, were not ready to forgo all their power and prestige. The Report of the Pay and Services Commission (set up by the ME and headed by Justice Cornelius) recommended that all cadres of the bureaucracy be unified into a Pakistan Administrative Service. They protested strongly and warned the ME that such reforms would result in 'psychological upheaval' and for 'many years to come the country and the administration would be busy settling problems introduced by these drastic changes and the drive for development would lose momentum and be neglected'.[35] They also pointed out to the ME that the 'present system which has stood the test of time, not only during the British regime but also during the tumultuous and important years since Independence should be permitted to continue with changes as experience has shown necessary'.[36]

They eventually managed to convince the ME that the structural changes envisaged by the Pay and Services Commission Report

would be detrimental to the new regime's development programmes. The report was duly shelved, and in 1964 Ayub stated that
national development was his first priority and, as such, nothing
should be done which 'might involve the risk of disrupting the
administrative fabric . . . the government has, therefore, come to
the conclusion that while no radical changes should be made in the
existing structure, all the public services should be enabled to make
their best possible contribution to the service of the nation in their
respective spheres.'[37] The BE had salvaged their position in the
Ayub regime, and Ayub's dependence on them was to prove his
undoing.

Some observers erroneously presume that there was a 'partner-
ship between the army and the civil service'.[38] This view could be
applied to the colonial period when the ME and BE had served the
same master—the British government. In the post-Independent
period the political situation was not the same, and the political
elites were the masters themselves. It was therefore nearer the truth
to say that the BE 'were frightened into submission'.[39]

By 1966, however, the BE had once again regained their political
strength. In a test case, a bureaucrat (Yazdani Malik) who had
physically assaulted an MPA (Makhdoom S. Gilani) in the National
Assembly, was acquitted, indicating that the BE could expect to
survive such actions.[40] They had also become an agency for socio-
economic development of the military regime and thereby had full
control over economic planning.[41]

Basic Democracy and the Presidential Election

The institutional framework of the Basic Democracy system
rested on a hierarchical order. At the bottom level were the union
councils which comprised of several villages making up one basic
unit. The union councillor (Basic Democrat) represented
1000–1500 voters. The second level constituted the tehsil councils
which were made up of several union councils. At the third level
were the district councils, made up of several tehsil councils, and the
final level was the divisional council composed of several district
councils. The chairman of each council was automatically a member
of the next higher council. The total number of Basic Democrats
was not more than 80,000. Half of these were from East Bengal,
and the whole system was intended to act as an electoral college to
elect the president and members of the National and Provincial
Assemblies.

The governing elites projected the objectives of the BD system as their attempt to 'develop local leadership' at grassroots level, so that democracy was not foisted on the people from above but grew from within.[42] The system, it was hoped, would free the situation from 'party intrigues, political pressures and tub-thumping politicians'.[43] Through the BD system Ayub sought to form a vertical alliance with the middle sectors, especially from the rural areas. This would have made him independent of his institutional base, the military.

By 1965 Ayub's regime had succeeded in developing horizontal alliances with the BE and IE, but other elite groups continued to oppose his rule. The Combined Opposition Party (COP) was formed to confront him in the 1965 elections. It was composed of the Council Muslim League (representing the LE faction), the Jamaat-i-Islami (representing the RE) and the Awami League (representing the EBPE); the WPPE were represented by members such as A. K. Brohi, H. S. Suhrawardhy and M. A. Kasuri. The nine-point programme put forward by the COP stood for the repeal of all political instruments devised by the ME and the restoration of the parliamentary system of government, with power invested in the legislature (national and provincial) rather than in the president (executive). It also asked for the economic reforms and the repeal of the Family Laws Ordinance (1961).

The results of the 1965 presidential elections are set out in Table 15. Ayub's victory was a foregone conclusion because the BE controlled the BD system and were able to manipulate the Basic Democrats by telling them that they would lose their position if a new government was installed. However, Miss Jinnah had more votes than Ayub in East Bengal, an indication that the EBPE had been more effective than their counterparts in West Pakistan.

Table 15: PERCENTAGE OF VOTES CAST IN THE PRESIDENTIAL ELECTIONS 1965

Candidates	Percentage of votes obtained		
	Pakistan	West Pakistan	East Pakistan
Ayub Khan	63.3	73.6	53.1
Miss Fatima Jinnah	34.4	26.1	46.6
Others	2.3	0.3	0.3
Total	100.00	100.00	100.00

Source: Adapted from Pakistan Election Commission, *Presidential Election Results,* 1965.

In an effort to bring together ethnically polarized groups the ME used the strategy of economic modernization. In this matter they were able to form a horizontal alliance with the IE. The ME had created an 'adequate infrastructure' and an 'adequate institutional framework' for encouraging economic development,[44] but had failed to distribute wealth. Their alliances with the BE and IE had led to uneven development and inequalities of income (see chapter 6).

Ayub had continuously dealt with the LE, and through his Land Reforms (1959) and other strategies tried to form an alliance with them. He retained the One-Unit Plan and had appointed powerful landlords, the Nawab of Kalabagh and Bhutto, as governor and cabinet minister respectively. However, under the strong political influence of the BE and IE, he tended to support capitalist rather than feudal vested interests. Members of his immediate family became industrial magnates,[45] and, following the same trend, many military officers were absorbed into private corporations.[46]

The LE believed that Ayub would share his power with them and gave him their full support in the 1965 elections. But the BE would not tolerate this horizontal alliance between the ME and LE, and sowed the seeds of distrust between them. By 1966, Ayub's disagreement with Punjabi and Sindhi LEs (like Nawab Kalabagh and Bhutto) led to their resignations. Ayub's downfall can be dated to the period when he formally lost LE support. After Kalabagh, no other governor could effectively control West Pakistan. Bhutto then formed the Pakistan People's Party which attracted LE support and also exploited the elite–mass gap created by Ayub's alliance with the IE and BE to mobilize the masses.

Ayub's gravest mistake was to alienate the military which had backed his coup d'état in 1958 to save the country from disintegration. After the 1962 Constitution he discarded his military colleagues, became head of a political party (the Convention Muslim League) and attempted to legitimize his political role by establishing his own support base through the BD system. He further upset the military by reducing its budget allocation,[47] but managed to keep the military in check, despite growing resentment, by posting generals whom he could trust. Table 16 shows how his defence expenditure during the years 1963–4 and 1964–5 had fallen to an all-time low as a proportion of total government spending.

In 1969, when the masses and other elite factions had turned against Ayub, he had no choice but to turn to the military for help. According to one of the officers interviewed by the author, he tried

Table 16:   DEFENCE EXPENDITURES AS PERCENTAGE OF TOTAL
GOVERNMENT EXPENDITURES,1948/49–1971/72
(MILLIONS OF U.S. DOLLARS)

Year	Defence expenditures	Total expenditures	Defence as % of total
1948–49	97.2	136.6	71.1
1949–50	131.7	180.0	73.3
1950–51	136.8	266.6	51.3
1954–55	133.7	246.7	54.1
1955–56	193.2	301.8	64.2
1956–57	168.2	279.4	60.2
1957–58	179.4	319.6	56.1
1958–59	209.9	410.9	51.0
1959–60	219.7	388.7	56.5
1960–61	234.2	398.8	58.7
1961–62	232.8	417.2	55.6
1962–63	200.4	377.0	53.1
1963–64	242.9	490.8	49.5
1964–65	265.7	576.0	46.1
1965–66	601.1	1,094.4	54.9
1966–67	482.8	792.7	60.9
1967–68	460.0	858.3	53.59
1968–69	510.9	920.2	55.52
1969–70	578.8	1,073.6	53.91
1970–71[a]	715.8	1,274.2	56.17
1971–72[a]	896.8	1,511.4	59.33
1972–73[b]	890.5	1,565.1	56.89

Source: Government of Pakistan, Finance Division, *Pakistan Economic Survey, 1971–72*
(Karachi: Manager of Publications, 1972), pp. 94–5.
Notes: *a* Revised figures
          b Estimates as of July–August 1972.

to 'play politics' in an effort to rally the support of the officer
corps.[48] He ordered General Yahya Khan to place the country
under martial law, but the latter did not respond owing to internal
military pressures. When it became apparent that the military
would not support him, Ayub was forced to hand over power to
General Yahya. The important point to note in this transfer of
power from one military head to another was that any political
leadership in Pakistan needed military support either to sustain or
dismantle it.

The Yahya Regime (1969–71)

General Yahya Khan took over the government of Pakistan in 1969 with a promise of 'protecting the country from utter destruction'.[49] His rule, like a military operation, was run more from the General Headquarters than from the presidential palace.[50] Political unrest came to an end, but the imposition of a second military regime had different impacts on various groups within the elites and masses. For the exploited masses, it was hoped that new leadership would alleviate poverty; while the ethnically exploited (particularly the Bengalis) looked on the new regime merely as a change from one military dictatorship to another.

Yahya Khan used a political rather than an economic approach to defuse the ethnic situation. His legal Framework Order of 1970 promised to give 'maximum autonomy' to the provinces and ensured that

(a) the people of all areas of Pakistan shall be enabled to participate fully in all forms of national activities;
(b) within a specified period, economic and all other disparities between the provinces and between different areas are removed by the adoption of statutory and other measures.[51]

Acting in fulfilment of the first clause, he used electoral power to decide the country's future leadership. He dismantled the One-Unit Plan and held the country's first elections on a 'one man, one vote' basis in December 1970. He was not himself a political contestant in these elections. The two major competing parties were the Pakistan People's Party in West Pakistan and the Awami League in East Pakistan. The two powerful leaders behind these parties were Bhutto and Mujibur Rahman respectively, and the results of the elections are shown in Table 17.

As the table indicates, the support for Mujibur Rahman was from East Bengal while Bhutto was backed in the Punjab. The 1970 election had become an ethnic contest. At the national level Mujib was clearly the leader voted for by the majority and was entitled to the office of prime minister. General Yahya Khan was willing to hand it to him, but Bhutto succeeded in creating a conflict where none existed. While all other minority parties accepted the Awami League domination, Bhutto demanded power-sharing, and this demand was rejected by Mujib.[52]

General Yahya's weakness lay in listening to Bhutto, rather than to Mujib. The sooner power had been handed over to Mujib, the

Table 17: RESULTS OF THE GENERAL ELECTIONS TO THE NATIONAL
ASSEMBLY, 1970 (NUMBERS OF SEATS WON)

Party	Punjab	Sind	NWFP	Baluchistan	East Bengal	Total
Awami League	0	0	0	0	160	160
Pakistan People's Party	62	18	1	0	0	81
Other parties*	15	6	17	4	1	43
Independent	5	3	7	0	1	16
	82	27	25	4	162	300

Source: Adapted from: *Report on General Elections, Pakistan, 1970–71,* vol. 1 (Islamabad: Election Commission, Government of Pakistan, 1972), pp. 204–5.

Note: *There were eight other political parties. These were: Pakistan Muslim League (Qayyum group), Pakistan Muslim League (Convention group), Council Muslim League, Jamiat-ul-Ulema-i-Islam, the Jamaat-i-Islam, National Awami Party, Markazi Jamiat-ul-Ulema-i-Pakistan and Pakistan Democratic Party.

better it would have been for Pakistan. As prime minister of Pakistan, it would have been very difficult for Mujib to find a cause for political secession. Besides, any attempt to do so on his part would have given the ME a justifiable cause for preventing it.

A careful study of the political talks held between Yahya, Mujib and Bhutto during the January to March 1971 period reveals that while Mujib demanded the transfer of power, Bhutto delayed it. When Yahya, in consultation with Mujib, declared 3 March 1971 as the date for the opening of the National Assembly, Bhutto threatened not only to boycott it but also to 'liquidate' the West Pakistani members who attended it.[53] Bhutto's political strategy was to play for time, to make himself the prime minister of, if not the whole, at least of West Pakistan. He knew that the East Bengalis would not tolerate another military regime and the delay could easily lead to a civil war between them and the Pakistan military. With the people of East Bengal fully backing Mujib, the army stood little chance of holding a balance, especially since Indian intervention was actively threatened. Yahya was unable to outbid Bhutto's strategies and at Bhutto's insistence postponed the National

Assembly. At this the smouldering ethnic nationalism of the Bengalis, who had come so near to acquiring political power, could no longer contain itself and civil war followed. Bhutto later tried to absolve himself of the blame by writing a book which rationalized the whole affair.[54]

The military, a victim of Bhutto's strategies, had no choice but to 'do its duty' to ensure the 'integrity, solidarity and security of Pakistan'.[55] The cost in terms of the loss of life and property was enormous. In the final outcome the military realized that it was not the Indian forces that had been their greatest foe, but the forces of ethnic nationalism.

The Military under Bhutto (1971–1977)

As the victor of the civil war, Bhutto did not allow the Yahya side of the Bangladesh affair to be publicized. Even the report of the commission (the Hamoodur Rahman Report), set up to inquire into the causes of the civil war, was never made public. Like the BE, the ME also could pose a threat to his power, so Bhutto tried to subordinate them politically.

While the ME nursed its wounds Bhutto took his chance to impose his control over this elite group. He fired some senior officers and placed persons trusted by himself in strategic posts. He abolished the position of commander-in-chief and replaced it with the office of chief of staff, so that ultimate authority would rest with the head of state. To avoid another coup d'état, he incorporated in his constitution the clause that any attempt to abrogate the constitution through force or conspiracy would be considered 'high treason'.[56] He did recognize the dual role of the military, however, and stated that it could defend Pakistan against external aggression and, 'subject to law', could act internally, 'in aid of civil power when called upon to do so'.[57]

Although the military was quick to reorganize itself, it could not wipe out the shame of its surrender. While negotiations were going on with the Indian government for the release of its prisoners of war there was considerable resentment among the young officers. They believed that it was better to have died on the battlefield than to have surrendered. Some of the senior officers interviewed by the author in 1975 thought that the whole battle strategy in East Bengal had been wrong. Instead of dispersing, the troops should have been concentrated in Dacca and then the Indian forces should have been invited to take them alive if they could. This might have led to ultimate defeat, but it would have been defeat with honour. Such thinking led to an unsuccessful coup d'état in 1973 in which it was planned to eliminate the most senior military officers as well as the politicians who were responsible for the East Bengal fiasco. In their trial in a military court (with General Zia-ul-Haq as the military judge) the conspiring officers were sentenced to long-term imprisonment. Bhutto was impressed by the loyalty of the military judge and later rewarded him with the position of chief of staff of the military establishment in March 1976.

Despite his apparent control over the ME Bhutto was aware that the only threat to his power in Pakistan was from this elite group. Without diverting the attention of the ME, as he had done previously in 1971, he could not transform Pakistan into a one-party state. Bhutto also knew the military's sensitivity towards ethnic nationalism and he exploited it (see chapter 9).

During Bhutto's regime, the military was given a 'development' role in Baluchistan. Its function was to:

(a) assist the civilian administration in restoring law and order in affected areas;
(b) apprehend hostile elements and recover unauthorized arms and instruments of warfare;
(c) maintain the security of the lines of communication in affected areas and undertake whatever action was necessary against hostile elements;
(d) assist the civil administration in various development and uplift projects in the Maari and Mengal areas of Baluchistan.[58]

In the post-1971 period the military were very reluctant to involve themselves in military solutions of ethnic problems. They knew the considerable uneasiness among the younger officers towards the Bhutto regime. They were also aware of the manner in which they had been involved in settling Bhutto's personal feud with the Baluchis in Baluchistan, and again, following the elections in March 1977, they had been used to control the masses and maintain Bhutto's crumbling regime. The July 1977 coup d'état was therefore not a spontaneous decision but a gradual culmination of a long period of disenchantment with the political leadership. Ethnic polarization had been created once again, and if another civil war had started the military would have become involved in it.

The Zia-ul-Haq Regime (1977–)

In his first speech after the coup d'état on 5 July 1977, General Zia-ul-Haq made it clear that the armed forces have always desired and tried for a political solution to a political problem. That is why the armed forces had stressed on the then government that they should reach a compromise with their political rivals without any loss of time . . . It must be quite clear to you now that when the political leaders fail to steer the country out of a crisis, it is an inexcusable sin for the armed forces to sit as silent spectators.[59]

The General made it clear that he had filled the 'vacuum created by the political leaders', as a 'soldier of Islam'.[60]

The political patterns of the new military regime have slowly begun to emerge. By comparison with previous military regimes it was more conservative than revolutionary with regard to Islam. Its prescriptive regulations for maintaining political order were strongly inclined towards the Nizam-i-Mustafa (Islamic political order), including the imposition of a partial set of Islamic punishments for civil offences. General Zia's regime indicated a serious desire to tackle the fundamental contradiction created by the previous governing elites of Pakistan, that is, their failure to bring about the political institutionalization of Islam. It also defused the ethnic situation by releasing the Pathan and Baluchi leaders who had been incarcerated, dismantling the trial of a group of dissidents for the Hyderabad conspiracy case and making it clear that the Baluchistan problem required a political and not a military solution.

In the present unstable political conditions the governing elites face many obstacles. Their immediate goal, however, should be to hold elections and hand over power to the political elites. The length of their stay in power depends on how skilfully they form horizontal and vertical alliances with the elites and masses.

The new eighteen-man Council of Ministers is indicative of two trends. First, that General Zia has forged horizontal alliances with the BE, PE and IE; secondly, that his present selection of ministers is conservative. These trends can lead the ME down blind alleys if they are not aware of the fact that similar horizontal alliances made by the Ayub regime proved detrimental to the egalitarian distribution of wealth. The interests of the IE and the masses contradict each other.

At the mass level, the vertical alliances of the ME with them are weak. The masses, whose expectations were raised high by the Bhutto regime, will continue to look to the regime to seek redress of their grievances. If the ME are unable to fulfil these demands their political frustration can be easily exploited by other elite groups or elite factions.

Above all, the military rulers must make changes within a framework which will lead to the integration of an Islamic nationhood. Instead of seeking to entrench themselves in the political arena until a strong political opposition is generated, they must try to keep intact the credibility of the military. Their political role must be one of patrolling the society from time to time, but not to govern it.

Conclusion

The role of the military, as the foregoing discussion shows, is closely interrelated with the political system of Pakistan. Whenever political crises have reached deadlock, the masses have looked to the military to come to their rescue. Such crises have strained the political system, largely through ethnic polarization. Given the military–state relationship, the ME, it can be predicted, will always take over the political arena whenever such crises threaten the state.

The military thus serves to act as a check on the system whenever some elite group (like Bhutto's) becomes dictatorial and does not share power with others. Without the support of the military, even Ayub, who had sought to entrench himself in the political arena, had to resign. On the basis of civil–military models of Western countries, the Pakistan military's role has often been termed as 'interventionist'. This, as stated earlier, does not apply in Pakistan, for the military is a part of the political system and has all the power it needs to take over the government of the country. It would therefore be in order to give the military a constitutional role, that is, to take over the political arena under certain conditions. These conditions would have to be carefully defined in the constitution. It would not mean giving the military a licence to rule; on the contrary, their role would be clearly defined for performing two functions: first, to remove the governing elites and, secondly, to remain in power for a limited period to resolve a political crisis. It is, however, beyond the scope of this study to deal with this subject in greater detail. Suffice it to say that the interests of the masses must be the main guiding factor in political coup d'états. The military must be the saviours and not the oppressors of the Pakistan masses.

In a political system where rulers have used political parties to extend their power, parliaments to rubber-stamp their decisions and all other political resources for their own ends, the checks and balances proposed above are essential.

9

The One-Party State and Political Conflict

In the post-1971 period, the shock of the break-up of Pakistan also aroused strong popular feeling for a new start in national political life. Such hopes had been pinned on a man who had promised to make Pakistan so strong that it could fight a thousand-year war with India. Bhutto's strategy, however, after gaining power was different. He tried to maximize his power in an absolute sense, and attempted to transform Pakistan into a one-party state.

Studies of one-party states have indicated that they normally act as alternatives to military regimes and are conducive to national integration, because 'the party, not the government, is the emanation of the people, that is, holds their loyalty and ties them to the state'.[1] Bhutto's aspirations for achieving this goal were embodied in his political organization, the PPP, and the other political resources at his command. These can be summarised as a new ideology (socialism), use of the state machinery (bureaucracy, military, judiciary, police, etc.) and political instruments (such as the Constitution of 1973). How he accomplished his goal and its impact on the ideological state will be the subject of this chapter.

Party Ideology

The policies of the Ayub regime, along with the agents of capitalism, the BE and IE, had led the country on a path of economic disaster which had resulted in uneven regional development and had widened the elite–mass gap. Ayub had sought to build his political constituency among the rural middle class, while Bhutto had politically mobilized the peasantry. Ayub had depended on the industrialists, Bhutto had incited the industrial masses. All this had been possible because Bhutto had used the new political ideology of socialism.

The use of ideology is a common strategy in many Third World countries. In some it has enjoyed the status of a 'political religion' which cannot be challenged.[2] In other states, like Ceylon and Burma, it was inspired by a sacred base (Buddhism).[3] In yet others it was secular. Ideologies in such states are therefore a coherent body of ideas which by skilful manipulation could be made to change the perception and goals of the masses.

In the ideological state, the role of ideology was supreme. This ideology was ensconced with Islam and was closely related to the creation of Pakistan. The ideological platform of a new party either had to coincide with conservative or revolutionary Islamic orientations or establish a secular base. Bhutto's ideology of socialism became popular because its 'action approach' appealed to the peasants and the industrial labourers. Bhutto argued that the capitalist mode of production, encouraged by the Ayub regime, had led to the establishment of a 'monstrous economic system of loot and plunder which the regime lauded as a free enterprise' which had made the 'poor poorer and the few richer'.[4] Capitalism was blamed for the ills of the country and socialism was projected as the panacea which would transform Pakistan into a classless society. This was to be done by curbing the power of the IE (see chapter 6).

Bhutto shifted the emphasis from religion because he felt that the struggle was not between 'Muslim and Muslim but between the exploiter and the exploited, between the oppressor and the oppressed'.[5] In fact, to attract the RE the word 'Islamic' was added to Bhutto's socialism.[6] Nevertheless, members of the RE had given 'fatwas' (religio–legal ruling), saying that socialism was 'kufr' (disbelief) and wrote slogans such as 'socialism kufr hai, Muslim millat ek ho' (Socialism is heresy, let the Muslim people remain one). The PPP reacted by stating that socialism was akin to Masawat-i-Mohammadi (Equality of the Prophet), because

> Islam and the principles of socialism are not mutually repugnant; Islam preaches equality and socialism is the modern technique of attaining it . . . Pakistan cannot last without the supremacy of Islam. A socialist form of government does not rival that supremacy. On the contrary, socialism will make the whole population the custodian of Islamic values.[7]

Sloganeering in Pakistani politics, as mentioned earlier, was an important channel of political communication, especially for mobilization of the masses. PPP slogans like 'Roti, Kapra and Makan' (food, clothing and shelter) were very effective in reaching the peasantry and industrial masses, as well as catching the imagination of the middle-sector urban groups. In one sense, as has been correctly pointed out, socialism was an ideology of 'protest' against the system which had been predominant for almost a decade.[8]

Bhutto's socialism, however, had several other aspects. It was a nationalist socialism because it offered to remove any inequalities within territorial boundaries. It was also humanist because it aimed at creating a society based on social justice and not the profit motive. At the same time, it was an elitist socialism because it did not emanate from the masses but from a privileged group which planned to implement such egalitarianism. In addition, it was a reactionary socialism which promised to strike at imperialism and protect the country from capitalist penetration and market forces. In reality, it was aimed at the politicization of the masses so that any elite group opposition could be countered with mass power. Bhutto's ideology was a facade to maximize his personal power, not one which practised what it preached. His life-style contradicted his socialism.[9]

To gain maximum support the PPP enlisted anybody who served its interests, irrespective of their political beliefs. The party thus attracted a diversity of groups, ranging from the peasantry and the industrial masses to capitalists and feudal landlords. Adherence to the principles of socialism was not a necessary condition for membership of the PPP. By monopolizing all political and economic resources the party organized a 'spoils' system through which material rewards, party tickets and party positions were awarded to those who could expand its political base. This could be said to have been to the regime's credit since it did succeed in making the masses very politically conscious.

Bhutto's objective was to merge the party with the state. This could not be done at once, but such a goal was evident in all the major strategies he employed. His main tactic had consistently been to concentrate all party power in his own person so that it was totally dependent upon him (as the Muslim League had been on Jinnah). Party propaganda, therefore, built a personality cult around him, as the man who had saved Pakistan from disintegration in 1971. Bhutto was placed on the highest political pedestal which hitherto had been reserved for the founder of the state. The latter was known as the Quaid-i-Azam (the great leader) and Bhutto became the Quad-i-Awan (the leader of the people). The only difference be-

tween the two titles was that while the former was bestowed on
Jinnah by a grateful nation, the latter was given by the PPP to
Bhutto. Such party propaganda to impress the masses was highly
resented by opposing political elites.[10]

Since Bhutto controlled the party and the state machinery, his
decisions were the party's decisions and they were executed by the
state machinery. Because of this arrangement, it became very difficult for the political opposition to articulate its demands. If they
opposed the party they opposed the government, and if they
opposed the latter they could be considered traitors. In other words,
in a civilian rule no effort was made to create a healthy political
atmosphere for the growth of political parties. Even internal opposition within the PPP was severely censored and dissidents were
forced to resign (e.g. Mubasher Hassan), physically beaten (e.g.
J. A. Rahim), imprisoned (e.g. Hanif Ramay) or discarded (e.g.
Mairaj Mohammad Khan).

The State Machinery

In the one-party state, the state machinery had to follow the purposes and goals of the dominant party. All important divisions of
the state machinery—the bureaucracy, judiciary and the military
—were brought under the centralized control of the party leader,
Bhutto, and thus became a parallel extension for imposing personalized control over the elites and masses.

How Bhutto dismantled the bureaucracy and introduced the
lateral entry system has been discussed above in chapter 4. Without
going into the merits and demerits of the lateral entry system, one
needs to examine closely how this system was used patrimonially to
create a bureaucrary within the bureaucracy, which would be loyal
to Bhutto. About 2796 lateral entry appointments were made in the
period 1972–7 to strategic positions in the federal government. Of
these, 1519 were from the Punjab, 650 from Sind, 451 from NWFP
and 60 in Baluchistan. The zeal of these appointees in part explains
the over-enthusiasm shown by the bureaucracy in rigging the 1977
elections to ensure Bhutto's success. The Zia regime was concerned
about such favouritism and announced an enquiry into such
appointments.[11]

The military was a difficult institution to penetrate through lateral entry systems. Bhutto therefore resorted to the more conventional tactics of purging anti-PPP generals or those with 'Bonapar-
tist tendencies'.[12] Political payoffs took the form of ambassadorial

appointments overseas, rapid promotions within the services and sometimes ministerial appointments.[13] In order to bind the military constitutionally the office of the commander-in-chief of the armed forces was abolished and replaced by the chiefs of staff of various services. Bhutto always felt insecure with regard to the military and kept a tight control on the political–military stratum. Just before his fall from power, Bhutto ordered all the chiefs of staff to affirm in public their support for his regime to show the PNA his strength. How far the military was ready to honour such a public commitment was another matter.

In case the military did not enforce his personalized rule, Bhutto had also formed a Federal Security Force, a paramilitary organization that could chastise or liquidate his political opponents. According to the banned *Punjab Punch* (8 July 1973), the total expenditure of the special police establishments increased 27 times during the Bhutto regime, and over 5000 persons were detained as political prisoners.

The Political Instrument

Constitutionalism has been thought necessary to impose limitations on the powers of government and as such is an antithesis of personalized rule.[14] Successive constitutions in Pakistan were perceived as instruments for the extension and legitimation of one man's power. The BE Constitution of 1956 was revoked by the ME, who replaced it with their own in 1962, which in turn was abrogated by the LE and replaced by their Constitution of 1973. Each constitution had not attempted to improve its predecessor through amendments but had completely discarded it.

According to the 1973 Constitution the prime minister was to be elected by a majority vote of the total membership of the National Assembly (Art. 91:3), and authority was vested in the office of the prime minister rather than the president, which made the former's decisions binding on the latter. With the president under his control as a mere figurehead, Bhutto was able to control the National Assembly by placing limitations on its powers to remove him from office. Resolutions for votes of no-confidence were allowed, but they could not be passed unless the Assembly named his successor (Art. 92:2). Such a resolution could be voted on within three days of having been moved in the NA, but no later than seven days. Within this period Bhutto could imprison all dissenting members, since the bill had to be passed by a 'majority of the total membership of the NA' (96:5). In order to prevent any dissenters from his own party voting for such a resolution Bhutto made the provision that such a vote would be disregarded if 'the majority of the members of that political party in the National Assembly had cast their votes against the passing of such a resolution' (96:5). If, however, such a resolution was not carried, a period of six months had to elapse before another vote of no-confidence could be proposed by the National Assembly (96:6).

This constitution also included clauses for safeguarding the legitimate rights of the minority groups and for giving them 'due representation' in the Federal and Provincial Services (Art. 36), and participation in the Armed Forces of Pakistan (Art. 39). With regard to the distribution of revenue between the centre and provinces, effective control rested with the former (Art. 160). Furthermore, the governor of each province was to be appointed by the centre. Also, in order to assure the political opposition that their economic interests would be safeguarded a Council of Common Interests (Art. 153) was to be set up, through which the provincial chief and federal ministers, under the chairmanship of Bhutto, could regulate policies. With members of the PPP holding the positions of governor and chief ministers in the provinces, the Council of Common Interests remained so in name only, with a one-way political communication, from centre to province.

The Constitution demanded 'loyalty to the State' as the basic duty of every citizen (Art. 5:1) and obedience to the Constitution as the 'basic obligation of every citizen' (Art. 5:2). It empowered the centre to issue a Proclamation of Emergency (Art. 232) if it was satisfied that the security of Pakistan or of any province was threatened with external aggression or internal disturbance 'beyond the power of a provincial government to control' (Art. 232). This last-mentioned clause was prematurely used by Bhutto in NWFP and Baluchistan, and it succeeded in alienating these provinces from the centre.

The governing elites, as always, considered themselves indispensable to the survival of Pakistan, a fact reflected in the type of constitutions that emerged. In Bhutto's constitution the checks on the removal of the prime minister allowed its incumbent to remain constantly in power. The emphasis on the 'majority of the total membership of the National Assembly' implied dependence on the elite majority from the Punjab. The centre's control over the Federal Legislative lists (fourth and fifth schedules of the Constitution) vested more economic control in its hands, making the provinces dependent on it for their economic development.

Old and sensitive issues such as provincial autonomy or the federal principle remained loosely defined in the Constitution. There was no change from the conventional paths taken by the past regimes. The NA still retained the power to amend any clauses relating to the provincial interests or the centre's powers to suspend provincial governments without a referendum of consent from the provinces concerned. The federal principle adumbrated in the Lahore Resolution (1940) and in the Objectives Resolution (1949) was not implemented and the vested interests of governing elites continued to take priority over national interests. The constitution remained, as stated earlier, an instrument for extension of personal power (see Fig. 4). In the light of this discussion, the constitutional organization of the government made Bhutto's position pivotal to all central and provincial arrangements. Those constitutional formulae which enhanced the power of the governing elites without the consensus of the elite groups and the support of the masses remained meaningless in the ideological state.

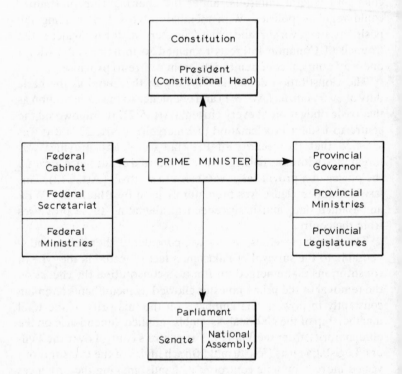

Fig. 4: Constitutional Map of the Bhutto Regime

Elite Factionalism and Political Conflict

Elite factionalism, as the reader must by now be aware, was a strong characteristic of Pakistan elite groups. It imposed the greatest strain on the political system when it developed along ethnic lines. Such factionalism, as analysed earlier, had split the PE into the WPPE and the EBPE. Similar factionalism in the LE group led to the ethnicization of political forces of the NWFP and Baluchistan on one side, and of Sind and Punjab on the other.

The pro-Bhutto LE faction ruled the Punjab and Sind provinces. The governor of Punjab was the Nawab of Bahawalpur (Mohammad Abbassi) and the chief minister (Sadiq Hussain Qureshi) was from a landed family of Multan. The governor of Sind was Nawab Dilawar Khanji and the chief minister (Ghulam Mustafa Jatoi) was also a landlord. These two provinces helped to perpetuate Bhutto's personalized rule. On the other hand, the NAP (a party of the LE faction from NWFP and Baluchistan) was the PPP's strongest rival in these provinces.

The NAP was originally under the control of Maulana Bashani (an East Bengali) and in 1967 had split into two factions. The Peking-oriented faction remained under the leadership of Bashani while the Moscow-oriented faction was led by Wali Khan and other landlords.[15] They believed in the federal principle and they were forced to politicize their ethnicity when their political rights were denied. Their slogan in 1970 was based on the concept of 'Paktoon Kwa' (a pure Pathan culture), provincial autonomy and freedom from Punjabi domination.[16]

The ideology of the Moscow faction of the NAP was a mixture of regionalism, secularism, socialism and all-Pakistan nationalism.[17] According to Wali Khan, Pakistan had been manipulated by the governing elites to suit their own political ends and, as such, the ideology of the Muslim League had been corrupted by the PPP. This change had caused conflicts between political elites. Nevertheless, he believed that there was

> one nation in this country and that is the Pakistani nation and that this Pakistani nation is composed of nationalities—who have their own distinct language and culture—there is no contradiction in the two, but these nationalities are like flowers who with their distinct colour and fragrance blend into a bouquet—manifesting their unity in diversity.[18]

Baluchi leaders also believed in the same ideology and reinforced it with another analogy. Here Pakistan was considered the home of four brothers who should be treated as brothers and not as slaves.[19] Both groups were opposed to the 'one-man' rule in Pakistan. In their typical manner they had warned Bhutto that 'not a ballot but a bullet can settle the issue'.[20] Bhutto therefore had no choice but to agree to a compromise (the 6 March 1972 Accord). The most important clauses in the accord assured the opposition that a constitutional political arrangement would allow them the freedom to form their own political governments and that the centre would not appoint provincial governors without their approval and consent.

Until April 1973 when the Constitution was passed by the majority in the NA, the NAP continued to oppose many clauses which did not offer a fair deal to the LE in these regions. They compromised in the end but not without forming a United Democratic Front one month before the Constitution came into force, to confront the governing elites if their legitimate rights were not restored or implemented.

Political conflicts, however, did not confine themselves to the national levels and they also continued in the provinces too. In Baluchistan, Ghaus Baksh Bizenjo (1972–3) was appointed governor and Ataullah Mengal (1972–3) chief minister. They were both tribal chieftains and members of the NAP. The Bhutto regime alleged that during their administration a tribal lashkar (war party) had been raised and issued with arms and ammunition from the government armoury. This lashkar had been used for settling personal and tribal feuds and attacking and killing Punjabi settlers in the area. It was also alleged that the lashkar was being trained by foreign agents in the art of guerilla warfare. When some arms were discovered in the Iraqi Embassy en route to the Baluchi insurgents, Bhutto used this as a final excuse to dismiss the NAP governors, following which the NAP chief ministers also resigned. Bhutto then appointed his own party members to these positions but made no serious attempt to bring a political solution to the Baluchi problem.

While political opposition increased instead of lessening in Baluchistan another threat was posed to Bhutto's regime from the military. Some young officers headed by a brigadier held Bhutto and his party henchman responsible for the creation of Bangladesh. They therefore planned a coup d'état which was discovered in 1973. Because of their court martial Bhutto knew that there was considerable resentment in the military against him. To prevent this resentment from becoming active again he reverted to his old strategy of 1971. This was to involve the military once more so that he could emerge triumphant. By provoking the Baluchis to insurgency through PPP rule in the province, he invoked the emergency powers in the Constitution and imposed a military solution to the Baluchistan problem. Such a solution in 1974 led the military into violent clashes with the tribal LE faction in the mountains. It again brought the military into disrepute with Baluchis and led to a further ethnicization of political issues.

In the NWFP the governor was Arbab Sikander (1972–3) of the NAP and the chief minister Mufti Mahmood (1972–3) of the JUI. This province was the stronghold of the NAP, and Bhutto needed new political strategies to bring about the fall of the NAP and its government lest they become powerful enough to threaten his own position. He therefore formed an alliance with Khan Abdul Qayyum Khan of the Muslim League (Qayyum group) by appointing him minister of the interior in his cabinet. The ML(Q) created disruptions at the elite level while the Kissan–Mazdoor party provoked disturbances at the mass level. In this province he also dismissed the governor and the provincial chief minister, and the ministry resigned in 1973. Bhutto's nominees to replace them were weak and without any grassroot following. With the military already deployed in Baluchistan in 1974, yet another strategy was needed to eliminate the NAP. The political assassination of Bhutto's nominee Hayat Mohammad Sherpao in March 1975 gave him the excuse he needed to pin the blame on the NAP.[21] The party was labelled 'anti-state' and 'anti-Islam' and was banned in 1975 by a judicial ruling. The leaders of the NAP were incarcerated and debarred from taking part in elections until 1980.

Just as Ayub had jailed almost all members of the Awami League and had induced the Agarthala conspiracy case, Bhutto repeated the same strategy with the leadership of the NAP and created the Hyderabad conspiracy case. A course of action that had previously led the country to a civil war was being reenacted.

In his passion to create a one-party state, Bhutto's political manoeuvring had placed the political system under ethnic strain. His failure to honour the March 1972 Accord in the Constitution, his dismissal of the provincial governments of NWFP and Baluchistan in 1973, his involvement of the military in Baluchistan in 1974 and the banning of the NAP in 1975 had eroded his political credibility in the provinces. The NWFP and Baluchistan continued in their anti-Bhutto stand through the formation of another party, the National Democratic Front in 1975. The IE, ME, RE and PE were becoming politically active and factionalism within his own party over his policies further threatened his own power. In such a situation he could not continue for long without going 'back to the electorate not only for a new mandate but also in search for legitimacy'.[22] This political legitimacy would have consolidated his position in the political arena and allowed him to reassert his control over all the provinces of Pakistan. More important than the holding of an election was the assurance of a complete victory in such an election. The time had come again to form a vertical alliance with the peasantry and industrial labour and a horizontal alliance with the elite groups.

The Elections of 1977

In March 1977 the political elites formed a coalition known as the Pakistan National Alliance (PNA) in an attempt to remove Bhutto from the political arena. The PNA was made up of the following organizations: National Democratic Party (NDP) Jamaat-i-Islami (JI), Jamiatul-Ulema-i-Islam (JUI), Jamiatul-Ulema-i-Pakistan (JUP), Tehriq-i-Istaqlal (TI), Pakistan Democratic Party (PDP), Pakistan Muslim League (PML), the Khaksar Tehrik and the All-Jammu and Kashmir Muslim Conference.

The PNA manifesto was based within an economic–religious framework which promised to give the IE the freedom of private enterprise and to denationalize certain industries. Furthermore, the PNA promised to bring out a 'clear-cut industrial policy which would ensure protection to labour and investment (capital) and sincere co-operation between the two so as to maximize production within the minimum possible time'.[23] In other words, the status quo of the capitalist system was to be maintained.

The PNA was a coalition of political parties with diverse interests but bound together by a common enemy in Bhutto. The NDP, which had replaced the NAP, represented the feudal interests of the khans and sardars of NWFP and Baluchistan. On the other hand there were the 'Islam-pasand' (religious) parties like the JI, JUI and JUP whose prime interest was to bring in the Nizam-i-Mustafa (the Islamic system). Apart from the Islamic ideology, they considered all others to be 'kufr' (disbelief). The TI and PML were centre of left, that is, between Islam and capitalism. The results of the March 1977 elections between these contestants are given in Table 18.

It was apparent from the allocation of seats to the provinces that Punjab was the lynchpin for attaining the political leadership of Pakistan. If a political leader could win all the seats in Sind (43),

Table 18:   RESULTS OF THE MARCH 1977 ELECTIONS
(NUMBERS OF SEATS WON)

Province	PPP		PNA		Independent*		Total
	Seats won	% of total	Seats won	% of total	Seats won	% of total	
Punjab	107	93.0	8	7.0	—	—	115
Sind	32	74.4	11	25.6	—	—	43
NWFP	8	30.8	17	65.4	1	3.8	26
Baluchistan	7	100.0	—	—	—	—	7
Islamabad	1	100.0	—	—	—	—	1
Tribal Areas	—	—	—	—	8	100.0	8
TOTAL	155	77.5	36	18.0	9	4.5	200

Source: *Overseas Weekly Dawn* (Karachi), 13 March 1977.
Note: *The independent seat in NWFP was won by the Qayyum Muslim League.

NWFP (26) and Baluchistan (7), he would still not emerge as the overall leader. Bhutto's position was secured by the Punjabi vote where he won 107 out of 115 seats. In the provincial elections the PPP had won 119 out of 186 seats in the Punjab, 30 out of 62 in Sind, 3 out of 42 in the NWFP and none out of 21 seats in Baluchistan. It is therefore appropriate to examine the nature of the support as well as the opposition to Bhutto rule in the Punjab which led to his downfall.

Bhutto's horizontal alliances with the Punjabi LE and vertical alliance with the Punjabi peasantry were the basis of his support. The Bhutto regime kept up a massive propaganda about the primacy of their interests. Some peasants interviewed by the author informed him that any concern shown for them by political leaders meant security for them. New slogans like 'Ghareebon ke majboori hay, Bhutto bohat zaroori hay' (the redeemer of the poor can only be Bhutto) were used to build high expectations among the exploited, as Bhutto promised to 'improve the quality of the common man's life'.[24] He had impressed his audiences that there were two Bhuttos, one present in him, the other in them, and the bond was unbreakable.[25] The peasants often clung to such emotional arguments and supported him. On the other hand, industrial labour was divided because of frustrations resulting from the economic policies of the regime. Labour leaders like Mukhtar Rana were imprisoned for disagreeing with the PPP and such action removed a great deal of the labour support away from Bhutto (also see chapter 6). The RE and the Punjabi PE had by this time joined the IE in their political opposition to the Bhutto regime.

Other horizontal alliances with the PE did not develop because some of its important factions did not agree with Bhutto's policies. One faction, composed of members who were more inclined to the left (e.g. Dr Mubasher Hassan, J. A. Rahim, Hanif Ramay, Khurshid Hassan Mir), was disappointed with Bhutto's compromise with socialism. As elections approached Bhutto de-emphasized his socialism and even promised to denationalize some of the industries he had taken into state ownership.

Yet other PE factions (e.g. M. A. Kasuri) genuinely believed that Pakistan 'has a future only as a genuine federation of the four provinces, each province being led by whoever is elected by its people'.[26] Without this, ethnic polarization could lead to the development of ethnic nationalism. Such views, held by elites outside the PPP as well as within it, made it weaker in the Punjab. In addition, the increasing incidence of political violence made the credibility of the Bhutto's one-party regime domination an obstacle to be removed.[27]

One-party states have often proved to be incompatible with democratic processes, particularly in multi-ethnic societies. Their prime problem is the 'creation of nations out of heterogeneous peoples'.[28] Democratic rule in such societies rested on the voting power of one ethnic group in the majority. Such a majority in Pakistan after 1971, as stated on several occasions, belonged to the Punjabis. In the pre-1971 period, when the Bengalis had held majority voting power, the Punjabi minority had resisted all attempts at an election based on a 'one man, one vote' principle. In the post-1971 period they advocated this principle because it gave them strong leverage and access to economic and political resources. Such a majority contradicted, in fact, the idea of democracy.

Bhutto's personalized rule in a multi-ethnic society was bound to create political crises. Since the Constitution did not ensure that all ethnic leaders would get an equal opportunity to become national leaders, the 'majority' principle of democracy became the tyranny of the minority. The governing elite, blinded by the power generated by their majority strength, failed to realize that it was an ethnic minority they were repressing and that the power of ethnicity had been tested in 1971.

Some one-party states have endeavoured to create national integration by accommodating regional ethnic parties through political participation.[29] Others have tried to eliminate all opposition to the regime.[30] Bhutto's one-party state had done nothing to integrate the minority provinces at a national level and in fact had added to the politicization of their ethnicity—which in the absence of a national identity created secessionist trends.

Bhutto's fall was therefore not due to the rigging of the elections—the furore over rigging was merely a symptom of the deep ethnic cleavages and elite polarization that had developed during his rule.[31] These caused sufficient strain on the political system to cause a violent eruption.

Studies have revealed that election processes differ from one political system to another and they can have both stabilizing and destabilizing effects.[32] In the Pakistani political system, elections were not vital to the system because of elitist rule. The system had been run for considerable periods without elections, and when they had been held by governing elites with vested interests (Ayub in 1965 and Bhutto in 1977) they did not allow the electorate to choose between candidates but only served to narrow the choice to one candidate—the contesting governing elite—and to perpetuate elite rule. The only 'fair' elections held in Pakistan had been those of 1970. In these elections the governing elites were not contesting. The aftermath of the March 1977 elections was conducive to another civil war. From April to July 1977, the political elites of the PNA showed their political strength through hartals (strikes) and piya-jam (wheel jam) strikes in cities, industrial strikes, bombings and processions organized by the RE and PE in Lahore. Large-scale demonstrations in Karachi, Hyderabad, Lahore, Multan, Rawalpindi and Peshawar led to serious clashes between the people and Bhutto's police forces. The stronger the political opposition became, the more ruthlessly was the state machinery used against them. Finally, Bhutto had to call in the army, whose action in opening fire on a crowd in Lahore led to the resignation of senior military officers. Martial law was imposed in many cities and economic activities came to a standstill. Some Arab countries tried to mediate, but Bhutto still held on to power.

There was only one force that could step in and resolve the crisis—the military. The military duly took over on 5 July 1977 and placed the country under its third martial law.

Conclusion

Many observers in Pakistan consider Bhutto an enigma. His orator-
ical style had impressed the masses; his skilful vertical and horizontal alliances had made the PPP powerful; his foreign policies and
international prestige diverted the attention of the people from
national politics and his socialist ideology had promised to build a
classless society. These were all new political strategies and it is to
Bhutto's credit that he helped to increase the political awareness of
the masses.

What the people failed to realize was that underneath his sophisticated veneer Bhutto was a member of the LE whose political
socialization as a feudalist was elitist and therefore incompatible
with democracy. His acute political foresight to capitalize on any
situation caused many to succumb to his influence without realizing
that he was one of the prime architects in the break-up of Pakistan.
His policies towards the NAP and its leaders were no different from
those of the previous regimes with the AL. With a lack of historical
vision, Pakistanis failed to discern that it was precisely policies like
these that would lead to the disintegration of the country.

This comment raises an important question about the type of a
political leader that Pakistan needs. An ideological state requires a
leader such as Caliph Omar (634–644 AD), the Commander of the
Faithful, who was known for his just administration. This ideal has
only been put forward to point out that the responsibility of the
nation's highest office should not be entrusted to politicians who
own large tracts of land and talk of land reforms or who claim to
want to safeguard the rights of the people when their own means of
production exploits the poor peasantry. Dynamic Islamic leadership demands Islamic responsibilities of the Muslim leaders, and the
establishment of an egalitarian society through the radicalization of
the social, political and economic framework of Pakistan.

The second important question is about the structure of Pakistan's leadership. Leadership based on the ethnic support of the
largest ethnic group will only lead to ethnic polarization since this
would deny political participation to minority ethnic leadership. A
parity principle must be devised to allow all four provinces to
participate equally in the political and economic development of the
country. The structure of leadership must be changed to the satis-
faction of the people of Pakistan.

10

Ethnic Nationalism and Imperialism

The task of nation-building has been held by scholars to be a multi-dimensional problem involving the forging of a sense of territorial nationality, the bridging of the elite–mass gap, the establishment of a national central authority, the creation of a minimum consensus of values and the devising of common integrative institutions and codes of behaviour.[1] Some studies of Asian and African nations have noted that they are 'not yet nations in being but only nations in hope'.[2] Political crises such as those of identity, legitimacy, penetration, participation, integration and distribution afflict these countries and must be overcome before the society can transform itself into a modern nation state.[3] When these factors are not adequately dealt with, problems arise in converting subnational groups into a nation state. Some political scientists have considered that before new states can evolve as viable national societies they must pass through an 'endless round of coups, conquests, revolutions and wars'.[4]

Pakistan has passed through coup d'états, civil wars, ethnic insurgencies and ethnic nationalism (as in Bangladesh), but has not yet had a political revolution. Whether such an eventuality is possible can only be determined by examining the vital political forces of feudalism, capitalism and Islam. While the latter has always remained at the ideal level, the forces of feudalism and capitalism have contiued to dominate the political arena. The political system has therefore suffered from a low degree of elite consensus and elite cohesion, and nation-building goals have not been seriously followed. Table 19 sums up the diverse transformations of the state that were attempted by the elite groups.

Table 19:   ELITIST TRANSFORMATIONS OF PAKISTAN

Elite group	Type of state transformation
Military elites	Praetorian state
Bureaucratic elites	Administrative state
Landowning elites	Feudal state
Industrial elites	Capitalist state
Professional elites	Democratic state
Religious elites	Islamic state

The net result of these various self-fulfilling political strategies was that there was considerable political strain on the Pakistani political system. Each elite group was continually engaged in mobilizing its resources to transform the state to safeguard its vested interests. With such transformations in mind, each regime emphasized some ideology to legitimize their systems. The Ayub regime was inclined towards capitalism, the Bhutto regime towards 'Islamic socialism' which was merely a form of progressive feudalism and Zia-ul-Haq's regime has turned towards the Nizam-i-Mustafa. It is true, however, that none of them have tried to proceed in any one exclusive direction and this could only happen if a political revolution brings about such changes.

Reinforcement of its resources had at times sent each elite group to external centres for help. Thus the RE looked to Saudi Arabia for religious inspiration, the BE and ME turned to the United States for foreign aid and arms. This in turn made inroads for imperialism.[5] The linkage of the BE with imperialism and its impact on ethnicity will be discussed in this section.

Imperialism and Ethnicity

The 'will to be modern' has been particularly strong in ex-colonial countries because of the elite groups that had emerged during the colonial period.[6] Modernization theorists have used 'traditional' and 'modern' dichotomies, and equate modernization with economic development and technological advancement. The Western industrial nations projected as examples of such modernization standardized the goal to be achieved by the Third World countries. In the pursuit of such modernization capitalism penetrated and reinforced the groups that aided its entrenchment in the country. Such modernization did not take place in isolation, but in the global context the processes of capitalism created the dependency of the Third World on Western industrialized countries.[7] Dependency in turn created a situation in which the economy of certain countries is conditioned by the development and expansion of another so that 'some countries (the dominant ones) can expand and be self-sustaining, while other countries (the dependent ones) can do this only as a reflection of that expansion'.[8] Pakistan was no exception to this rule.

The nature and extent of Pakistan's dependency has varied in different periods. Before Partition, the sub-continent as a whole was dependent upon the colonizing power for its development. After Partition, it came under U.S. hegemony.

The BE were the first group to invite support from the U.S. in 1947 by assuring them that 'communism was incompatible with Pakistan's Islamic way of life'.[9] During Ghulam Mohammad's regime the Americans made a 'dramatic entry' into the political arena and went so far as to influence the appointment of Bogra (the U.S. Ambassador) as prime minister of Pakistan.[10] The BE, ME and IE all had ties with imperialist powers but each for a different reason. The ME wanted to increase their fighting machinery, the IE their economic power and the BE their administrative power. The BE's role was most significant in the country's economic development.

The role of the United States as the 'organizer and leader of the world imperialist system'[11] has been well documented and does not need elaboration. Pakistan was strategically important for the maintenance of U.S. domination in South Asia. On the other hand, it was a new market for capitalist expansion, and U.S. personnel started coming into the country from 1948 onwards. Table 20 gives their numbers in both wings.

As is apparent from the table, most of the U.S. personnel were concentrated in West Pakistan since this was the centre of the powerholders in the country. The most significant impact of U.S. imperialism in this area was on economic development. In order to monopolize economic decision-making, a group of experts was installed in the Planning Board (which later came to be known as the Planning Commission) in 1954. This was the highest economic planning body in the country and the American advisors came to be known as the Harvard Advisory Group (HAG). The function of this group was to

Table 20:   NUMBERS OF U.S. OFFICIALS STATIONED IN PAKISTAN
1948–1971

Year	West Pakistan	East Pakistan
1948	19	0
1949	26	1
1950	28	2
1951	41	3
1952	43	3
1953	56	4
1954	116	5
1955	169	9
1956	190	21
1957	214	45
1958	231	45
1959	229	39
1960	216	39
1961	205	38
1962	239	40
1963	271	36
1964	269	44
1965	260	45
1966	119	119
1967	166	68
1968	188	67
1969	193	58
1970	160	52
1971	146	34
Totals	3,675	692

Source: Adapted from R. LaPorte Jr., *Power and Privilege* (Berkeley: University of California Press, 1975), p. 169.

help it conduct research for, and organize and draft a long range development plan for use of the nation's resources;
strengthen its capacity to provide analyses and recommendations to the government on major economic-policy questions;
help train a staff of professionals in economics, finance, agriculture, industry and other important areas of national planning.[12]

The HAG remained in Pakistan from 1954 to 1970. It was funded by the Ford Foundation until 1965, the World Bank from 1965 to 1968 and the United Nations Organization from 1968 to 1970.[13] Its programme was under the supervision of the Graduate School of Public Administration until 1962 after which a Development Advisory Service was set up at the Center for International

Affairs at Harvard to supervise the economic development of Pakistan.

The abundance of advisors did not mean that Pakistan's political, economic, social and religious problems were being resolved. The group was essentially interested in implementing Western capitalist doctrines, and their impact on economic development (on majority provinces like East Bengal) was ignored. One study states that

> underdeveloped countries do not really need people to come and give them counsel on what to do. There are times when a particular piece of expert guidance is needed in order to decide on some technical detail, but in general it is all too obvious what needs to be done.[14]

For the governing elites, however, such advice was needed to rationalize policies they had already decided on for the economic development of West Pakistan. They consulted the HAG 'on all important economic decisions'.[15] Internally, the Planning Commission was dependent on it. HAG influence involved 'the direct transfer of economic knowledge to the highest policy levels of the government'.[16] The HAG thus 'quickly earned for itself acceptance, respect and substantive influence with those making critical development decisions in Pakistan'.[17]

The direct role of the HAG can be seen by examining its impact on the Five Year plans devised for the country. In drafting the First Five Year Plan (1955–1960), the advisors were 'under pressure to produce a good plan' and they did the 'substantive work themselves resulting in the Harvard Group preparing most of the important sections of the ... Plan'.[18] In the Second Five Year Plan (1960–1965), 'the character of the final product and its timing was materially influenced by the HAG ... by advice, background papers, comments on staff papers and by actual drafting or redrafting of sections of the Plan ... their participation was indispensable'.[19] In the Third Five Year Plan (1965–70) there was a much greater 'coordinated effort of all the agencies involved, with the Planning Commission in charge of the work'.[20]

Imperialism, as stated earlier, encouraged internal colonialism. The BE and IE, rationalizing the one-economy thesis, developed only those areas that they inhabited. Such developments were further compounded by foreign aid which reinforced the economic and political power of these elite groups (see Table 21).

The table shows that as grants decreased, loans increased. Irrespective of the form of aid, the important question was not how it was going to be used but who was going to use it. The governing elites

Table 21:   FOREIGN ECONOMIC ASSISTANCE TO PAKISTAN
1950–1970

Time/Period	Grants		Loans		Total million U.S. $
	million U.S. $	% total	million U.S. $	% total	
Pre-First Plan (1950–1955)	251	67.5	120	32.5	371
First Five Year Plan (1955–1960)	573	59.4	417	40.6	990
Second Five Year Plan (1960–1965)	345	14.5	2,023	85.5	2,368
Third Five Year Plan (1965–1970)	193	6.8	2,507	93.2	2,700
TOTAL	1,362	21.2	5,067	78.8	6,429

Source: Dickson K. Smith, 'Foreign Aid and Economic Development in Pakistan : The Ayub Years (1958–1969)', unpublished Ph.D. dissertation, Department of Economics, University of Utah (1974), p. 288.

were in control of it and East Bengal did not receive more than 35 per cent of this assistance overall.[21]

As mentioned earlier, ethnicity is an important variable in Third World political systems and the forces of ethnic nationalism have led to civil wars in countries such as the Congo (1960) and Nigeria (1967). In the case of Pakistan, the lack of a national identity had created contradictions in the ideological state which in turn manifested themselves as an internal dualism—the ethno-Islamic and the ethno-national.[22] The former defined an ethnic group's identification with religion, while the latter defined its relationship with the state. In other words, the ethnic groups in Pakistan were united by a common religious base, Islam, while on the other hand each had its own language, history, literature and territorial unit. Since religion had not been institutionalized in the state, the ethnic groups found it difficult to relate to the national boundaries of the state.

Ethnicity, therefore, contained four elements which can be listed, in one commentator's words, as

(1) certain objective characteristics with common ancestry, such as language, territory, cultural practices and the like . . . ;
(2) which are perceived by both insiders and outsiders as important indicators of identity;
(3) so that they can become the basis for mobilizing social solidarity; and
(4) which, in certain situations, result in political activity.[23]

Ethnicity only became apparent in certain situations in Pakistani society. As Muslims, the tendency of the ethnic groups was to establish an egalitarian order, but in the absence of this they tended to politicize the only identity left to them—their ethnicity. It therefore acted as a powerful force for unifying the group when intergroup conflicts had excluded some groups from economic development or political participation.

The effect of this in Pakistan was to allow old inequities to continue and to promote modernization in a grossly unbalanced manner, which only served to maintain the dominance of the elite order and certain ethnic groups. The governing elites had unilaterally accepted the growing influence of economic imperialism but were unaware that modernization was instrumental in the politicization of ethnicity.[24] Furthermore, as modernization raised the political and economic aspirations of the ethnic groups it led to increased ethnic competition, tension and alienation between groups. Thus, the BE and IE who belonged to various ethnic groups (the Punjabis and Muhajirs) had no scruples in helping their own groups. The imperialists and the ethnic groups had both helped themselves in Pakistan.

The HAG came to an end in 1970, but not without having influenced the break-up of Pakistan. In 1971 some of the imperialist powers intervened, as the USSR backed India but the USA remained neutral. Imperialism will always seek to serve its own interests before those of the countries it penetrates, especially Third World countries.

Conclusion

The major points that emerge from this discussion of ethnicity in Pakistan can therefore be summed up as follows: first, the level of ethnic discord varied directly with the extent of the uneven economic development of the geographical areas occupied by the ethnic groups; secondly, the level of ethnic discord varied directly with the degree of political participation of each ethnic group within the political arena. As long as ethnic groups dominate and exploit other groups in the ideological state, Pakistan will always be threatened with disintegration and military rule will be inevitable to hold the provinces together.

Within the grip of imperialism, elite groups tend to become aligned towards the world capitalist system. The more dependent Pakistan becomes on other countries, the less control it will have on its internal political processes. This dependence will be determined within the country by the emerging class structures. Whether this class will overcome ethnic discords depends on how they distribute economic and political power among ethnic groups. One thing is certain, however, that as class structures, emanating from Western imperialism, became clearly defined, it will be inclined towards secularism. In such a situation, not only will the rich be exploiting the poor, but Muslims will exploit other Muslims. The new class structure will not only widen the gap between the elites and the masses but through it the forces of Western cultural and political imperialism will weaken national identity. Every conscientious Pakistani must work towards building a national identity through Islamic democratization and integration of ethnic groups. In this lies the only hope for the future of the state.

Islamization is a process for the implementation of the Islamic view of life. Islam gives both the message and an outline of the methods for bringing about such a transformation of a society.[25] Islamization has not taken place in the ideological state because, as already indicated in this study, the political elites kept Islam on an unapproachable pedestal and adopted non-Islamic methods to safeguard their vested interests. Their elite politics hindered the redistribution of wealth which would have given the poverty-ridden masses a better deal in life irrespective of their ethnicity. If Islamization is not implemented then the time is not far when the masses will revolt against their oppressors, in a manner similar to that of the East Bengalis in 1971. The political role of the military has therefore been a particularly difficult one when the political elite groups have time and again led the country to the brink of a civil war. Bhutto's pseudo-socialism raised the political consciousness and expectations of the people, but since it was secular and not based on Islam it could not bind the people together. It is therefore, high time that the political elites of Pakistan realize that a new generation of people has been born in the country and, for them, a new system of power-sharing and political participation must be devised. The pursuit of Western models of development will lead not only to the loss of a national identity but even cause the loss of the country.

Epilogue

Military regimes in Pakistan have always legitimated their coups by resorting to the 'doctrine of necessity'. This formula enables them to take political action when elite groups fail to resolve their political differences. In the case of the present military takeover, the two opposing forces in March 1977 were the PPP and the PNA.

More than a year has elapsed since the takeover by the military regime and during this period it has made some significant elite coalitions. These will be examined briefly and their implications for the future pointed out.

A general assessment of the political performance of the present military regime might conclude that it has been struggling to stabilize its position in the political arena. It has been threatened by three main problems: the trial and fate of Z. A. Bhutto who is still in jail on a murder charge; the general elections which have been promised but are still to be held; and the ushering in of the Nizam-i-Mustafa.

With regard to Z. A. Bhutto, certain elite groups still retain their loyalty for him, and some segments of the masses (peasants and labour) who were politicized by Bhutto still also support him. The extent of this backing became evident when the military had to postpone the elections in October 1977 because the PNA leaders were unsure of a victory.

On the first anniversary of the military regime (5 July 1978) a new Federal Cabinet was appointed. The elite group distribution within this cabinet is indicated in Table 22. The table suggests that elite selection had two objectives: to make coalitions with two important elite groups (LE and PE) and to gain the support of

Pathan and Baluchi elites. The former strategy was intended to divide the loyalties of the Punjabi and Sindhi LE which had supported Bhutto. It was also necessary to split the PE, as some of its members (e.g. Yahya Bakhtiar) were strong defenders of the political actions of the ex-premier. Men like Sharifuddin Pirzada and A. K. Brohi were selected to counteract the supporters of Bhutto in the PE and to legitimize the actions of the government. In order to attract the Pathan and Baluchi elites the Hotis, Habibullahs, Jogezais and M. Baluch were included in the Cabinet.

Table 22:   ELITE GROUP DISTRIBUTION IN THE FEDERAL CABINET
(5 July 1978)

ELITE GROUP	NUMBER
Military Elites	4
Bureaucratic Elites	1
Landowning Elites	5
Professional Elites	4
Industrial Elites	2
Total	16

Source: *Crescent International Biweekly* Canada), 15 July 1978
Note: Ministers of State have not been included.

Table 23:   ELITE GROUP DISTRIBUTION IN THE FEDERAL CABINET
(22 August 1978)

ELITE GROUP	NUMBER
Landowning Elites	7
Professional Elites	5
Industrial Elites	3
Religious Elites	5
Bureaucratic Elites	1
Total	21

Source: *The Jhang* (London), 24 August 1978
Note: Ministers of State have not been included.

This coalition cabinet, however, was a weak one which it could tackle neither the problems of future elections nor of the imposition of the Nizam-i-Mustafa. Subsequently, on 22 August 1978 another coalition cabinet was appointed. Its elite group distribution is indicated in Table 23. There were three significant changes in this cabinet. First, apart from General Zia-ul-Haq, all military cabinet ministers were withdrawn. This was done to dispel the general impression of a militarized regime. Indirectly, however, the power of the ME remained intact. Secondly, to weaken Sindhi elite support for the PPP, several Sindhis were selected for cabinet appointments (e.g. Talpurs, Khoses). Thirdly, to counter the threat from the socialistic ideology of the PPP a coalition was formed with the RE. This was done by the inclusion of men like Professor Ghafoor Ahmad, Chaudhri Rehmat Illahi and Mohammad Azam Farooqi. The RE were given further economic power by the appointment of a very competent Islamic economist (Professor Khurshid Ahmad) as the deputy chairman of the Planning Commission.

The formal entry of the RE into the political arena is an important step as it is the first time in history of Pakistan that an ME–RE coalition has been formed. How far such a coalition will succeed in bringing about the political institutionalization of Islam in the state remains to be seen. On the basis of the present political arrangements some future political trends can be predicted. First, Islamization has to take place within the politico-economic context of Pakistan. Its success will depend on the nature and degree of specifically Islamic changes introduced into the political system. Secondly, if these changes are not fundamental but a mere patchwork the impact of Islamization will be negligible. Nothing short of a complete revolution is needed to accomplish it. Thirdly, the success of the implication of such changes will depend upon how much support the ME–RE coalition can obtain from other elite groups, particularly the PE, BE and IE. The IE is quite capable of inviting imperialist intervention if Islam is seen as unduly restricting their business enterprises. Fourthly, the solidarity of the PNA has begun to weaken. The TI party has disassociated itself from the PNA and has accused the ME of perpetuating their rule.[1] The ME in turn have used the PE to defend their political actions. In a recent television interview, Mr A. K. Brohi stated that the Constitution of 1973 did not become defunct when General Zia-ul-Haq became president. On the contrary, the constitution permitted martial law as a necessity to enable the ME to hold elections and to administer the country 'conformably, as far as practicable, with the tenets of the Constitution'.[2] Fifthly, elite coalitions with the Pathans and Baluchis are still weak since the elites chosen from those groups do not have much local political influence. The Pathan leader Wali Khan, for example, has not joined the ME. One of the leaders of the Marri tribe (Sher Mohammad Marri) has threatened that the Baluchistan problem must be resolved soon or the Baluchis would have to resort to force.[3] Discontent is widespread among the Sindhis because Bhutto's daughter Benazir has been detained while his wife is being kept under house arrest. Recent political violence among Sindhi students has resulted in the closure of the universities in Sind.[4] Some members of the PPP and the TI have also been arrested.[5]

Lastly, elections have been promised for 1979, and the legitimation of the present political arrangements and of the Nizam-i-Mustafa depend on their outcome. All the reforms the government is introducing now must be legitimated by an election in the future. If the ME misuse their power or try to perpetuate their rule indefinitely one may expect the kind of retaliation or reaction that brought about the downfall of the Ayub Khan (1969) and Yahya Khan (1971) regimes. The military is a part of the political system of Pakistan, but their role is limited by the 'doctrine of necessity' and for their failures as political leaders they must not be exempt from political accountability.

Notes & References

Chapter 1: *The Ideological State*

1   F. Abbot, *Islam and Pakistan* (New York: Cornell University Press, 1968), p. 45.

2   R. Martin, *The Sociology of Power* (London: Routledge & Kegan Paul, 1977), p. 85.

3   See: S. M. Akram, *Muslim Civilization in India* (New York: Columbia University Press, 1964), p. 213.

4   W. Irvine, *The Army of the Mughals* (Delhi: Eurasian Publishing House, 1962), p. 6.

5   B. Davey, *The Economic Development of India: A Marxist Analysis* (Nottingham: Spokesman Books, 1975), p. 29.

6   E. Wolf, *Peasants* (Englewood Cliffs, N. J.: Prentice-Hall, 1966), pp. 50–5.

7   I. Habib, *The Agrarian System of Mughal India 1556–1707* (Bombay: Asia Publishing House, 1963). See chapter IX.

8   See: I. Habib, 'Potentialities of Capitalist Development in the Economy of Mughal India', *Journal of Economic History,* vol. XXIX, no. 1 (March 1969), pp. 53–4.

9   A. Maddison, *Class Structure and Economic Growth in India: India and Pakistan since the Mughals* (New York: Norton, 1971), pp. 23–4.

10   Davey, *Economic Development of India,* p. 29.

11   The cases of Tippu Sultan of Mysore and Nawab Mir Kasim of Bengal during the eighteenth century are relevant here.

12   See: F. Abbot, 'Decline of the Mughal Empire and Shah Waliullah', *The Muslim World,* vol. LII, no. 2 (April 1962), pp. 115–23. Also see: A.

Ahmad, 'Political and Religious Ideas of Shah Waliullah of Delhi', *The Muslim World*, vol. LII, no. 1 (January 1962), pp. 26–8.

13   See: C. H. Enloe, 'The Military Uses of Ethnicity', *Millenium*, vol. 4, no. 3 (Winter 1975–6), pp. 220–34.

14   Quotation from Lord Macaulay's 1835 Minute of Education, in Maddison, *Class Structure in India*, p. 41.

15   Lord William Bentinck's statement. Quoted in: A. Hoogvelt, *The Sociology of Developing Societies* (London: The Macmillan Press, 1976), p. 102. Chap. 5 gives an excellent analysis of the transformation of indigenous structures under colonialism.

16   *Ibid.*, p. 103.

17   *Ibid.*, p. 72.

18   See: T. E. Weisskopf, 'Capitalism and Underdevelopment in the Modern World', in R. C. Edward, M. Reich and T. E. Weisskopf (eds), *The Capitalist System* (Englewood Cliffs, N.J.: Prentice-Hall 1972), pp. 442–57.

19   M. B. Brown, 'A Critique of Marxist Theories of Imperialism', in R. Owen and B. Sutcliffe (eds), *Studies in the Theory of Imperialism* (London: Longman, 1972), p. 46.

20   Sir Syed Ahmed Khan's address to Lord Ripon in the Viceroy's Council on 12 January 1883.

21   Sir Mohammad Iqbal, *The Reconstruction of Religious thought in Islam* (London: Oxford University Press, 1934), pp. 155–60.

22   Speech addressed to the All India Muslim League on 21 March 1932. See: M. T. Titus, *Islam and India* (Calcutta: Y.M.C.A. Publishing House, 1959), p. 80.

23   Quoted in: Wilfred C. Smith, *Modern Islam in India* (Lahore: Minerva Press, 1943), pp. 115–18.

24   M. A. Jinnah, *Letters of Iqbal to Jinnah* (Lahore: Sh. Mohammad Ashraf, 1956), pp. 17–18.

25   Aziz Ahmad and G. E. von Grunebaum (eds), *Muslim Self-Statement in India and Pakistan, 1957–1968* (Wiesbaden: Otto Harrassowtiz, 1970), p. 148.

26   Aziz Ahmad, 'The Shrinking Frontiers of Islam', *International Journal of Middle East Studies*, vol. 7, no. 2 (April 1976), p. 148.

27   Sarojini Naidu, *Mohammah Ali Jinnah: Ambassador of Unity: His Speeches and Writings, 1912–1917* (Madras: Ganesh Publishers, 1918), p. 7.

28   K. B. Sayeed, *Pakistan: The Formative Phase* (Karachi: Pakistan Publishing House, 1960), pp. 192–3.

29   Wayne A. Wilcox, 'Ideological Dilemmas in Pakistan's Political Cul-

ture' in D. E. Smith (ed.), *South Asian Politics and Religion* (Princeton, N. J.: Princeton University Press, 1966), pp. 342–3.

30 Sayeed, *Pakistan*, pp. 192–3.

31 See: Z. H. Faruqi, *The Deoband School and the Demand for Pakistan* (London: Asia Publishing House, 1963), pp. 84–9, 124–6. Also see: A. Maudoodi, *Nationalism and India* (Pathankot: Maktabe-e-Jamaat-e-Islami, 1947), p. 28. Also see: K. Siddiqui, *Conflict, Crisis and War in Pakistan* (New York: Praeger Publishers, 1972), p. 70.

32 The very word 'Pakistan', when originally formulated by Choudhury Rehmat Ali (1897–1951), encompassed the areas of the Punjab, Afghania (North West Frontier Province), Kashmir, Iran, Sind (including Kutch and Kathiawar), Tukharistan, Afghanistan and Baluchistan. Rehmat Ali had classified Bengal and Assam as a separate federation to be known as 'Bang-e-Islam'; in south India he had proposed 'Usmanistan' from the princely states of Hyderabad (Deccan). For details see: Siddiqui, *Conflict, Crisis, and War in Pakistan*, pp. 39–46.

33 Ahmad and Grunebaum, *Muslim Self-Statement*, pp. 153–5.

34 Jinnah's letter to M. K. Gandhi, 1 January 1940. See: J. Ahmed (ed.), *Speeches and Writings of Mr Jinnah*, vol. 1 (Lahore: Sh. Muhammad Ashraf, 1960).

35 Ahmad and Grunebaum, *Muslim Self-Statement*, pp. 153–5.

36 Arif Hussain, *Pakistan: Its Ideology and Foreign Policy* (London: Frank Cass, 1966), p. 155.

37 I. Stephen, *Pakistan*, (London: Ernest Benn, 1967), p. 30. In 1947 Maulana Maudoodi defined the Ideological State as a state based on Islamic principles. See his book *The Process of Islamic Revolution* (Lahore: Islamic Publications, 1970).

38 D. E. Smith, *India as a Secular State* (Princeton, N. J.: Princeton University Press, 1963), p. 4.

39 Werner Levi, 'Pakistan, The Soviet Union and China', *Pacific Affairs*, vol. xxxv, no. 3 (Fall 1962), pp. 211–22.

Chapter 2: *The Political System*

1 This terminology has been adapted from A. Carter, *Elite Politics in Rural India* (Cambridge: Cambridge University Press, 1974), p. 101.

2 Speech in Dacca, 28 March 1948. See: *Jinnah Speeches: As Governor-General of Pakistan, 1947–1948* (Karachi: Pakistan Publications n. d.), p. 104.

3 *Ibid.*, p. 111.

4 Myron Weiner, *Political Science and South Asian Studies* (Bloomington: Indiana University Press, 1975), p. 137.

5   D. N. Wilber, *Pakistan: Its People, Its Societies, Its Culture* (New Haven: HRAF Press, 1964), p. 65.

6   See: J. W. Spain, 'Pathans of the Tribal Areas', in S. Maron (ed.), *Pakistan: Society and Culture* (New Haven: HRAF, 1957), p. 62.

7   F. Barth, 'Pathan Identity and its Maintenance', in F. Barth (ed.), *Ethnic Groups and Boundaries* (Boston: Little Brown, 1969), pp. 117–34.

8   A. S. Ahmed, *Social and Economic Change in the Tribal Areas* (Karachi: Oxford University Press, 1977), pp. 20–1.

9   See an excellent study on Ghaffar Khan by Mohammad Said Khan, *Abdul Ghaffar Khan: The Pakhtoon Khudai–Khidmatgar* (forthcoming).

10   Interview with Khan Abdul Ghaffar Khan, Jan. 1978, in Peshawar.

11   'The Baluchistan Puzzle', *The Pakistan Times* (Lahore), 25 November 1973.

12   Interview with a tribal chieftain of Baluchistan, Dec. 1977, in Karachi.

13   Bhutto's speech to heads of diplomatic missions who were invited to Kalat. See *Pakistan Times* (Lahore), 20 April 1974.

14   See: *Census of Pakistan 1951* (Karachi: Government of Pakistan, 1951), vol. I, p. 31.

15   Marvin Olson (ed.), *Power in Societies* (London: The Macmillan Company, 1970).

16   This definition has been adapted for this study from the following authors: J. Walton, *Elites and Economic Development* (Austin: University of Texas Press, 1977), pp. 80–1; A. M. Orum, *Introduction to Political Sociology* (Englewood Cliffs, N. J. : Prentice-Hall, 1978), p. 127.

17   Walton, *Elites and Economic Development*, p. 80.

18   Orum, *Introductory to Political Sociology*, p. 127.

19   M. Palmer, *The Interdisciplinary Study of Politics* (New York: Harper & Row, 1974), p. 31.

20   *Ibid.*, p. 32.

Chapter 3: *The Landowning Elites*

1   *Population Census of 1961,* Census Bulletin No. 2 (Government of Pakistan, Ministry of Home Affairs), p. 14.

2   See: *Report of the Land Reforms Commission for West Pakistan* (Lahore: Superintendent Government Printing, 1959).

3   See: M. A. Ali, *The Mughal Nobility under Aurangzeb* (London: Asia Publishing House, 1966).

4   'Mahal' means a village in the Punjab while 'Bhaichara' means brotherhood in the NWFP region.

5   See: H. N. Gardezi, 'Neocolonial Alliances and the Crises of Pakistan' in K. Gough and H. P. Sharma (eds), *Imperialism and Revolution in South Asia* (New York: Monthly Review Press, 1973), pp. 130–44.

6   D. N. Wilber, *Pakistan: Its People, Its Society, Its Culture* (New Haven, Conn., HRAF Press, 1964), p. 219.

7   Pakistan, Ministry of Food and Agriculture, Agricultural Census Organization, *Pakistan Census of Agriculture, East Pakistan,* vol 1 (1962) Table 3, p. 33.

8   J. S. Migdal, *Peasants, Politics and Revolution: Pressures Towards Political and Social Change in the Third World* (Princeton, N. J.: Princeton University Press, 1973), pp. 34–5.

9   *Report of the Land Reforms Commission for West Pakistan 1959,* p. 14.

10   Z. Eglar, *A Punjabi Village in Pakistan* (New York: Columbia University Press, 1960), p. 44. Also see: M. R. Raza, *Two Pakistani Villages: A Study of Social Stratification* (Lahore: University of the Punjab, Department of Sociology, 1969), p. 55.

11   Saghir Ahmed, *Class and Power in a Punjab Village* (New York: Monthly Review Press, 1977), p. 101.

12   *Ibid.,* p. 129.

13   Mao Tse-Tung, *Selected Works,* vol. I (Peking: Foreign Languages Press, 1967), pp. 13–21, 23–59, 137–43.

14   T. Ali, *Pakistan: Military Rule or People's Power?* (New York: William Morrow, 1970), p. 170.

15   H. Alavi, 'Peasants and Revolution', in Gough and Sharma (eds), *Imperialism and Revolution in South Asia,* pp. 291–337.

16   Saghir Ahmad, 'Peasant Classes in Pakistan', in Gough and Sharma, *ibid.,* pp. 212–15.

17   *Report of the Government Hari Enquiry Committee 1947–1948* (Government of Sind, n.d.), p. 7.

18   Planning Board, Government of Pakistan, *The First Five Year Plan, 1955–1960,* vol. II (Karachi: Manager of Publications, 1958), p. 118.

19   S. M. Akhtar, *Pakistan: A Developing Economy,* vol. I (Lahore: Publishers United, 1967), p. 151.

20   H. H. Kizilbash, 'Local Government: Democracy at the Capital and Autocracy in the Villages', *Pakistan Economic and Social Review,* vol. XI, no. 1 (Spring 1973), pp. 104–24.

21   *Ibid.,* p. 117.

22   *Ibid.,* p. 119.

23   *Ibid.*

24   S. M. Akhtar (ed.), *Village Life in Lahore District: Selected Political*

Aspects (Lahore: Social Science Research Centre, University of Punjab, 1960), pp. 16–17.

25   R. N. Pehrson, *The Social Organization of the Marri Baluch* (Chicago: Aldine Publishing, 1966), p. 20.

26   Akbar S. Ahmed, *Social and Economic Change in Tribal Areas* (Karachi: Oxford University Press, 1977), pp. 7–8.

27   See the account of such politics in K. B. Sayeed, 'Collapse of Parliamentary Democracy in Pakistan', *The Middle East Journal*, vol. 13, no. 4 (1959), p. 393.

28   Mushtaq Ahmed, *Government and Politics in Pakistan* (Karachi: Space Publishers, 1970), pp. 127–8.

29   See: Feroz Khan Noon, *From Memory* (Lahore: Ferozesons, 1966).

30   Speech at Dacca, 21 March 1948. See: *Jinnah Speeches as Governor General of Pakistan 1947–1948* (Karachi: Pakistan Publications, n.d.), p. 84.

31   K. Callard, *Pakistan: A Political Study* (London: Allen & Unwin, 1957), p. 43.

32   The Constitution of the Islamic Republic of Pakistan, 1956, Appendix I, Article 15, noted in Callard, *ibid.*, p. 332.

33   Ayub Khan, *Friends Not Masters* (New York: Oxford University Press, 1967), p. 43.

34   Address to the Planning Board Staff, 12 May 1958. Quoted in M. Ahmed, *Government and Politics in Pakistan*, p. 71.

35   W. Bredo, 'Land Reform and Development in Pakistan', in W. Froehlich (ed.), *Land Tenure, Industrialization and Social Stability* (Wisconsin: The Marquette University Press, 1971), p. 267.

36   H. Feldman, *Revolution in Pakistan* (London: Oxford University Press, 1967), p. 59.

37   K. B. Sayeed, 'Pakistan's Constitutional Autocracy', *Pacific Affairs*, vol. XXVI, no. 4 (Winter 1963–4), p. 365.

38   *Ibid.*, p. 365.

39   M. Ahmed, *Government and Politics in Pakistan*, p. 236.

40   S. J. Burki, 'West Pakistan's Rural Works Program: A Study in Political and Administrative Response', *The Middle East Journal*, vol. 23, no. 3 (1969), p. 333.

41   See: Government of Pakistan, *Year Book of Agricultural Statistics, 1969*. Quoted in D. A. Khan and H. A. Chaudhari, 'Income Impact of the Green Revolution', *Pakistan Economic and Social Review*, vol. XI, no. 1 (Spring 1973), pp. 68–9.

42   P. Lieftinck *et al.*, *Water and Power Resources of West Pakistan: A Study in Sector Planning* (Baltimore: The Johns Hopkins Press, 1968), p. 23.

43   Khan and Chaudhari, *'Income Impact of the Green Revolution,'* pp. 79–80.

44   *Election Manifesto of the Pakistan People's Party* (1970), p. 28.

45   *Land Reform Regulation 1972* (Karachi: Printwell Publications, 1972), pp. 1–17.

46   *People's Rule: The First Year* (Islamabad: Ministry of Information and Broadcasting, 1972).

47   *The Pakistan Times* (Lahore), 19 December 1976.

48   *Pakistan Affairs* (Washington, D.C., Embassy of Pakistan), 1 February 1977, p. 2.

49   P. C. Joshi, 'Land Reforms and Agrarian Change in India and Pakistan since 1947: I', *The Journal of Peasant Studies,* vol. I, no. 2 (January 1974), p. 170.

50   K. B. Sayeed, 'How Radical is the Pakistan People's Party?', *Pacific Affairs,* vol. I, no. 48 (Spring 1975), p. 52.

51   Bruce J. Exposito, 'The Politics of Agrarian Reform in Pakistan', *Asian Survey,* vol. XIV, no. 5 (May 1974), p. 438. Also see: W. E. Gustafson, 'Economic Reforms under the Bhutto Regime', *Journal of Asian and African Studies,* vol. VIII, nos. 3 and 4 (1973), p. 249.

52   M. G. Weinbaum, 'The March 1977 Election in Pakistan: Where Everyone Lost', *Asian Survey,* vol. XXII, no. 7 (July 1977), p. 604.

53   *Ibid.*

54   N. Sanderatne, 'Landowners and Land Reforms in Pakistan', *South Asian Review,* vol. 17, no. 2 (January 1974), pp. 133–4.

Chapter 4: *The Bureaucratic Elites*

1   S. C. Dube, 'Bureaucracy and Nation-Building in Transitional Societies', in J. L. Finkle and R. W. Gable (eds), *Political Development and Social Change* (New York: John Wiley, 1971), p. 326.

2   *Ibid.,* p. 327.

3   Muneer Ahmed, *The Civil Servant in Pakistan* (Karachi: Oxford University Press, 1964), p. 125.

4   G. Birkhead (ed.), *Administrative Problems in Pakistan* (New York: Syracuse University Press, 1966), p. 11.

5   K. B. Sayeed, 'The Political Role of Pakistan's Civil Service', *Pacific Affairs,* vol. 31, no. 2 (1958), p. 131.

6   *Ibid.,* p. 137.

7   H. F. Goodnow, *The Civil Service of Pakistan* (New Haven, Conn.: Yale University Press, 1964), p. 173.

8   R. Braibanti, 'The Higher Bureaucracy in Pakistan', in R. Braibanti (ed.), *Asian Bureaucratic Traditions Emergent from the British Imperial Tradition* (Durham, N. C.: Duke University Press, 1966), p. 327.

9   National Assembly of Pakistan, Parliamentary Debates, 15 February 1957, pp. 344–5. Quoted in Braibanti, *Asian Bureaucratic Traditions,* p. 134.

10   K. B. Sayeed, *Pakistan: The Formative Phase* (Karachi: Pakistan Publishing House, 1960), p. 392.

11   Ahmed, *The Civil Servant in Pakistan,* pp. 112–13.

12   Dube, 'Bureaucracy and Nation-Building', p. 328.

13   L. Ziring, *The Ayub Khan Era: Politics in Pakistan 1958–1969* (New York: Syracuse University Press, 1971), p. 121.

14   Sir Francis Modie, Governor of Punjab (1947–9), Sir George Cunningham, Governor of NWFP (1947–8), Sir Ambrose Dundas, Governor of Sind (1948–9), and Sir Frederick Bourne, Governor of East Bengal (1947–50).

15   According to Sayeed, Jinnah had called upon the governors and civil servants to keep a close watch over Cabinet meetings and other activities of politicians. See Sayeed, *Pakistan: The Formative Phase,* p. 282.

16   Jamiluddin Ahmed (ed.), *Speeches and Writings of Mr Jinnah,* vol. ii (Lahore: Sh. Mohammad Ashraf, 1964), pp. 528–9.

17   *Ibid.,* pp. 501–2. Speech delivered to gazetted officers in Chittagong, 25 March 1948.

18   H. F. Goodnow, *The Civil Service of Pakistan,* p. 131.

19   Chaudhri Mohammad Ali, *The Emergence of Pakistan* (New York: Columbia University Press, 1967), pp. 356–63.

20   Constituent Assembly of Pakistan, Debates ii, no. 1 (24 February 1948), pp. 6–7. Quoted in K. B. Sayeed, *The Political System of Pakistan* (Boston: Houghton Mifflin 1967), p. 64.

21   This study was headed by a senior bureaucrat, Akhtar Hussain. *Report of the Provincial Administration Commission* (Lahore: Government of Pakistan, 1960), p. 3.

22   G. A. Heeger, 'Bureaucracy, Political Parties and Political Development', *World Politics,* vol. 25, no. 4 (April 1973), p. 600.

23   *Dawn (*Karachi), 10 April 1953.

24   Section 10(1) of the Government of India Act (1935) stated: 'The Governor General's Ministers shall be chosen by him, shall be sworn as members of the Council and shall hold office during his pleasure.'

25   H. S. Suhrawardhy, Address to the Nation, delivered in Dacca, 8 May 1953. Quoted in Ahmed Hussain, *Politics and People's Representation in Pakistan* (Lahore: Ferozesons, 1972), p. 37.

26   R. Jahan, *Pakistan: Failure in National Integration* (New York: Columbia University Press,1972), p. 45.

27   See Fatima Jinnah's statement in *Pakistan Standard* (Independence Day Number), 14 August 1954.

28   R. Park and R. S. Wheeler, 'East Pakistan Under Governors' Rule', *Far Eastern Survey*, no. 23 (1954), p. 133.

29   Constituent Assembly of Pakistan, Debates xvi (15 September 1954), p. 361.

30   I. Jennings, *Constitutional Problems of Pakistan* (Cambridge: Cambridge University Press, 1957), p. vii.

31   Justice Muhammad Shahabuddin, *Recollections and Reflections* (Lahore: PLD Publications, 1972), p. 119.

32   *Dawn* (Karachi), 21 and 22 March 1955 and 26 May 1956.

33   K. Callard, *Pakistan: A Political Study* (London: Allen & Unwin, 1957), p. 190.

34   *Ibid.,* p. 121.

35   Constitution of the Islamic Republic of Pakistan, Part iv, Article 6. Quoted in Callard, *Pakistan: A Political Study*, pp. 333–4.

36   Jahan, *Pakistan: Failure in National Integration*, p. 92

37   In 1961, 59% of the District Commissioners in Pakistan came from the CSP. In 1964 there were 53% . Their age range was between 26 and 40 years. See: Minhajuddin, 'Some Aspects of District Administration', in Inayatullah (ed.), *District Administration in West Pakistan* (Peshawar: Academy for Rural Development, 1964), pp. 27–41.

38   S. A. Jillani, 'The Civil Service of Pakistan', unpublished M. A. thesis, Department of Political Science, University of Punjab (Lahore, 1956), pp. 122–3.

39   Electoral Reform Commission, *Report on Malpractices of Government Officials*. Quoted in Munir Ahmed, *Legislatures in Pakistan 1947–1958* (Lahore: University of Punjab, 1960), p. 107.

40   R. Egger, *The Development of Public Administration in Pakistan* (Karachi: Inter Services Press, 1953), pp. x–xi.

41   Government of Pakistan, *Report of Reorganization of Pakistan Government for National Development* (Karachi, 1955).

42   See: H. Feldman, *From Crisis to Crisis* (London: Oxford University Press, 1972), p. 304. He writes that after Bhutto left, 'Ayub had need of some highly literate person who could fill the gap in his own knowledge and reading. Bhutto did this capably until he broke off with Ayub Khan and, upon his departure, Altaf Gauhar, who had already displayed his own talent and energy, was there at hand.'

43   *Pakistan Times* (Lahore), 1 April 1973.

44   C. I. Eugene Kim and L. Ziring, *An Introduction to Asian Politics* (New Jersey: Prentice-Hall, 1977), pp. 231–2.

45   Bhutto's Broadcast to the Nation from Radio Pakistan, 23 August 1973.

46   See: Baseer Alam's article, 'Civil Service: Implementation of Reforms', *Dawn* (Karachi), 9 January 1978.

Chapter 5: *The Religious Elites*

1   R. D. Campbell, *Pakistan: Emerging Democracy* (New Jersey: D. van Nostrand, 1963), p. 90.

2   K. Siddique, *Conflict, Crisis and War in Pakistan* (New York: Praeger Publishers, 1972), p. 106.

3   Maulana Maudoodi has been a prolific writer throughout his life, and his books and his Islamic movement have spread to the Middle East, Africa and Europe.

4   The anti-colonial struggle led by these pirs at provincial levels ought to be investigated by South Asian scholars. The Hur movement was crushed by the British in the 1940s. Its leader, the late Pir of Pagaro, was hanged in 1943 and his sons were sent to England for further education. One of them is the present Pir of Pagaro. The Faqir of Ipi's name was Haji Mirza Ali Khan and he belonged to the Utmanzai Wazirs. He had engaged the British in tribal warfare in Waziristan in the 1930s. Campaigns against him had led to the mobilization of some 32,000 regular troops and 5000 scouts, at a cost of approximately £1,200,000 to £1,500,000. For details see: Peter Mayne, *The Saints of Sind* (New York: Doubleday, 1956). Also see: J. W. Spain, *The Pathan Borderland* (The Hague: Mouton, 1960).

5   The slogan in Urdu was 'Abdul Majid ko detay ho ya Quran Majid to detay ho'. Another slogan was 'Hamid Ullah ko detay ho ya Khuda-wan-ta-Allah ko detay ho' which meant 'will you vote for Hamid ullah or Allah?'

6   For the above information I am indebted to Professor Khurshid Ahmed's lectures on the JI given at the Islamic Foundation, Leicester, in August 1978.

7   K. B. Sayeed, 'The Jamaat-i-Islami Movement in Pakistan', *Pacific Affairs*, vol. xxx, no. 2 (March 1957), p. 64.

8   C. J. Adams, 'The Ideology of Maulana Maudoodi', in D. E. Smith (ed)., *South Asian Politics and Religion* (Princeton, N. J.: Princeton University Press, 1966), pp. 380–1.

9   Interview with Prof. Khurshid Ahmed, Director-General, Islamic Foundation. See his excellent study: K. Ahmed (ed.), *Islam: Its Meaning and Message* (Leicester: The Islamic Foundation, 1976).

10   Quaid-i-Azam Mohammad Ali Jinnah; *Speeches as Governor-General of Pakistan, 1947–1948* (Karachi: Pakistan Publications, n.d.), p. 9.

11   *Ibid.*, p. 58.

12   *Ibid.*, p. 65.

13   S. Mahmood, *A Political Study of Pakistan* (Lahore: Sh. Mohammad Ashraf, 1975), pp. 210–1.

14   See: G. E. von Grunebaum, *Modern Islam* (Berkeley: University of California Press, 1962), p. 230. Also see: I. Lichtenstadter: *Islam and the Modern Age* (London, 1959) and E. J. Rosenthal, *Islam in the Modern National State* (Cambridge: Cambridge University Press, 1965).

15   Some of the most controversial discussions on the Objectives Resolution were held behind closed doors. See: S. M. Akram, 'Religion in Pakistan', unpublished paper presented at the Conference on *Pakistan Since 1958*, held at the Islamic Studies Department, McGill University, Montreal, 17–19 June 1964, pp. 1–9.

16   See speech given by I. H. Qureshi at the Institute of Islamic Culture in Lahore. Also see speech given by A. K. Brohi on 'Thoughts on the Future Constitution of Pakistan', quoted in L. Binder, *Religion and Politics in Pakistan* (Berkeley: University of California Press, 1961), pp. 153, 278.

17   Sayeed, 'The Jamaat-i-Islami Movement', p. 61.

18   *Ibid.*, p. 66.

19   Lecture given to Law College Students at Lahore on 18 February 1948. Quoted in Binder, *Religion and Politics in Pakistan,* p. 103.

20   Sayeed, 'The Jamaat-i-Islami Movement', p. 68.

21   Binder, *Religion and Politics in Pakistan,* pp. 369–70.

22   Wayne A. Wilcox, 'Ideological Dilemmas in Pakistan's Political Culture', in D. E. Smith (ed.), *South Asian Politics and Religion,* p. 350.

23   F. Abbot, *Islam and Pakistan* (Ithaca, N.Y.: Cornell University Press, 1968), p. 193.

24   A. Maudoodi, *The Qadiani Problem* (Lahore: Markazi-Shobe e-Nashr-e-Ishaat, Jamait-e-Islami, 1953), p. 33.

25   *Report of the Court of Inquiry constituted under Punjab Act III of 1954 to inquire into the Punjab Disturbances of 1953* (Lahore: Government Printing Press, 1954), p. 243.

26   K. B. Sayeed, 'Religion and Nation-Building in Pakistan', *The Middle East Journal,* vol. 17, no. 3 (1963), pp. 384–5.

27   Mohammad Ayub Khan, *Speeches and Statements* (Karachi: Pakistan Publications, 1960–1), p. 5.

28   F. Abbot, 'Pakistan and the Secular State', in D. E. Smith (ed.), *South Asian Politics and Religion,* p. 370.

29   Article 204(a), *The Constitution of the Republic of Pakistan, 1962.* Quoted in A. Ahmad and G. E. Von Grunebaum (eds), *Muslim Self-Statements in India and Pakistan: 1857–1947* (Wiesbaden: Otto Harrassowitz, 1970), pp. 214–20.

30 *Ibid.,* p. 219.

31 Manzoor Ahmed, 'Islam as State Policy in Pakistan', unpublished paper presented in Mexico City, at the 30th International Congress of Human Sciences in Asia and North Africa, 3–8 July 1976. This paper gives an excellent discussion on the political implications of Islam. The author, who works in the Department of Philosophy, Karachi University, was interviewed again in December 1977 in Pakistan.

32 C. J. Adams, 'The Ideology of Maulana Maudoodi', in D. E. Smith (ed.), *South Asian Politics and Religion,* p. 379.

33 *The Pakistan Times* (Lahore), 18 June 1964.

34 *Pakistan Observer* (Dacca), 3 October 1964.

35 K. B. Sayeed, 'Pakistan's Constitutional Autocracy', *Pacific Affairs,* vol. xxxvi, no. 4 (1963–4), p. 369.

36 *Report of the Activities of National Reconstruction, East Pakistan* (Dacca: Government Press, 1962), pp. 2–5 and 36–7.

37 Javed Iqbal, *The Ideology of Pakistan and Its Implementation* (Lahore: Shaikh Ghulam Ali, 1959), p. xii.

38 Abbot, *Islam and Pakistan,* pp. 217–21.

39 *The Central Institute of Islamic Research* (Karachi: The Central Institute of Islamic Research, 1963), p. 3.

40 F. Rahman, *Islam* (New York: Holt, Rinehart & Winston, 1966), p. 249.

41 K. B. Sayeed, *The Political System of Pakistan* (Boston: Houghton Mifflin, 1967), p. 104.

42 Derek Lovejoy, 'Islam in Islamabad', *Asian Review,* vol. 1, no. 2 (1968), p. 117.

43 Abbot, *Islam and Pakistan,* p. 193.

44 *Political Parties: The Election Program* (Issued by the Embassy of Pakistan, Washington D.C., 1970).

45 For an analysis of the 1970 elections see: C. Baxter, 'Pakistan Votes', *Asian Survey,* vol. xi, no. 3 (March 1971). p. 221.

46 G. W. Choudhury, 'Bangladesh: Why it Happened', *International Affairs,* vol. 48, no. 2 (1972), p. 247.

47 K. B. Sayeed, 'Islam and National Integration in Pakistan', in D. E. Smith (ed.), *South Asian Politics and Religion,* p. 408.

48 Speech made by the Amir (leader) of the Jamaat-i-Islami on 18 February 1973. See: *The Pakistan Times* (Lahore), 23 February 1973.

49 Article 227, *The Constitution of the Islamic Republic of Pakistan, 1973.*

50 *The Pakistan Times* (Lahore), 19 January 1972.

51 *Ibid.*

52 K. B. Sayeed, 'How Radical is the Pakistan People's Party?', *Pacific Affairs,* vol. I, no. 48 (September 1975), p. 55.

53 Anwar H. Syed, 'Pakistan in 1976: Business as Usual', *Asian Survey,* vol. XVII, no. 2 (February 1977), pp. 183–4.

54 *Dawn* (Karachi), 25 January 1977.

55 Gen. Zia-ul Haq's speech, *Dawn* (Karachi), 2 January 1978.

56 The members of the Council of Islamic Ideology are: Chairman, Justice M. A. Cheema; Secretary, T. H. Hashi; Members: Justice S. Ahmad, A. K. Brohi, K. M. Ishaq, Maulana S. S. Kakakhel, Mufti J. H. Mujtahid, Maulana M. H. Nadvi, Maulana Z. A. Ansari, Maulana M. T. Usmani, Mufti M. H. Naeemi, Dir Q. Sialvi and Dr Z. Ahmad.

57 The influential members attending it were: Maulana O. Anwar, Maulana M. Usmani, Maulana Mahmood, Maulana Z. Qasmi, Maulana Ropari, Maulana Poya (Shia leader), Maulana Razaque, Maulana Chinioti, Maulana Haq, Maulana S. Dinpuri, Maulana Ajmal, Maulana H. Qasmi, Maulana Alvi, Maulana H. Jalandhri, Maulana Wasaya, Maulana Zaheer, Maulana Jama Ullah, Maulana Bakshi, Mufti Rehman Qazi, Allah Yar, S. Rizvi (advocate), and Agha Shorish Kashmiri. See *Daily News* (Karachi), 31 December 1977.

58 *Dawn* (Karachi), 1 January 1978.

59 *Report of the Constitution Commission* (Karachi: Government of Pakistan Press, 1962), p. 72.

60 Guy Hunter, *Modernizing Peasant Societies: A Comparative Study in Asia and Africa* (London: Oxford University Press, 1969), p. 17.

Chapter 6: *The Industrial Elites*

1 *The First Five Year Plan, 1955–1960* (National Planning Board, Government of Pakistan, Karachi, 1958), p. 7.

2 See: H. Papanek, 'Pakistan's Big Businessmen: Muslim Separatism, Entrepreneurship and Partial Modernization', *Economic Development and Cultural Change,* vol. 21, no. 1 (1972), pp. 1–32.

3 *Twenty Years of Pakistan: 1947–1967* (Karachi: Pakistan Publications, 1967), p. 182.

4 See: Government of Pakistan, *Economy of Pakistan 1948–1968* (Islamabad: Ministry of Finance, 1968), p. 74.

5 K. Siddiqui, *Conflict, Crises and War in Pakistan* (New York: Praeger Publishers, 1972), p. 60.

6 S. Richard, 'A View of Pakistan's Industrial Development', *Asian Survey,* vol. V, no. 12 (1968), p. 591.

7   Timothy and L. Nulty, 'Pakistan: The Busy Bee Route to Development', *Transaction,* vol. 8 (February 1971), pp. 18–26.

8   G. F. Papanek, 'Pakistan's Industrial Entrepreneurs: Education, Occupational Background and Finance', in W. P. Falcon and G. F. Papanek (eds), *Policy II: The Pakistan Experience* (Cambridge Mass.: Harvard University Press, 1971), p. 239.

9   See: R. Miliband, *Marxism and Politics* (London: Oxford University Press, 1977), pp. 108–9. Also see H. Alavi, 'The State in Post-Colonial Societies: Pakistan and Bangladesh', in K. Gough and H. P. Sharma (eds), *Imperialism and Revolution in South Asia* (New York: Monthly Review Press, 1973), pp. 145–73.

10   M. Weiner, 'The Politics of South Asia', in G. Almond and J. Coleman (eds), *The Politics of Developing Areas* (Princeton, N. J.: Princeton University Press, 1962), p. 12.

11   A. Lee Fritschler, 'Business Participation in Administration', in G. S. Birkhead (ed.), *Administrative Problems of Pakistan* (New York:Syracuse University Press, 1966), p. 75.

12   Dickson K. Smith, 'Foreign Aid and Economic Development in Pakistan: The Ayub Years (1958–1969)', Unpublished Ph. D. thesis, Department of Economics, University of Utah (1974), p. 167.

13   M. H. Khoja, 'Agricultural Development in Pakistan', in A. M. Ghouse (ed.), *Pakistan in the Development Decade: Problems and Performance* (Lahore: Economic Department Seminar, 1968), p. 251.

14   Mahbub-ul-Haq, *The Poverty Curtain* (New York: Columbia University Press, 1976), p. 15.

15   H. Feldman, *Revolution in Pakistan* (London: Oxford University Press, 1967), p. 25.

16   See: *Report of the Economic Appraisal Committee* (Karachi: Ministry of Economic Affairs, 1953), p. 179.

17   Feldman, *Revolution in Pakistan,* pp. 51–2.

18   The main branch had regional chambers of commerce and 41 trade and industry associations. See: R. S. Wheeler, *The Politics of Pakistan* (Ithaca, N. Y.: Cornell University Press, 1971), p. 291.

19   The inter-marriage link between the IE and other elite groups is an important one which has not been sufficiently explored by political scientists in Pakistan.

20   *New York Times,* 4 January 1972.

21   Gunnar Myrdal, *Asian Drama* (New York: The Twentieth Century Fund, 1968), vol. I, p. 335. Most of these were small businessmen and contractors who participated in the Basic Democracy scheme. In the Basic Democracy elections of 1964, 73.61% of urban businessmen and contractors were elected from East Bengal. For details see: Rehman Sobhan, *Basic Democracies, Works Programmes and Rural Development in East Pakistan*

(Dacca: Oxford University Press, 1968), p.82. According to another study, 32% of East Pakistani and 19% of West Pakistani members of the Provincial and National Assemblies of 1962 and 1965 were businessmen, contractors and industrialists. In the Constituent and National Assemblies of 1947 to 1958, only 4% of East Pakistanis and 3% of West Pakistanis belonged to the entrepreneurial classes. See: T. Maniruzzaman, 'Crisis in the Political Development and the Collapse of the Ayub Regime in Pakistan', in *The Journal of Developing Areas,* vol. v, no. 2 (1971), p. 227.

22 See: H. Feldman, *From Crisis to Crisis* (London: Oxford University Press, 1972), pp. 287 and 305.

23 G. F. Papanek, *Pakistan's Development: Social Goals and Private Incentives* (Cambridge, Mass.: Harvard University Press, 1967). These quotations are the subtitles in the book.

24 Arthur MacEwan, 'Capitalist Expansion, Ideology and Intervention', in R. C. Edwards, M. Reich and T. E. Weisskopf (eds), *The Capitalist System* (Englewood Cliffs, N.J.: Prentice-Hall, 1972), pp. 409–20.

25 M. Friedman, *Capitalism and Freedom* (Chicago: University of Chicago Press, 1962), pp. 161–2.

26 T. E. Weisskopf, 'Capitalism and Inequality', in Edwards, Reich & Weisskopf, *The Capitalist System,* pp. 125–33.

27 *The Poverty Curtain,* pp. 7–8.

28 Papanek, 'Pakistan's Development', p. 242.

29 Mahbub-ul-Haq, *The Strategy of Economic Planning* (New York: Oxford University Press, 1963), pp. 1–3.

30 Mahbub-ul-Haq, speech delivered at the Second Management Convention in Karachi, quoted in *The Business Recorder,* 25 April 1968.

31 Haq, *The Poverty Curtain,* p. 6.

32 Siddiqi, *Conflict, Crises and War in Pakistan,* p. 60.

33 According to H. Papanek, there were '29 largest houses (of family oriented enterprise groups) ranked in terms of net worth', but of these only two were owned by East Bengalis. Quoted in R. Jahan, *Pakistan: Failure in National Integration* (New York: Columbia University Press, 1972), p. 62.

34 For details, see the following: A. R. Khan, 'What's Been Happening to the Real Wages in Pakistan?', *The Pakistan Development Review,* vol. vii, no. 3 (1967), pp. 317–47; S. R. Bose, 'Trends of Real Income of the Rural Poor in East Pakistan 1949–1966', *The Pakistan Development Review,* vol. viii, no. 3 (1968), pp. 452–88; Jahan, *Pakistan:Failure in National Integration,* pp. 67–89.

35 G. F. Papanek, 'The Location of Industry', *The Pakistan Development Review,* vol. x, no. 3 (1970), p. 300.

36 See: A. Matin, 'Location of Industries in West Pakistan', in A. M. Ghouse (ed.), *Pakistan in the Development Decade,* pp. 142–3.

37   K. Griffith and A. Rahman (eds), *Growth and Inequality in Pakistan* (London: The Macmillan Press, 1972), p. 3.

38   *Outline of the Fourth Five Year Plan, 1970–1975* (Planning Commission, Government of Pakistan, 1975), p. 15.

39   *Ibid.*, p. 15.

40   See: Jahan, *Pakistan: Failure in National Integration,* pp. 68–89.

41   R. Amjad, *Industrial Concentration and Economic Power in Pakistan* (Lahore: South Asian Institute, University of the Punjab, 1974), pp. 17–18.

42.   M. Anisur Rahman, *East and West Pakistan: A Problem in the Political Economy of Regional Planning* (Cambridge, Mass.: Centre for International Affairs, Harvard University Press, 1968), p. 35.

43   The seven deadly sins of economic development were: number games, excessive controls, investment illusions, development fashions, divorce between planning and implementation, neglect of human resources and growth without justice. Haq, *The Poverty Curtain,* pp. 14–26.

44   Jahan, *Pakistan: Failure in National Integration,* p. 7.

45   *The Pakistan Observer* (Dacca), 31 May and 22 June 1968. See the editorials.

46   Speech of A. S. M. Sulaiman, in the N.A. See: *Pakistan National Assembly Debates,* vol. II, 22 June 1966, pp. 1281–2.

47   Pakistan Central Statistical Office, *Pakistan Statistical Yearbook 1963* (Karachi: Manager of Publications, 1964), p. 67.

48   *Area Handbook of Pakistan* (Washington, D.C.: American University, 1971), p. 425.

49   See: Z. Y. Ahmad, 'Mass Movement 1968–69', unpublished M.A. thesis, Department of Political Science, University of the Punjab, March 1976.

50   *The Pakistan Times* (Lahore), 31 January 1969.

51   For an excellent discussion of job opportunities created for the labour force, see: S. J. Burki, 'Employment Strategies for Economic Stability in Pakistan: New Initiatives', unpublished paper delivered at the Jinnah–Iqbal International Seminar on Pakistan, Columbia University, New York, on 9–11 March 1978. Quoted here with the kind permission of the author.

52   The principal cities were Karachi, Lahore, Hyderabad, Lyallpur and Multan. See Burki, *ibid.,* p. 21.

53   *New York Times,* 22 December 1971. These were later returned. *The Pakistan Times* (Lahore), 6 June 1972.

54   'Pakistani Tycoon Arrest Heralds Economic Battle', *The Washington Post,* 3 January 1972.

55   Amjad, *Industrial Concentration and Economic Power in Pakistan*, p. 53.

56   W. E. Gustafson, 'Economic Reforms Under the Bhutto Regime', *Journal of Asian and African Studies*, vol. VIII, no. 3–4 (1973), pp. 241–58.

57   *The Pakistan Times* (Lahore), 4 February 1973.

58   S. A. Kochanek, *Business and Politics in India* (Berkeley: University of California Press, 1974), p. 13.

59   S. K. Basu, *The Managing Agency System: Its Prospects and Retrospect* (Calcutta: World Press, 1958), pp. 4–5.

60   L. J. White, *Industrial Concentration and Economic Power in Pakistan* (Princeton, N.J.: Princeton University Press, 1974), p. 143.

61   *The Pakistan Times* (Lahore), 17 January 1972.

62   S. J. Burki, 'Economic Decision-Making in Pakistan', in L. Ziring, R. Braibanti and W. H. Wriggins (eds), *Pakistan: The Long View* (Durham, N. C.: Duke University Press, 1977), p. 164.

63   Burki, *ibid.*, p. 164.

64   'Bhutto Follows a Capitalist Path', *The New York Times*, 4 June 1972.

65   *The Pakistan Times* (Lahore), 4 February 1973.

66   *Viewpoint* (Lahore), vol. 2, no. 45, 17 June 1977.

Chapter 7: *The Professional Elites*

1   R. Braibanti, *Research on the Bureaucracy of Pakistan* (Durham, N. C.: Duke University Press, 1966), p. 257.

2   P. B. Calkin, 'A Note on Lawyers in Muslim India', *Law and Society*, vol. III, nos 2 and 3 (Nov. 1963–Feb. 1964), p. 303.

3   Edward Shils, 'The Intellectual in the Political Development of the New States', in H. G. Kehshull (ed.), *Politics in Transitional Societies* (New York: Appleton-Century-Crofts, 1968), p. 175.

4   Braibanti, *Research on the Bureaucracy of Pakistan*, pp. 248–9.

5   Karl von Vorys, *Political Development in Pakistan* (Princeton N.J: Princeton University Press, 1965), p. 136.

6   Such a conception of democracy is based on the writings of J. A. Schumpeter's *Capitalism, Socialism and Democracy* (New York: Harper and Row, 1950), pp. 240–96.

7   For conception of 'representative democracy' or 'participatory democracy', see: R. Weissberg, *Political Learning, Political Choice and Democratic Citizenship* (Englewood Cliffs, N.J.: Prentice-Hall, 1974), pp. 176–8. Also see the following: J. R. Pennock, *Liberal Democracy: Its Merits and Prospects* (New York: Rinehart, 1950); T. E. Cook *et al.* (eds), *Participatory Democracy* (San Francisco: Canfield Press, 1971).

8   R. Jahan, *Pakistan: Failure in National Integration* (New York: Columbia University Press, 1972), p. 39. Also see: F. R. Khan, *Sociology of Pakistan* (Dacca: Shirin Publications, 1966), pp. 199–203.

9   Von Vorys, *Political Development in Pakistan*, p. 137.

10   S. Mahmood, *A Political Study of Pakistan* (Lahore: Sh. Muhammad Ashraf, 1975), pp. 210–1.

11   *The Pakistan Times* (Lahore), 11, 12 January 1953.

12   Mahmood, *A Political Study of Pakistan*, p. 54.

13   M. B. Naqvi, 'West Pakistan's Struggle for Power', *South Asian Review*, vol. 4, no. 3 (April 1971), p. 219.

14   Mahmood, *A Political Study of Pakistan*, p. 51.

15   *The Times* (London), 30 October 1954.

16   M. A. Gurmani, the Governor, was not eligible for this office for the Presiding Officer, by convention, was a member of the Assembly. See: Muneer Ahmed, *Legislatures in Pakistan* (Lahore, Department of Political Science, University of the Punjab, 1960), pp. 41–2.

17   This party is alleged to have been formed in the Government Houses at Karachi and Lahore. See: *Dawn* (Karachi), 16 March 1957.

18   M. Rashiduzzaman, *Pakistan: A Study of Government and Politics* (Dacca: The University Press, 1967), p. 121.

19   See the Draft of the Awami League Manifesto under the first General Secretary, Shamsul Haq.

20   *Dawn* (Karachi), 3, 11 October 1957.

21   *Dawn* (Karachi), 22 August 1957.

22   *Dawn* (Karachi), 19 November 1956.

23   *Dawn* (Karachi), 5 March 1957. This speech was made at the annual dinner of the Federation of Chamber of Commerce where Mirza was the chief guest.

24   *Dawn* (Karachi), 10 October 1957. For an excellent discussion on this matter, from which my inferences are drawn, see: T. Maniruzzaman, 'Group Interest in Pakistan Politics (1947–1958)', *Pacific Affairs*, vol. xxxix, nos 1 and 2 (Spring–Summer 1966), pp. 83–98.

25   Delegation led by an industrialist, M. A. Rangoonwalla. *Dawn* (Karachi), 2 November 1957.

26   Maniruzzaman, 'Group Interest in Pakistan Politics', p. 91.

27   General Ayub Khan's comment. Quoted in K. B. Sayeed, 'Pakistan's Constitutional Autocracy', *Pacific Affairs*, vol. xxxvi, no. 4 (1963), p. 370.

28   See: Justice Shahabuddin's *Reflections and Recollections* (Lahore: PLD Publishers, 1972,) In chapter 15, Shahabuddin gives a good account of how his constitutional proposals were not incorporated in the Constitution.

29 *Report of the Constitution Commission* (Karachi, Government of Pakistan Press, 1962), p. 6.

30 *Ibid.,* p. 13.

31 Burki mentions some judges like M. K. Kayani and ex-civil service members, who actually supported the BE against the ME. See: S. J. Burki, 'Twenty Years of Civil Service in Pakistan: a Re-evaluation', *Asian Survey,* vol.ix, no. 4 (1969), pp. 239–54.

32 *The Pakistan Times* (Lahore), 4, 7, 9 August 1962.

33 H. Feldman, *From Crisis to Crisis* (London: Oxford University Press, 1972), p. 2.

34 N. J. Newman, 'Democracy Under Control', *The Times* (London), 16 March 1962.

35 Braibanti, *Research on the Bureaucracy of Pakistan,* p. 255.

36 *The Pakistan Code,* vol. xiv (Karachi: Government of Pakistan Press, 1967), p. 308.

37 R. S. Wheeler, *The Politics of Pakistan* (Ithaca, N.Y.: Cornell University Press, 1970), p. 293.

38 Braibanti, *Research on the Bureaucracy of Pakistan,* p. 28.

39 *Dawn* (Karachi), 5 October 1964.

40 Under this Act a person was neither charged, nor tried nor told the reason for his detention. *The New York Times,* 31 January 1962.

41 *Dawn* (Karachi), 5 October 1962.

42 *Dawn* (Karachi), 30 September 1962.

43 Some of the prominent supporters of the NDF were: Maulana Maudoodi, Yusuf Khattak, Ayub Khuhro, Mumta Daultana, Ghulam Ali Talpur, Sardar Bahadar, Z. H. Lari, Abu Hussain, Sarker and Fazlur Rahman.

44 *Dawn* (Karachi), 8 January 1963.

45 *Dawn* (Karachi), 26 January 1964.

46 P. C. Sederberg, 'Sheikh Mujib and Charismatic Politics in Bangladesh', *Asian Forum,* vol. iv, no. 3 (June–Sept. 1972), p. 2.

47 *Viewpoint* (Lahore), vol. i, no. 26 (6 February 1976), pp. 11–12.

48 *Ibid.*

49 *Ibid.*

50 Z. Siddiqui, 'Rape of the Law', *Herald* (Karachi), vol. 9, no. 1 (January 1978), pp. 33–6.

51 Lahore High Court: *Judgement in Murder Trial, State* v. *Zulfiqar Ali Bhutto and others* (Lahore: The Pakistan Times Press, 1978), p. 131.

Chapter 8: *The Military Elites*

1   Ayal Al Qazzaz, 'Army and Society in Israel', *Pacific Sociological Review*, vol. 16, no. 2 (April 1973), p. 144.

2   R. E. Ward and D. Rustow (eds), *Political Modernization in Japan and Turkey* (Princeton, N.J.: Princeton University Press, 1964), p. 352.

3   E. Beeri, *Army Officers in Arab Politics and Society* (New York: Praeger, 1970), p. 281.

4   Brig. Gulzar Ahmed, 'Armed Forces of an Ideological State', *Pakistan Army Journal*, vol. xi, no. 1 (June 1969), pp. 31–2.

5   Maj.-Gen. F. M. Khan, *The Story of the Pakistan Army* (Karachi: Oxford University Press, 1963), p. 63.

6   Lt.-Col. A. H. Qureshi, 'Some Psychological Aspects of Motivation', *Pakistan Army Journal*, vol. xv, no. 1 (July 1973), p. 26.

7   Maj. S. Shami, 'Random thoughts for an Officer and his Wife', *Infantry* (Quetta), vol. iii, no. 1 (July 1974), p. 31.

8   The major exponent of the 'martial race' theory was Lord Roberts, Commander-in-Chief of the B.I.A. from 1885 to 1893. Others who reinforced the theory included Gen. O'Moore Creagh, Commander-in-Chief of B.I.A. from 1909 to 1914. For more information see: S. P. Cohen, *The Indian Army* (Berkeley: The University of California Press, 1971).

9   Col. M. Ahmed, *My Chief* (Lahore: Longmans Green, 1960), p. 21.

10   *Dawn* (Karachi), 16 November 1965.

11   K. B. Sayeed, 'The Role of the Military in Pakistan', in J. van Doorn (ed.), *Armed Forces and Society* (The Hague: Mouton, 1968). Also see: *Dawn* (Karachi), 18 May 1966.

12   Ayub Khan's hometown in Hazara District was modernized during his rule, as was Larkhana, Bhutto's hometown in Sind.

13   Privileged information.

14   Privileged information.

15   A mimeographed copy of the paper was given to the author by the Research and Development Department of the GHQ in July 1975.

16   *Ibid.*, p. 2.

17   *Ibid.*

18   See: M. Janowitz, *The Military in the Development of New Nations* (Chicago: The University of Chicago Press, 1971). Many essays in J. J. Johnson (ed.), *The Role of the Military in Underdeveloped Countries* (Princeton, N.J.: Princeton University Press, 1972), follow the same line of thought.

19   E. B. Shils, 'The Military in the Political Development of New States', in Johnson (ed.), *ibid.*, p. 31.

20   See: S. E. Finer, *The Man on Horseback* (London: Pall Mall, 1962); M. Price, 'A Theoretical Approach to Military Rule in New States', *World Politics,* vol. 23 (April 1971), pp. 399–430; Amos Perlmutter, 'The Praetorian State and the Praetorian Army: Towards a Taxonomy of Civil-Military Relations in Developing Polities', in J. L. Finkle and R. W. Gable (eds), *Political Development and Social Change* (New York: John Wiley, 1971), pp. 284–304. Other works referring to the same theme include: R. Emerson, *From Empire to Nation* (Boston: Beacon Press, 1970); M. Halpern, 'Middle Eastern Armies and the New Middle Class', in Johnson (ed.), *Role of the Military in Underdeveloped Countries,* pp. 277–316; A. R. Zolberg, 'Military Rule and Political Development in Tropical Africa: A Preliminary Report', in van Doorn (ed.), *Military Profession and Military Regimes,* pp. 157–74; C. E. Welch Jr., *Soldier and State in Africa* (Evanston: Northwestern University Press, 1970); S. P. Huntington, *Political Order in Changing Societies* (New Haven: Yale University Press, 1969).

21   Perlmutter, 'The Praetorian State', pp. 284–304.

22   Interview with a Major-General, July 1975.

23   See: R. A. Moore, 'The Army as a Vehicle for Social Change in Pakistan', *The Journal of Developing Areas,* vol. ii (October 1967), pp. 57–74. Also see: D. W. Chang, 'The Military and Nation-Building in Korea, Burma and Pakistan', *Asian Survey,* vol. ix, no. 2 (November 1969), pp. 818–30.

24   The articles of the Association of the Army Welfare Trust had listed plans for expansion into major business ventures like textile machinery, banking, insurance, shipping, hotel building and the car industry. See: Memorandum and Articles of the Army Trust, Rawalpindi. In a personal interview with Major-General Khadim Hussain Raja in July 1975, the author was told that the army's welfare concerns for its servicemen were superior to any other within the country.

25   In the post-1971 period, its managing directors have been Major-General (retired) Mumtaz Nawaz Malik and Major-General Rao Farman Ali. Its major production items are sugar, yarn and cloth, and its total assets have shown a continuous increase, from 161 million Rupees in 1971 to 337 million Rupees in 1972, 454.53 million Rupees in 1973 and increasing to 578.87 million Rupees in 1974. See: K. Zuberi, 'Fauji Foundation: A Profile in 1975', *Pakistan Economist,* vol. 15, no. 8 (February 1975), pp. 14–26.

26   S. P. Cohen, 'Security Issues in South Asia', *Asian Survey,* vol. xv, no. 3 (March 1975), pp. 202–14.

27   'A Short Appreciation of Present and Future Problems of Pakistan', memorandum written by General Ayub Khan in October 1954 in London. Quoted in Col. M. Ahmed, *My Chief,* p. 85. Also see: General Ayub Khan's broadcast to the nation as its Chief Martial Law Administrator, on 18 October 1958.

28   Interview with a Brigadier, Jan. 1978.

29   Gen. Ayub's Broadcast to the Nation, 8 October 1958.

30   The leaders of the Awami League were jailed or detained as security risks and disqualified until December 1966.

31   S. M. Qureshi, 'Party Politics in the Second Republic of Pakistan', *The Middle East Journal*, vol. 20, no. 4 (1966), p. 460.

32   Lt.-Gen. K. M. Shaikh's address to probationers from the Civil Service of Pakistan in Lahore in 1960. Quoted in S. J. Burki, 'Twenty Years of the Civil Service in Pakistan: A Re-evaluation', *Asian Survey*, vol. IX, no. 4 (April 1969), p. 247.

33   Speech by Gen. Ayub Khan. Quoted in R. Braibanti, *Research on the Bureaucracy of Pakistan* (Durham N. C.: Duke University Press, 1966), pp. 350–1.

34   Statement of Aziz Ahmed, a senior government official. *Dawn,* (Karachi) 8 March, 1959.

35   Government of Pakistan, *Report of and Services Commission 1959–1962* (Karachi: Government of Pakistan Press, 1962), p. 447.

36   *Ibid.*, p. 447.

37   *Dawn* (Karachi), 22 April 1964.

38   K. B. Sayeed, *Pakistan: The Formative Phase* (Karachi: Pakistan Publishing House, 1960), pp. 402–3.

39   A. Gorvine, 'The Civil Service Under Revolutionary Government in Pakistan', *The Middle East Journal*, vol. XIX, no. 3 (Summer 1965), p. 324.

40   This case has been discussed in L. Ziring, *The Ayub Khan Era: Politics in Pakistan 1958–1969* (New York: Syracuse University Press, 1971), pp. 134–7.

41   R. Jahan, *Pakistan: Failure in National Integration* (New York: Columbia University Press, 1972), p. 93.

42   See: *Future Role of Basic Democracies* (Government of Pakistan Press, Rawalpindi, 1961), p. 1.

43   Speech given by Ayub Khan. Quoted in Jahan, *Pakistan: Failure in National Integration*, p. 111.

44   Pakistan Planning Commission, *Socio-Economic Objectives of the Fourth Five Year Plan, 1970–1975*, p.12.

45   For the estimates of the wealth of Guahar Ayub, see: H. Feldman, *From Crisis to Crisis*, pp. 305–6.

46   Officers of the Pakistan Armed Forces occupied senior positions in The Pakistan Oil and Gas Corporation, Pakistan Press Trust, West Pakistan Industrial Development Corporation, West Pakistan Agricultural Corporation, Small Industries Corporation, Karachi Development Authority, Karachi Port Trust, National Shipping Corporation, Pakistan International Airlines, National Oil, Burmah Shell, Sui Northern Gas, and Batala

Industries. See: K. B. Sayeed, 'The Role of the Military in Pakistan', in van Doorn (ed.), *Armed Forces and Society,* p. 297.

47   R. Laporte Jr., *Power and Privilege: Influence and Decision-Making in Pakistan* (Berkeley: The University of California Press, 1975), p. 68.

48   Interview with a Major-General (July 1975).

49   General Yahya Khan's first Broadcast to the Nation on 26 March 1969.

50   See: F. M. Khan, *Pakistan's Crises in Leadership* (Islamabad: National Book Foundation, 1973), pp. 28–31.

51   Legal Framework Order. See: S. G. M. Badruddin, *Election Handbook 1970* (Karachi: Publishing and Marketing Associates, 1970), p. 128.

52   R. Jahan, 'Elite in Crisis: The Failure of Mujib–Yahya–Bhutto Negotiations', *Orbis*, vol. XVII, no. 2 (Summer 1973), pp. 575–97.

53   *Ibid.,* p. 588.

54   See Z. A. Bhutto, *The Great Tragedy* (Karachi: Vision Publishers, 1971).

55   General Yahya Khan's Broadcast to the Nation on 26 March 1971. Quoted in Zafrullah Khan, *The Agony of Pakistan* (Oxford: Alden Press, 1973), p. 148.

56   The Constitution of the Islamic Republic of Pakistan, 1973, Article 6, (1), (2) and (3).

57   *Ibid.,* Article 245.

58   See: Government of Pakistan, *White Paper on Baluchistan* (Islamabad, Printing Corporation of Pakistan, 1974), p. 25.

59   General Zia-ul-Haq's Broadcast to the Nation on 6 July 1977.

60   *Ibid.*

Chapter 9: *The One-Party State and Political Conflict*

1   I. Wallerstein, *Africa: The Politics of Independence* (New York: Vintage Books, 1961), pp. 97–8.

2   D. Apter, 'Political Religion in The New Nations', in C. Geertz (ed.), *Old Societies and New States* (New York: The Free Press, 1963), pp. 57–104.

3   W. Howard Wriggins, *The Rulers' Imperative* (New York: Columbia University Press, 1969), p. 135.

4   *Foundations and Policy: Pakistan People's Party* (n.d.). Quoted in H. A. Rizvi, *Pakistan People's Party: The First Phase 1967—71* (Lahore: Progressive Publishers, 1973), p. 7.

5   A. H. Khan, *Political Parties: Their Policies and Programs* (Lahore: Ferozesons, 1971), pp. 213–34.

6   Rizvi, *Pakistan People's Party,* p. 7.

7   Z. A. Bhutto, *Political Situation in Pakistan* (Lahore: Pakistan People's Party Political Series, No 1, 1968), pp. 14–15.

8   G. A. Heegar, 'Socialism in Pakistan', in H. Desfosses and J. Levesque (eds), *Socialism in The Third World* (New York: Praeger Publishers, 1975), pp. 291–309.

9   See K. B. Sayeed, 'How Radical is the Pakistan People's Party?', *Pacific Affairs,* vol. XLVIII, no. 1 (Spring 1975), p. 52.

10   M. G. Weinbaum, 'The March 1977 Elections in Pakistan: Where Everyone Lost', *Asian Survey,* vol. XVII, no. 7 (July 1977), p. 13.

11   See Gen. Zia-ul-Haq's statement: *Dawn* (Karachi), 4 Jan. 1978.

12   The removal of Gen. Gul Hassan and Air Marshall Rahim Khan was on these grounds.

13   General Tikka Khan was elevated to the position of a cabinet minister. After Bhutto's fall he led a procession in Lahore in favour of Bhutto, defying martial law restrictions. In some quarters this was taken as a signal for a counter coup d'état of pro-Bhutto generals against the Zia-ul-Haq regime.

14   B. O. Nwabueze, *Constitutionalism in the Emergent States* (London: Hurst, 1973), p. 1.

15   See M. Rashiduzzaman, 'The National Awami Party of Pakistan: Leftist Politics in Crises', *Pacific Affairs,* vol. XLII, no. 3 (Fall 1970), p. 399.

16   J. K. Bashir, *NWFP Elections of 1970: An Analysis* (Lahore: Progressive Publishers, 1973), p. 3.

17   H. Malik, 'Emergence of the Federal Pattern in Pakistan', *Journal of Asian and African Studies,* vol. VIII, nos. 3–4 (1973), p. 207. For Wali Khan ideology, see A. Muzdakiy, *Wali Khan Key Siyasat* (Lahore: Tariq Publishers, 1972).

18   *Government of Pakistan Supreme Court Judgement on Dissolution of NAP Rawalpindi* (Information and Broadcasting Division: Directorate of Research, Reference and Publication, Islamabad, 30 October 1975), pp. 27–9.

19   Statement by Khair Baksh Marri: *Daily News,* 1 January 1978.

20   Statement by Wali Khan: *The Pakistan Times* (Lahore), 15 October 1974.

21   A relative of Sherpao stated to the author that he strongly suspected Bhutto's involvement in this political assassination of his best friend in order to find a cause for getting rid of the NAP.

22   S. J. Burki, 'The Elections of 1977: The Ongoing Search for Legitimacy', 6 May 1977 (unpublished paper sent to the author by Burki). It is

the most comprehensive analysis yet made of the March 1977 elections. Burki's help in sending some published as well as unpublished papers to the author is gratefully acknowledged.

23   *Viewpoint* (Lahore), vol. ii, no. 30 (4 March 1977), p. 14.

24   *Ibid.*, p. 14.

25   A. H. Syed, 'The Pakistan People's Party: Phases One and Two', in L. Ziring, R. Braibanti and W. H. Wriggins (eds), *Pakistan: The Long View* (Durham, N. C.: Duke University Press, 1977), p. 75.

26   For this view, see article by I. H. Rehman, 'The Three Voices of the Punjab', *The Herald* (Karachi), vol. 19, no. 1 (January 1978), pp. 31–2.

27   Syed, 'The Pakistan People's Party', p. 103. This paper has an excellent discussion on the PPP's factionalism and political corruption.

28   W. A. Lewis, 'Beyond African Dictatorship: The Crises of the One Party State', *Encounter,* vol. xxv, no. 2 (August 1965), pp. 3–18.

29   I. Wallerstein, 'The Decline of the Party in Single Party African States', in J. LaPalambara and M. Weiner (eds), *Political Parties and Political Development* (Princeton, N.J.: Princeton University Press, 1969), p. 208.

30   W. J. Foltz, 'Political Opposition in Single Party States of Tropical Africa', in R. A. Dahl (ed.), *Regimes and Oppositions* (New Haven, Conn.: Yale University Press, 1973), pp. 143–70.

31   Some observations have been made by correspondents on the rigging of the March 1977 elections. See: *The Guardian,* 11 March 1977, and *The Times* (London), 5 April 1977. Some eyewitnesses informed the author that the elections were rigged through such measures as coercion, false voters' lists, the change of ballot boxes, and groups of women voters in veils being taken from one voting booth to another. For an exposé of such malpractices, see the report compiled by the ME: *White Paper on the Conduct of the General Elections in March 1977* (Islamabad: Printing Corporation of Pakistan Press, July 1978).

32   N. D. Palmer, *Elections and Political Development: The South Asian Experience* (London: Hurst, 1975), p. 7.

Chapter 10: *Ethnic Nationalism and Imperialism*

1   For details see: Myron Weiner, 'Political Integration and Political Development', in *The Annals of the American Academy of Political and Social Sciences,* vol. cclvii (1965), pp. 52–64.

2   Rupert Emerson, *From Empire to Nation* (Cambridge, Mass.: Harvard University Press, 1960), p. 94.

3   Clifford Geertz (ed.), *Old Societies and New States* (New York: Free Press, 1963), pp. 105–57.

4   Joseph R. Strayer, 'The Historical Experience of Nation Building in Europe', in K. W. Deutsch and W. J. Foltz (eds), *Nation Building* (Chicago: Aldine Atherton Press, 1971), pp. 17–26.

5   Here only the Pakistani initiatives towards attracting U.S. aid have been taken into account.

6   E. Shils, 'Political Development in New States', *Comparative Studies in Society and History,* vol. 2 (1959–60), pp. 265–91.

7   See: P. Baran, *The Political Economy of Growth* (New York: Monthly Review Press, 1957). Also see: A. G. Frank, *Capitalism and Underdevelopment in Latin America* (New York: Monthly Review Press, 1969).

8   Dos Santos, 'The Structure of Dependence', *American Economic Review,* vol. 60 (May 1970), p. 231.

9   Said Hassan, *Pakistan: The Story Behind its Economic Development* (New York: Vantage Press, 1971), pp. 91–3. The influence of such members of the BE as Ghulam Mohammad and Choudhary Mohammad Ali is evident here, and their influence persuaded Liaquat Ali Khan to invite American aid. These men from the Finance Services had wielded strong influence in the political arena since 1947. The latter also reorganized the Civil Service of Pakistan and both men, as we have seen, became members of the governing elite.

10   Hamza Alavi and Amir Khusro, *Pakistan and the Burden of U.S. Aid* (Karachi: Syed and Syed, 1965), pp. 10–11. Eisenhower was President of the U.S. at the time, and Dulles was the Secretary of State.

11   H. Magdoff, *The Age of Imperialism* (New York: Monthly Review Press, 1969), p. 40.

12   *Design for Pakistan* (a report on Assistance to the Pakistan Planning Commission by the Ford Foundation and Harvard University, February 1965), p. 2.

13   Dickson K. Smith, 'Foreign Aid and Economic Development in Pakistan: The Ayub Years (1958–1969)', unpublished Ph.D. thesis, Department of Economics, University of Utah (1974), p. 106.

14   A. Curle, *Planning for Education in Pakistan: A Personal Case Study* (Cambridge, Mass.: Harvard University Press, 1966), p. 6.

15   G. F. Papanek, *Pakistan's Development: Social Goals and Private Incentives* (Cambridge, Mass.: Harvard University Press, 1967), p. 85.

16   A Report to the Ford Foundation of the Committee to Review the Development Advisory Service, E. D. Edwards (Chairman), March 1971, p. 13. Quoted in D. Smith 'Foreign Aid and Economic Development in Pakistan: The Ayub Years (1958–1969), June 1974.

17   *Ibid.*

18   A. Waterson, *Planning in Pakistan: Organization and Implementation* (Baltimore: Johns Hopkins Press, 1963), pp. 34–5.

19   *Ibid.,* p. 98.

20   W. Tims, *Analytical Techniques for Development Planning: A Case Study of Pakistan's Third Five Year Plan* (Karachi: P.I.D.E. Special Publication Series, 1968), p. 4.

21   N. Islam, 'Foreign Assistance and Economic Development: The Case of Pakistan', *The Economic Journal*, vol. 82 (1972), p. 522.

22   A. Hussain, 'Ethnicity, National Identity and Praetorianism: The Case of Pakistan', *Asian Survey*, vol. XVI, no. 10 (October 1976), pp. 923–4.

23   N. Kasfir, *The Shrinking Political Arena* (Berkeley: University of California Press, 1976), p. 44.

24   See: C. Enloe, *Ethnic Conflict and Political Development* (Boston: Little Brown, 1973). Also see: R. H. Bates, 'Ethnic Competition and Modernization in Contemporary Africa', *Comparative Political Studies*, vol. 6, no. 4 (January 1974), p. 458.

25   Gaafar S. Idris, *The Process of Islamization* (Indiana: MSA Publication, 1977), pp. 1–2.

Epilogue

1   *The Times* (London), 19 September 1978.

2   *The Times* (London), 3 October 1978.

3   *The Times* (London), 25 September 1978.

4   *The Times* (London), 4 October 1978.

5   *The Times* (London), 9 October 1978.

Select Bibliography

This select bibliography is intended to give a comprehensive list of works on Pakistan's politics from all theoretical viewpoints (Marxist, non-Marxist, elitist, etc.)

A. Books

Abbot, F. K., *Islam and Pakistan* (Ithaca: Cornell University Press, 1968).

Ahmad, A. and G. E. von Grunebaum, *Muslim Self-Statements in India and Pakistan, 1857–1968* (Wiesbaden: Otto Harrassowitz, 1970).

Ahmad, I., *Pakistan General Elections 1970* (Lahore: South Asian Institute, Punjab University, 1976).

Ahmad, Khurshid, *Islam: Its Meaning & Message* (Leicester: The Islamic Foudation, 1976).

Ahmed, A. S., *Social and Economic Change in Tribal Areas* (Karachi: Oxford University Press, 1977).

Ahmed, Muneer, *Legislature in Pakistan 1947–1958* (Lahore: Department of Political Science, University of Punjab, 1960).

Ahmed, Mushtaq, *Government and Politics in Pakistan* (Karachi: Space Publishers, 1972).

Ali, Tariq, *Pakistan: Military Rule or People's Power* (New York: William Morrow, 1970).

Bhutto, Z. A., *The Great Tragedy* (Karachi: Vision Publications, 1971).

Binder, L., *Religion and Politics in Pakistan* (Berkeley: University of California Press, 1961).

Birkhead, Guthrie (ed.), *Administrative Problems in Pakistan* (Syracuse, N.Y.: Syracuse University Press, 1966).

Bolitho, H., *Jinnah: Creator of Pakistan* (London: John Murray, 1954).

Braibanti, R., *Research on the Bureaucracy of Pakistan* (Durham, N. C.: Duke University Press, 1966).

Burki, S. J., *Social Groups and Management: A Case Study of Pakistan* (Berkeley: University of California Press) (forthcoming).

Callard, K., *Pakistan: A Political Study* (London: Allen & Unwin, 1957).

Choudhury, G. W., *The Last Days of United Pakistan* (London: Hurst, 1974).

Davey, B., *The Economic Development of India: A Marxist View* (Nottingham: Spokesman Books, 1975).

Falcon, W. P. & G. F. Papanek (eds), *Development Policy II–The Pakistan Experience* (Cambridge, Mass.: Harvard University Press, 1971).

Feldman, H., *Revolution in Pakistan* (London: Oxford University Press, 1972).

From Crisis to Crisis (London: Oxford University Press, 1972).

The End and the Beginning: Pakistan 1969–1971 (London: Oxford University Press, 1975).

Goodnow, H. F., *The Civil Service of Pakistan* (New Haven, Conn.: Yale University Press, 1964).

Gough, K. & H. P. Sharma, *Imperialism and Revolution in South Asia* (New York: Monthly Review Press, 1973).

Hassan, Said, *Pakistan: The Story Behind its Development* (New York: Vantage Press, 1971).

Hussain, Arif, *Pakistan: Its Ideology and Foreign Policy* (London: Frank Cass, 1966).

Jahan, Raunaq, *Pakistan: Failure in National Integration* (New York: Columbia University Press, 1972).

Khan, Gen. Ayub, *Friends Not Masters* (New York: Oxford University Press, 1967).

Khan, Major-Gen. F. M., *The Story of the Pakistan Army* (Karachi: Oxford University Press, 1963).

Pakistan's Crises in Leadership (Islamabad: National Book Foundation, 1973).

Laporte, Robert, *Power and Privilege: Influence and Decision-Making in Pakistan* (Berkeley: University of California Press, 1975).

Lewis, S. R., *Pakistan: Industrialization and Trade Policies* (London: Oxford University Press, 1970).

McDonough, S., *Mohammad Ali Jinnah* (Lexington, Mass.: D. C. Heath 1970).

Maddison, A., *Class Structure and Economic Growth: India and Pakistan since the Mughals* (New York: W. W. Norton, 1971).

Palmer, D. P., *Elections and Political Development: The South Asian Experience* (London: Hurst, 1975).

Papanek, G. F., *Pakistan's Development: Social Goals and Private Incentives* (Cambridge, Mass.: Harvard University Press, 1967).

Pehrson, R. N., *The Social Organization of the Marri Baluch* (Chicago: Aldine Publishing, 1966).

Quaid-i-Azam Mohammad Ali Jinnah, *Speeches as Governor General of Pakistan, 1947–1948* (Karachi: Pakistan Publications, n.d.).

Qureshi, I. H., *The Struggle for Pakistan* (Karachi: University of Karachi, 1969).

Rizvi, H. A., *The Military and Politics in Pakistan* (Lahore: Progressive Publishers, 1974).

Sayeed, K. B., *The Political System of Pakistan* (Boston: Houghton Mifflin, 1967).

   Pakistan: The Formative Phase (Karachi: Pakistan Publishing House, 1960).

Siddiqui, K. B., *Conflict, Crises and War in Pakistan* (New York: Praeger Publishers, 1972).

Smith, D. E. (ed.), *South Asian Politics and Religion* (Princeton, N. J.: Princeton University Press, 1966).

Smith, W. C., *Modern Islam in India* (Lahore: Minerva Press, 1943).

Stephen, I., *Pakistan* (London: Ernest Benn, 1967).

Stevens, R. D., Hamza Alavi and P. J. Bertocci (eds), *Rural Development in Bangladesh and Pakistan* (Hawaii: The University Press of Hawaii, 1976).

Von Vorys, Karl, *Political Development in Pakistan* (Princeton, N. J.: Princeton University Press, 1965).

Weekes, R., *Pakistan: Birth and Growth of a Muslim Nation* (Princeton: Van Nostrand, 1964).

Wheeler, R. S., *The Politics of Pakistan* (Ithaca, N.Y.: Cornell University Press, 1970).

White, L., *Industrial Concentration and Economic Power in Pakistan* (Princeton, N.J.: Princeton University Press, 1974).

Wilcox, W. A., *Pakistan: The Consolidation of a Nation* (New York: Columbia University Press, 1964).

Williams, L. F. Rushbrook, *Pakistan Under Challenge* (London: Stacey International, 1975).

Zirling, L., *The Ayub Khan Era: Politics in Pakistan 1958–1969* (Syracuse, N. Y.: Syracuse University Press, 1971).

et al., Pakistan: The Long View (Durham, N. C.: Duke University Press, 1977).

B. Papers

Burki, S. J., 'Twenty Years of the Civil Service of Pakistan: A Re-evaluation', *Asian Survey,* vol. IX, no. 4 (1969), pp. 239–54.

'The Elections of 1977: The Ongoing Search for Legitimacy', unpublished paper sent by Burki to the author.

Exposito, B. B., 'The Politics of Agrarian Reform in Pakistan', *Asian Survey,* vol. XIV, no. 5 (May 1974), pp. 429–38.

Gorvine, A., 'The Role of the Civil Service under the Revolutionary Government', *The Middle East Journal,* vol. XIX (1965), pp. 321–6.

Gustafson, W. E., 'Economic Reforms under the Bhutto Regime', *Journal of Asian and African Studies,* vol. 8 (1973), pp. 241–58.

Heegar, G. A., 'Socialism in Pakistan', in H. Desfosses and J. Levesque (eds), *Socialism in the Third World* (New York: Praeger Publishers, 1975), pp. 291–309.

Jahan, R., 'Elite in Crisis, The Failure of Mujib–Yahya–Bhutto Negotiations', *Orbis,* vol. XVII, no. 2 (Summer 1973), pp. 575–97.

Laporte Jr., R., 'Regionalism and Political Opposition in Pakistan: Some Observations of the Bhutto Period', *Asian Thought and Society,* vol. 1, no. 2 (September 1976), pp. 215–26.

'The Leadership crisis in Pakistan: Analysis of the March 1977 Election and its Aftermath', *Asian Thought and Society,* vol. 2, no. 2 (September 1977), pp. 257–61.

Levak, A., 'Provincial Conflict and Nation-Building in Pakistan', in W. Bell and W. E. Freeman (eds), *Ethnicity and Nation-Building* (Beverley Hills, Calif.: Sage Publications, 1974), pp. 203–21.

Malik, H., 'Emergence of the Federal Pattern in Pakistan', *Journal of Asian and African Studies,* vol. VIII, nos. 3–4 (1973), pp. 205–15.

Maniruzzaman, T., 'Group Interests in Pakistan's Politics, 1947–1958', *Pacific Affairs,* vol XXXIX, nos. 1–2 (1966), pp. 83–98.

Qureshi, S. M. M., 'Party Politics in the Second Republic of Pakistan', *The Middle East Journal*, vol. 20, no 4 (Autumn 1966), pp. 456–72.

Rahman, F., 'Islam and the New Constitution of Pakistan', *Journal of Asian and African Studies*, vol. VIII, (1973), pp. 190–204.

Rashiduzzaman, M., 'The National Awami Party in Pakistan: Leftist Politics in Crises', *Pacific Affairs*, vol. XLII, no. 3 (Fall 1970), pp. 394–409.

Sayeed, K. B., 'The Jamait-i-Islami Movement in Pakistan', *Pacific Affairs*, vol. xxx,no. 2 (March 1957), pp. 59–68.

'Religion and Nation-Building in Pakistan', *The Middle East Journal*, vol. 17, no. 3 (1963), pp. 279–91.

'How Radical is the Pakistan's People's Party?', *Pacific Affairs*, vol. 48, no. 1 (1975), pp. 42–59.

Syed, A. H., 'Bureaucratic Ethic and Ethos in Pakistan', *Polity*, vol. 4, no. 2 (1971), pp. 159–94.

'Pakistan in 1976: Business as Usual', *Asian Survey*, vol. XVII, no. 2 (February 1977), pp. 181–90.

Weinbaum, M. G., 'The March 1977 Elections in Pakistan: Where Everyone Lost', *Asian Survey*, vol. XVII, no. 7 (July 1977), pp. 599–618.

Wilcox, W., 'Political Change in Pakistan: Structures, Functions, Constraints and Goals', in C. E. Welch Jr. (ed.), *Political Modernization* (Belmont, Calif.: Wadsworth Publishing, 1971), pp. 278–92.

Wright Jr., T. P., 'Indian Muslim Refugees in the Politics at Pakistan', *The Journal of Commonwealth Comparative Politics*, vol. XII, no. 2 (July 1974), pp. 189–205.

Ziring, L., 'Pakistan: The Campaign before the Storm', *Asian Survey*, vol. XVII, no. 7 (July 1977), pp. 581–98.

Index

A

Adamjee family, 93, 95, 104
Administrative Reforms Committee, 76–7
Advisory Council of Islamic Ideology, 86, 89
Afghanistan, 46
Agarthala Conspiracy Case, 64, 122, 155
Agriculture, 44, 47, 97–8, 138 n46, 164; modernization, 46, 56–7, 60, 118; see also Land Reforms
Ahmad, Ghafoor, Professor, 171
Ahmad, Khurshid, Professor, 171
Ahmadiya sect, 90, 91; see also riots
Ahmed, Aziz, 68
Akbar, Emperor, 22
Ali, Caliph, 40, 81
Ali, Chaudhri Mohammad, 68, 72, 117, 163 n9
Ali, Syed Amjad, 104
Ali, Wazir, family, 93, 95
Ali, Yaqub, 124
All-India Muslim League (1907–47), 25, 26, 27, 28, 44; see also Jinnah, Mohammad Ali; Pakistan Muslim League
All-Jammu and Kashmir Muslim Conference, 156
All-Pakistan Confederation of Labour, 105
All-Pakistan Khatim-i-Nabuwat Conference, 91
All-Pakistan Lawyers Conference, 122
Amin family, 95, 104
Army, 71, 99, 126–30, 133–4, 136, 138–9, 142, 146, 149–50, 151, 154–5, 159; Mughal period, 126–8; British Indian Army (BIA), 23, 46, 61, 126–7, 128–9, 132; officer corps,
14, 127, 128, 129, 130–2, 133, 138, 142, 159; Army Welfare Trust, 134; Fauji Foundation, 134; see also Elites, military; martial law; military rule
Assemblies, Provincial, 71, 99, 136, 137, 155; see also Governors, Provincial
Assembly, Constituent, 69, 70, 72, 73, 74, 82, 112, 117, 118, 123
Assembly, National (NA), 43, 51, 56, 99, 112, 119, 136, 137, 141–2, 150–1, 152, 154; see also Constitutions; Elections
Audits and Accounts Service, 63
Awami League (AL), 70–1, 104, 117, 118, 120–2, 135 n30, 137, 140, 160
Ayub Khan, Mohammad, see Khan, Mohammad Ayub

B

Bahawalpur, Nawab of (Mohammad Abbassi), 153
Bakhtiar, Yahya, 170
Bakr, Hazrat Abu, Caliph, 124–5
Baksh, Pir Illahi, 52
Baluch, M., 170
Baluchis/Baluchistan, 48, 51; colonial period, 24, 93; post-Independence, 15, 41, 71, 103, 116, 129, 143, 144, 149, 151, 153–4, 156–7, 170, 171; conflict (1971), 154–5
Baluchistan Liberation Movement, 41
Bangladesh, 39, 89, 122, 134, 142, 154, 161; see also Civil war (1971); East Bengal Banking, 106, 134 n24
Bara, 51
Bashani, Maulana, 70, 153
Basic Democracy system (BD), 114, 118, 136–7, 138

Basic Principles Committee: Interim Report (1950), 115, 116; Report (1952), 115, 116

Bawany family, 95

Bengal, 93, 128; *see also* East Bengal; West Bengal Bhutto, Zulfikar Ali, 160; and PPP, 42, 88, 108, 138, 146; and socialism, 146–9, 162, 168; in Ayub's cabinet, 42, 75, 138; election (1970), 140; civil war (1971), 88–9, 146; rise to power, 140–1; regime (1971–7), 98, 146; administrative reforms, 75–8, 135; labour reforms, 106, 107; land reforms (1972), 57–60; use of state machinery, 122–5, 146, 149–50; use of constitution, 122–5, 146, 150–2; and IE, 98, 106–9; and army, 14–15, 142–3, 145, 154–5; and RE, 89–90, 133; and Baluchis, 41, 153–5; and NWFP, 153, 155; and Punjab 153, 170; and Sindhis, 39, 80, 153, 170; opposition to, 122, 153, 155–6; election (1977), 90, 156–7, 159; fall, 43, 149 *n*13, 159; imprisonment and trial, 124–5, 169, 172

Biharis, 109

Bizenjo, Ghaus Baksh, 154

Bogra, Mohammad Ali, 54, 69–70, 71–2, 74, 116, 163

Bohra community, 94, 95, 96

Bombay, 94, 95

Bourgeoisie, 37, 80, 104

Bourne, Frederick, Sir, 66 *n*14

British in India, *see* colonialism; army, British Indian Army; Indian Civil Service

Brohi, A. K., 137, 170, 171

Bugti, A. N., 15

Bureau of National Reconstruction, 87

Bureaucracy, 61–78, 99, 107, 109, 121, 122, 135, 146, 149; *see also* elites, bureaucratic

Burgess, Geoffrey, 64

Burma, 94, 147

C

Cabinet Secretariat, 67, 68, 72, 73, 152; *see also* Central Government Cabinet

Calcutta, 93, 95

Capitalism, 34, 93; and colonialism, 22–3, 24–5, 41; and Islamic law, 32, 83, 92; post-Independence, 15, 60, 92, 93–4, 97, 99–106, 109–10, 113, 138, 146, 147, 148, 156, 160, 161, 162–3; and US imperialism, 162–4, 168; *see also* industry

Central Excise Service, 63

Central Government Cabinet, 14, 35, 67, 112

Central Intelligence Agency, 77

Central Islamic Research Institute, 87

Central Superior Services, 13, 63

Ceylon, 147

Chakwal, 95

Chalna, 39

China, 77, 86, 153

Chinioti, 94, 95

Chittagong, 39

Choudhury, Hamidul Huq, 68

Chundrigar, I. I., 118

CIA, *see* Central Intelligence Agency

Civil Service Academy, 64–5

Civil Service Act (1973), 77

Civil Service of Pakistan (1947–73) (CSP), 61, 62–5, 67, 68, 73, 75, 76, 77, 99, 135–6, 163 *n*9

Civil war (1971), 13, 39, 89, 102, 114, 141–2, 148, 160, 161, 167; *see also* Bangladesh

Class structure, 38, 168

Code of Criminal Procedure (Amendment) Act (1963), 120

Colonialism: and Mughal decline, 21–2; rebellion (1857), 46; and feudalism, 24–5, 32, 44, 45–6, 93; and capitalism, 22–3, 24–5, 32, 93–4, 163; and elites, 36, 42, 65, 80, 136; and Independence movement, 25–9; heritage of, 34, 36, 39, 53, 61–3, 64, 65, 73, 77, 82, 111–12, 123, 128–9, 132, 162; *see also* army, British Indian Army; Indian Civil Service

Colony family, 95

Combined Opposition Party (COP), 87, 120, 137

Communism, 31, 163

Conciliation Courts Ordinance (1961), 120

Constituent Assembly, *see* Assembly, Constituent

Constitution Commission (1961), 91, 119

Constitutions, 113, 115, 119, 122–3, 124, 127–8, 145, 150; (1956), 54, 69, 72–3, 83, 85, 89, 119, 128, 150; (1962), 83, 86, 89, 119–20, 128, 138, 150; amendments (1963), 86; Accord (1972), 154, 155; (1973), 141, 146, 150–2, 154, 158, 171 corruption, 98, 133, 135

Council of Common Interests, 151

Council of Islamic Ideology, 91, 92

Coups d'etat, 161; (1958), 128, 134; (1973), 143, 154–5; (1977) 143–4

Crescent family, 95, 104

Cunningham, George, Sir, 66 *n*14

Customs Service, 63

D

Dacca, 39, 142

Daultana, Mian Mumtaz, 52, 53, 85

Dawood family, 95, 99, 104, 106
Defence expenditure, 138–9
Delhi, 21, 41, 95
Democracy: and colonialism, 26, 28, 111; and Islamic law, 30–1, 32, 82, 83, 85, 92; and the ideological state, 33, 79; post-Independence, 53, 70, 112–15, 116, 117, 119–20, 158–9, 160; see also Basic Democracy system
Deoband Academy for Theology, 28
Din-i-Illahi, 22
Dogras, 128
Dundas, Ambrose, Sir, 66 n 14

E

East Africa, 94, 95
East Bengal: colonial period, 46, 93; Permanent Settlement Act (1793), 46; post-Independence, 38–9, 41, 66 n14, 67, 68–71, 72, 73, 79, 89, 90, 94–5, 101, 102–3, 104, 109, 114, 116, 117, 118, 121–2, 129, 134, 136, 137, 140, 141, 164, 165, 166; and CSP, 64–5; Acquisition and Tenancy Act (1953), 46; secession, 123, 140–2, 158; see also Agartharla Conspiracy Case; Bangladesh; civil war; East Bengal professional elite; language controversy
East Bengal professional elite (EBPA), 64, 70–1, 74, 94, 104, 113–14, 116, 119, 120, 121–2, 135, 137, 153
East Pakistan, see East Bengal
Economy: Mughal period, 20–2; colonial period, 22–5; post-Independence, 89, 92, 93–109, 117–18, 136, 137, 138, 146, 147, 163, 164; see also agriculture; capitalism; feudalism; industry
Education, 62, 63–4, 92, 111
Eggar Report, 74–5
Elections, 113, 159, 172; (1937), 27; (1945), 70–1, 114; (1962), 56; (1965), 56, 87, 137, 138, 159; (1970), 88, 99, 106, 114, 140, 159; (1977), 43, 77, 90, 143, 149, 159, 169
Electoral Bodies Disqualification Order (1958) (EBDO), 135
Elites: bureaucratic (BE), 13, 35, 36, 37, 39, 41, 52, 54, 61–78, 80, 82, 91, 97, 98, 112, 114, 115, 117, 119, 130, 133, 135–6, 137, 138, 144, 147, 150, 162, 163, 165, 167, 170, 171, see also bureaucracy; governing, 35, 36, 37, 40, 43, 51, 78, 81, 83, 91, 97, 98, 102, 104, 112, 113, 114–15, 124, 125, 144, 151, 152, 153, 158–9, 166, 167; industrial (IE), 13, 35, 36, 37, 41, 44, 60, 80, 92, 93–107, 112, 114,

118, 121, 137, 138, 144, 146, 147, 155, 156, 162, 163, 165, 167, 170, 171; landowning (LE), 13, 35, 36, 37, 39, 40, 41, 44–60, 66, 70, 71, 74, 75, 82, 88, 94, 97, 98, 106, 112, 114, 116, 117, 121, 122, 124, 130, 135, 137, 138, 150, 153, 154, 155, 157–8, 160, 162, 169, 170, see also landlords; military, 13, 14–15, 35, 36, 37, 39, 40, 41, 55–7, 73, 75, 80, 85–8, 90, 94, 97, 98–9, 112, 114, 115, 119–22, 126–45, 150, 155, 159 n31, 162, 163, 170, 171, 172, see also army; political, 14, 34–8, 42–3, 75, 113, 114, 117, 136, 144, 156, 159, 168; professional (PE), 35, 36, 37, 39, 41, 66, 80, 82, 83, 87, 90, 91, 111–25, 153, 155, 162, 169, 170, 171, see also EBPE, WPPE; religious (RE), 28, 35, 36, 37, 41, 74, 79–92, 94, 97, 121, 133, 137, 147, 155, 158, 159, 162, 170, 171
Emergency Powers, 123
Ethnicity, 23, 38–43, 64–5, 68–9, 74, 77, 92, 93, 94–6, 101–4, 109–10, 114, 115–17, 118, 120, 121, 128, 129–30, 131–2, 134, 140, 141, 143, 144, 145, 148, 151–2, 153, 154–5, 166–8; and democracy, 158–9, 160; and imperialism, 161–8; ethnic nationalism, 13, 15, 53, 89, 114, 122, 142; see also individual provinces; language controversy

F

Family Laws Ordinance (1961), 86, 137
Fancy family, 95, 107
Farooqi, Mohammad Azam, 171
Fazlullah, Kazi, 52
Federal Security Force, 124, 150
Federal Service Commission Act (1973), 77
Federal Unified Grades, 76, 77
Federation of the Chambers of Commerce and Industry, 98–9
Feudalism: Mughal period, 20–3, 45, 61; colonial period, 24–5, 45–7; post-Independence, 41, 44, 74, 94, 97, 107, 116, 138, 148, 156; and Islamic law, 32, 83, 92; and politics, 51–5, 56, 71, 72, 106, 113, 160, 161; heritage of, 34, 45–6; see also landlords; peasants
Five Year Plans: First (1955–60), 50, 101, 165, 166; Second (1960–5), 101, 165, 166; Third (1965–70), 101, 103, 165, 166; Fourth (1970–5), 103–4
Ford Foundation, 164
Foreign aid, 104, 118, 134, 162, 165–6
Foreign investment, 102
France, 22, 24

G

Ganatantri Dal Party, 70–1; *see also* United Front
Gandhi, Mahatma, 27
Gardezi family, 56
Gauhar, Altaf, 75 *n*42
Germany, 24
Gilani, Makhdoom S., 136
Gladieux Report, 75
Government of India Act (1935), .66–7, 69, 72, 115; amendments (1954), 72
Governors-General, role of, 66–7, 68, 69, 72, 116
Governors, Provincial, 66, 68, 119, 151, 154, 155
Governor's Rule, 67; (1949–51), 52; (1954), 71
Gujrat, 41, 94, 129
Gurkhas, 128

H

Habib family, 93, 95
Habibullah family, 170
Hanif, Mohammad, 108
Haris, *see* peasants
Haroon group, 52, 99
Harvard Advisory Group (HAG), 104, 163–5, 167
Hassan, Mubasher, Dr, 108, 149, 158
Hindus: under Caliphs and Sultans, 19; Mughal period, 19, 20, 21, 22; colonial period, 26, 27, 28–9, 46, 93, 117, 128; post-Independence, 89, 128
Holland, 22, 24
Hoti family, 56, 60, 170
Housing, 101, 106, 148
Huq, A. K. Fazlul, 70, 71
Huq, S. A., Justice, 123
Hur movement, 80 *n*4
Hussain, Akhtar, 68 *n*21
Hussan, Gul, General, 149 *n*12
Hyderbad, 159
Hyderbad Conspiracy Case, 144, 155
Hyeson family, 95

I

Ideological state, concept of, 33–4; *see also* democracy; Islam and state formation
Illahi, Chaudhri Rehmat, 171
Imperialism, 161–8, 171; *see also* United States of America
Income Tax Service, 63
Independence (1947), 23, 25, 36, 41, 42, 46, 61, 115
India, 122, 134, 141, 142, 146, 167; *see also* civil war; West Bengal
Indian Administrative Service, 61

Indian Civil Service (ICS), 23, 61, 62–3, 64
Indian Congress Party, 27, 41
Industrial Relations Ordinance (1969), 105
Industry, 93–100, 138 *n*46, 156, 164; cement, 96, 106, 108; chemicals, 94, 96, 106; electricals, 106; electricity, 106; engineering, 106, 111; fertilizers, 108; food, 96, 97; gas, 106, 138 *n*46; jute, 38, 94, 96, 97; metals, 96, 106, 108; paper, 96; petrochemicals, 96, 106, 138 *n*46; sugar, 94, 96, 134 *n*25; textiles, 94, 96, 97, 134 *n*25; vehicles, 96, 106, 134 *n*24; wood, 96; *see also* elites, industrial; nationalization
Insurance companies, 106, 134 *n*24
Investment, 108–9; *see also* banking, foreign investment
Iqbal, Javaid, 87
Iqbal, Mohammad, 26
Iraq, 154
Islam: establishment of, 19, 39, 86, 126; under Mughals, 19–22, 36, 126; and capitalism, 156; and Hinduism, 19, 20, 25–9; and nationalism, 25–32; and socialism, 147, 162; and state formation, 25–9, 30–2, 79, 80, 81, 82–92, 115, 117, 127–8, 130–3, 134, 144, 147, 160, 161, 162, 166, 167, 168, 171; *see also* Islamic law
Islamabad, 15, 88, 98
Islamic Council, 89, 90
Islamic law, 22, 26, 29, 30–2, 68, 78, 80, 81, 82–6, 89–90, 111, 124, 125, 156, 169, 171, 172; Shias, 81; Sunnis, 81
Ismaili sect, 80
Isphani family, 93, 104
Israel, 126

J

Jagirdars, *see* landlords
Jamaat-i-Islam (JI), 80–1, 85, 89, 137, 156–7; *see also* Pakistan National Alliance
Jamiatul-Ulema-i-Islam (JUI), 80, 155, 156–7; *see also* Pakistan National Alliance
Jamiatul-Ulema-i-Pakistan (JUP), 80, 91, 156–7; *see also* Pakistan National Alliance
Jatoi family, 60, 153
Jinnah, Fatima, 87, 137
Jinnah, Mohammad Ali, 25, 27–29, 38, 44, 53–4, 66, 69, 82, 112, 148
Jogezais family, 170
Joint Labour Council (1969), 105
Judiciary, 62, 90, 91, 92, 120, 123–4, 146, 149; *see also* elites, professional

K

Kalabagh, Nawab of, 56, 138
Karachi, 15, 41, 88, 94, 95, 98, 103, 105, 138 n46, 159
Karim, A., 98, 104
Kashmir dispute, 128, 133
Kasim, Nawab Mir, 22n
Kasuri, M. A., 122, 137
Kathiawar, 94, 95
Kayani, M. R., Justice, 123
Khaksar Tehriq, 156; see also Pakistan National Alliance
Khaliquzzaman, Chaudhri, 54
Khan, Aga, 80
Khan, Akbar, Major-General, 133
Khan, Khan Abdul Ghaffar, 15, 40
Khan, Liaquat Ali, 53, 54, 66, 82, 133, 163 n9
Khan, Mohammad Ayub, 133; regime (1958–69), 42, 128, 134–9, 146–7, 162; constitution, 91, 119–20; election (1965), 159; land reforms, 55–7, 60; and BE, 75, 77, 98: and IE, 92, 99; and industrial masses, 105, 107; and PE, 64; and RE, 80, 86–8; and Baluchis, 41; and NWFP, 80; opposition to, 120–1; resignation, 43, 132, 139, 145, 172; see also Agarthala Conspiracy; Basic Democracy Scheme
Khan, Nur, Air Marshall, 105
Khan, Rahim, Air Marshall, 149 n12
Khan, Syed Ahmed, Sir, 25
Khan, Tikka, General, 14, 130, 149 n13
Khan, Wali, 153, 172
Khan, Yahya, General, 88, 98, 105, 114, 122, 132, 135, 139, 140–2, 172
Khan, Zafrullah, 85
Khanji, Dilawar, Nawab, 153
Khoja community, 94, 95, 96
Khoso family, 171
Khuhro, M. A., 52
Kissan-Mazdoor Party, 15, 155
Krishak Sramik Party, 70–1
Kudai-Khidmatgars movement, 40

L

Labour reforms, 106, 107
Lahore, 15, 94, 95, 139 n13, 159
Lahore Resolution, see Pakistan Resolution (1940)
Land reforms, 54, 55, 58; (1959), 55–7, 60, 138; (1972), 57–60; (1976), 58–60
Land Reforms Commission (1961), 47–8
Landikotal, 51
Landlords: Mughal period, 20–1, 45; colonial period, 23–4, 45–6, 74; post-Independence, 15, 47–8, 49, 54, 55–7, 58, 99, 114, 158, 153; see also elites, landowning

Language controversy, 41, 69, 88, 92, 114, 153
Law Reform Commission, 120
Legal Framework Order (1970), 122, 140
Legal profession, 111–12, 120, 122–3; see also elites, professional
Liaquat, see Khan, Liaquat Ali
Lucknow, 41

M

Madras, 95
Mahmood, Mufti, 155
Malik, Yazdani, 136
Mamdot, Khan of, 52
Managing Agency and Election Directors Orders (1972) 107
Mansabdars, see Mughals
Mao Tse-tung, 49
Martial law, 71, 85–6, 98, 159, 171; see also army; elites, military; military rule
Maudoodi, Maulana, 80, 81, 83–4, 85, 87
Maulvis, 79–80, 90
Medical profession, 111; see also elites, professional
Memon community, 94, 95
Mengal, Ataullah, 154
Middle East, 106
Military rule, 75, 11–22, 159, 168, 169–72; concept of, 126, 127–8, 130–4, 142, 143–5, 169; see also army; elites, military; Khan, Mohammad Ayub; Khan, Yahya; martial law; Zia-al-Haq
Minimum Wages Ordinance (1961), 105
Ministry of Religious Affairs, 90
Mir, Khurshid Hassan, 158
Mirza, Iskander, 54–5, 71, 72, 117–18
Modie, Francis, Sir, 66 n14
Mohammad, Ghulam, 68–9, 71, 72, 117, 123, 163
Mohammad, Shulam, 133
Mughals (1526–1857), 19–20, 111, 128; and feudalism, 20–2, 45; elites, 36, 42, 82; mansabdari system, 20, 21, 61; decline, 21–2; cultural heritage of, 41
Muhajirs, 40, 41, 64–5, 68, 94–5, 99, 104, 105, 129, 167
Mujib, see Rahman, Mujibur
Multan, 159
Munir, Justice, 123
Muslim League, see Pakistan Muslim League
Muslims, see Islam

N

National Assembly (NA), see Assembly, National

National Awami Party (NAP), 41, 122, 123, 153–4, 155, 156, 160
National Democratic Front (NDF), 121, 155
National Democratic Party (NDP), 156–7; see also Pakistan National Alliance
National Development Corporation, 106
National Development Volunteer Corps, 106
Nationalism, 25–6, 27–9
Nationalization, 106–7, 109, 156, 158
Nazimuddin, Khawaja, Sir, 54, 66, 68–9, 70, 85
Niazi, Maulana, 91
Nizam-i-Islam Party, 70
Nizam-i-Mustafa (Islamic system), see Islam and state formation; Islamic law
Noon family, 52, 53, 54, 56, 60
Noorani, Maulana, 91
North West Frontier Provinces (NWFP): colonial period, 24, 45n, 80, 93; post-Independence, 45, 51, 56, 60, 66 n14, 67, 71, 72, 80, 103, 105, 116, 129, 149, 151, 153, 155, 156–7

O
Objectives Resolution (1949), 82–3, 85, 86, 115–16, 152
Okarvi, Maulana, 91
Omar, Caliph, 160
One-Party State, 123, 146–60 passim
One-Unit Plan, 71–2, 117, 138, 140
Othman, Caliph, 40

P
Pakistan Democratic Party (PDP), 156–7; see also Pakistan National Alliance
Pakistan Foreign Service (PFS), 63
Pakistan Industrial Development Corporation (PIDC), 75, 104
Pakistan Movement, 93
Pakistan Muslim League (PML), 52, 53, 54, 68, 70–1, 82, 99, 113, 114, 148, 153; Council group, 137; Convention group (PMLC), 138, see also Khan, Mohammad Ayub; Quyyum group (PMLQ), see also All-India Muslim League; Sind Muslim League
Pakistan National Alliance (PNA), 15, 43, 80, 90, 91, 109, 133, 149, 156–7, 159, 168, 171
Pakistan Peoples Party (PPP), 15; and Bhutto, 42, 138, 146, 149, 151, 160; and socialism, 76, 88, 122, 147–8; election (1970), 88–9, 140–1; land policy, 57; and administrative

reform, 76–7; economic policy, 108–9; in Baluchistan, 153–4, 157; in NWFP, 157; in Punjab, 157–8; in Sind, 157; in tribal areas, 157; military regime (1977–), 133, 167, 171, 172; see also Bhutto
Pakistan Resolution (1940), 25, 28, 152
Partition, see Independence
Pathans, 15, 40, 41, 109–10, 128, 129, 144, 153, 170, 171
Pay and Services Commission Report, 135–6
Peasants: Mughal period, 20–1; colonial period, 23–4, 46–7; post-Independence, 15, 37, 46, 47–51, 55–7, 58, 79, 105, 106, 109–10, 114, 144, 145, 146, 147, 148; and Bhutto, 155, 157–8, 169; see also feudalism; landlords
People's Public Works Department, 106
Peshawar, 15, 129, 159
Pirs (spiritual leaders), 79, 80
Pirzada, Hafiz, 122
Pirzada, Sharifuddin, 170
Planning Commission, 163, 165, 171
Police, 15, 146, 150, 159; Police Service of Pakistan, (PSP), 63, 77; All-Pakistan Unified Grade, 77
Political Parties Act (1962), 56, 121; Amendment (1963), 121
Portugal, 22
Presidents, role of, 73, 77, 85, 119, 125, 137, 140, 150, 152
Press, 15, 98, 99, 111, 118, 138 n46; censorship, 71
Prime Ministers, role of, 66, 67, 68, 69, 72, 73, 116, 125, 150, 151, 152
Provincial Assemblies, see Assemblies, Provincial
Provincial Governors, see Governors, Provincial
Provincialism, see ethnicity
Public and Representative Offices Disqualification Act (1949) (PRODA), 53, 72
Public Service Commission (PSC), 63–4
Public Shipping Corporation, 118
Punjab/Punjabis: colonial period, 24, 45n, 46, 93, 129; post-Independence, 14, 39, 41, 48, 51, 52, 53, 56, 60, 64–5, 66 n14, 67, 68, 69, 70, 71, 85, 94, 95, 99, 103, 104, 105, 109, 116, 129, 130, 138, 140, 141, 149, 151, 153, 154, 167; election (1977), 156–7, 158, 170
Punjab Punch, 150

Q
Qasim, Mohammad Ibn, 19
Qizilbash family, 60

Quadir, Manzur, 119–20, 122
Quereshi family, 60, 153
Quran, see Islamic law

R

Rahim, J. A., 149, 158
Rahman, Fazlur, 87–8
Rahman (Justice Hamoodur) Report,
    123, 142
Rahman, Mujibur, 99, 120, 121, 122,
    140–1
Rajputs, 128
Ramay, Hanif, 149, 158
Rana, Mukhtar, 158
Rangoon, 95
Rangoonwala, M. A., 98
Rashid, Sardar Abdur, 72
Rawalpindi, 15, 88, 159
Rawalpindi Conspiracy Case (1948),
    133
Rehmat Ali, Choudhury, 28n
Republican Party, 54, 113, 117, 118;
    see also Sahib, Khan
Riots: (1946) 89; Ahmadiya (1953),
    69, 85–6; (1977), 159

S

Sahib, Khan, 117
Saigol family, 95
Sattar, Pirzada Abdus, 52, 72
Saudi Arabia, 162
Security of Pakistan Act, 120
Service Tribunals Act (1973), 77
Shahabuddin, M., Justice, 123
Sheik, Naseer A., 104
Sherpao, Hayat Mohammad, 155
Shipping, 118, 134 n24, 138 n46
Sikander, Arbab, 155
Sikhs, 128
Sind/Sindhis, 41, 48; colonial period,
    19, 24, 46, 80, 93; post-
    independence, 39–40, 41, 48, 52–3,
    56, 60, 66 n14, 67, 71, 72, 77, 80,
    94, 95, 103, 116, 129, 138, 149,
    153; Tenancy Act (1950–), 50;
    election (1977), 156–7, 170, Zia
    regime, 171, 172
Sind Muslim League, 52
Sirhindi 22, 29
Six Point Programme, 121; see also
    Mujibur, Rahman
Socialism, 89, 90, 91, 107, 108, 109,
    122, 146–7, 153, 158, 160, 171; see
    also Bhutto; PPP
Soomro family, 60
Steel Corporation of Pakistan Ltd, 107
Strikes, 159
Suhrawardhy, H. S., 70, 117–18,
    120–1, 137; see also Awami League
Sumar, A. K., 98
Supreme Court of Pakistan, 123
Surat, 94

T

Talpur family, 56, 60, 171
Tehriq-i-Istaqlal (TI), 156–7, 171,
    172; see also Pakistan National
    Alliance
Third World, 33, 132, 147, 162–3, 167
Tilak, B. G., 27
Tippu, Sultan of Mysore, 22n
Tiwana family, 56
Trade, 103, 104, 109, 118
Trade associations, 97, 98–9
Trade unions, 105
Transport, 101
Tribalism, 41, 48, 51, 52, 79, 93, 120,
    130, 155
Tufail, Mian Mohammad, 133

U

Ulema, 79, 80, 86, 87, 88, 90
Union of Soviet Socialist Republics,
    46, 153, 167
United Democratic Front, 154
United Front, 70–1
United Nations, 164
United Provinces, 41
United States of America, 100, 118,
    134, 162, 163–5, 166, 167
Urdu, see language controversy
Usmani, Maulana Shabbir Ahmed, 82

V

Valika family, 95

W

Waliullah, Shah, 22, 29
Waziristan, 80 n4
West Bengal, 41
West Pakistan, 56, 64–5, 68, 73, 79,
    94, 101, 102–3, 104, 118, 129, 137,
    138, 140, 141, 164; see also
    Baluchistan; NWFP; Punjab; Sind
West Pakistan Industrial Relations
    Ordinance (1960), 105
West Pakistan Power and Develop-
    ment Authority (WPPDA) 75
West Pakistani professional elite
    (WPPE), 113, 114, 119, 120, 121,
    137, 153
Working class (urban/industrial), 15,
    37, 79, 99–101, 104, 105–6, 109–10,
    140, 144, 145, 147, 148; and
    Bhutto, 156, 157–8, 169
World Bank, 164

Y

Yahya, see Khan, Yahya, General

Z

Zamindars, see landlords
Zia-ul-Haq, General, 135, 143–4, 149,
    162, 169–72